Tracts of the Sun

an Earth-Orbit of Vajrayana Expressions

Tracts of the Sun

an Earth-Orbit of Vajrayana Expressions

Ngakpa Chögyam *&* Khandro Déchen

Quotations selected by
Naljorpa Druk-tsal Dorje *&* Naljorma Kha'drön dPa'mo

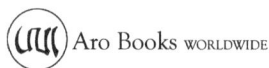

Aro Books WORLDWIDE

2022

Aro Books WORLDWIDE,

PO Box 111, 5 Court Close,

Cardiff, Wales, CF14 1JR

© 2022 by Ngakpa Chögyam & Khandro Déchen

Thangka of Kharchen Nyi-ma 'ö-Zèr by Thar'phen Lingtsang.
Cover design by Victor Howard Simmerson.
Cover photograph of Ngakpa Chögyam and Khandro Déchen by Ngakpa Trö-rig / Jack Webb.
Line drawings by Khandro Déchen.
Caligraphies by Ngak'chang Rinpoche.

First Edition 2022

ISBN: 978-1-898185-28-4 (paperback)
ISBN: 978-1-898185-32-1 (ePub)

For further information about Aro Books WORLDWIDE please see
http://aro-books-worldwide.org/

To obtain copies of all our publications please visit
https://www.lulu.com/spotlight/arobooksworldwide

The apparel of linguistic quotation, reveals wondrous meaning –
The textile quotations that are apparel, reveal the meaning of wonder.
Ngak'chang Rinpoche & Khandro Déchen

Vajra Guru Nyima 'ö-Zer *(nyi ma 'od zer)*

Preface

We did not consider it possible. We were wrong. We would therefore like to thank Naljorpa Druk-tsal Dorje and Naljorma Kha'drön dPa'mo for instigating this book – and for enthusiastically engaging in the immense task of compiling and introducing these quotations.

We are honoured to include a quotation for each month of the year from His Eminence Ögyen Dro'dül Thrin-lé Kunkyab Rinpoche, the Yangsrid of gTértön Drukdra Dorje – and from his esteemed father Khar-trül Wangchuk Rig'dzin Rinpoche. Both Lamas are our dear friends and this book is significantly enhanced by their generous contributions.

We were astonished to see how much Druk-tsal and Kha'drön collected. We can only see this plethora of quotations as a tribute to our Tsawa'i Lamas: Kyabjé Düd'jom Rinpoche Jig'drèl Yeshé Dorje; Kyabjé Künzang Dorje Rinpoche and Jomo Sam'phel Déchen Rinpoche; and 'Khordong gTérchen Tulku Chhi'mèd Rig'dzin Rinpoche.

Their speech remains a superb stream of quotable expressions – many of which appear in our books. We do not intend this as humility – because we are not given to humility. Hopefully, we're not given to arrogance either. This is merely an explanation of our inspiration.

Kyabjé Düd'jom Rinpoche Jig'drèl Yeshé Dorje was astonishing in everything he said and wrote. He was utterly encyclopædic in terms of the Nine Vehicles – and brilliant in the simplicity of his expression. We have included direct quotations from him in each month of the book.

We both still hear Kyabjé Künzang Dorje Rinpoche saying *"O yah"* – and giving those words a wide array of meaning according to the tone of his voice, his eyes, and hands.

Once when asked if we—as a sangha—could bring him anything from the West that he would like, he replied *"Don't ask me what I want – I want everything. There's no limit to my desire. Just come and visit us. That is all we want."*

'Khordong gTérchen Tulku Chhi'mèd Rig'dzin Rinpoche—in speaking of a certain person—said *"Yah, yah, yah… when mantra chanting, then only 'Om Money Pay-me Soon!' knowing."* His grasp of English humour was always delightful.

Having had such wonderful Tsawa'i Lamas—and still hearing their voices—often allows us to express Vajrayana[1] in ways that would not otherwise have occurred to us.

As Lamas dedicated to teaching through *the Arts*—as part of our presentation—we act as *life-style choreographers*: for those who are open to our *theatrical stage management*.

To interest Western Vajrayana students in the secular Art has been a challenge – but it is one in which we have persevered at the instruction of Kyabjé Düd'jom Rinpoche.

We are thus delighted by the way in which Kha'drön and Druk-tsal have embraced the *Art of Sartorialism*. Clothing is dominated by fashion – and the possibility of breaking free of the chains of fashion, is something they understood immediately.

---

1   *rDo rJe theg pa* / རྡོ་རྗེ་ཐེག་པ་

That *personal appearance* is an act of generosity in terms of *inspiring authentic appreciation and authentic individuality*, is something with which they have engaged in a remarkable way. They have enthused others who had laboured under the misconception that *the Arts* were only what society dictated. This can only be understood as an act of changchub sem[2] – active compassion.

Ngak'chang Chö-ying Gyamtso *&* Khandro Déchen Tsédrüp Rolpa'i Yeshé

ʃ *sNgags 'chang chos dByings rGya mTsho* ʅ dang ʃ *mKha' 'gro bDe chen tshe grub rol pa'i ye shes* ʅ

ʃ སྔགས་འཆང་ཆུ་མཚོ་ ʅ དང་ ʃ མཁའ་འགྲོ་བདེ་ཆེན་ ʅ

---

2   *byang chub sems* / བྱང་ཆུབ་ སེམས་ / *bodhicitta* – usually translated as 'compassion', but it means: mind directed towards pure and total presence; awakened heart; and the primordial state of pure and total presence.

Kharchen Nyima 'ö-Zer *(khar chen nyi ma 'od zer)*

The Art of Quotation

The apparel of linguistic quotation, reveals wondrous meaning –
The textile quotations that are apparel, reveal the meaning of wonder.
Ngak'chang Rinpoche & Khandro Déchen

The quotations in this book are taken from the teachings Ngak'chang Rinpoche and Khandro Déchen have given since 1981.

The idea of collecting these quotations came during the COVID-19 pandemic. It struck us that it would be fantastic if people could be inspired each day – and find appreciation and upliftment in their everyday lives. Ngak'chang Rinpoche and Khandro Déchen kindly agreed to this idea and supplied a title for the book: *Tracts of the Sun*. We enjoyed this title because of the play on words. Such linguistic devices are often employed by Ngak'chang Rinpoche and Khandro Déchen in their written and oral teachings. As we are non-native English speakers, we sometimes miss instances of playful language – but our Lamas always explain them when we meet as a sangha. This is often a source of mirth. *Tracts of the Sun* is a play on *the track of the sun* – where the track is the orbit of 365 days of the earth around the sun. The word tract is a *section of writing*. So, with this double meaning we have a book of quotations for each day of the year.

Playfulness is mirrored in most of Ngak'chang Rinpoche and Khandro Déchen's writings. Their view of life as Art—and our lives as Artists—is apparent in their linguistics in both prose and poetry. Their playfulness teases and tickles duality – and in so doing, reveals the natural state itself. They choose their words carefully: as painters choose colour, shape, and texture – or as composers arrange the notes of the chromatic scale in composition.

Their vocabulary is vast. Ngak'chang Rinpoche used to learn a new English word every few days during his youth. He had an excellent English teacher who was kindly yet strict in his discipline with regard to grammar and accurate word-usage. He gave Ngak'chang Rinpoche out-of-hours poetry tutelage and specialised writing tasks. Ngak'chang Rinpoche says that this was an extremely important foundation for his life as a Lama and writer.

Ngak'chang Rinpoche and Khandro Déchen's writing is crisp and clear. Their sentences tend to be stripped of unnecessary language – but at the same time rich in their expansion of meaning. We often find that transmission lies in the flow of the words and the dynamics of the language. The vocabulary is often so precise, that it is almost painful. Sometimes the surgical precision of their writing is visible in how they combine certain word pairs, like *sonorously scintillating; whimsically rigorous;* and, *panoramic curiosity.* These word pairs create a slight tension that facilitates a poetic ignition of perception.

In terms of Vajrayana, we have here an example of the mechanisms of nonduality as the inseparability of emptiness and form. In terms of Ngak'chang Rinpoche and Khandro Déchen's more poetic sections of writing, *form* equates to *linearity* which is married with *emptiness* in terms of *laterality.*

Emptiness is the implosion of dualistic sense-making. In terms of the Vajrayana view—when observing reality—one notices form arising out of emptiness and dissolving into emptiness again.

In the written material of Ngak'chang Rinpoche and Khandro Déchen, landscapes of linear comprehensible structures arise and then dissolve into nondual expositions which defy the dualistic rationale. It is almost as if one had immersed one's senses in Surrealism. In surrealism there is often no sense making. However, with Ngak'chang Rinpoche and Khandro Déchen's Surrealism – reality sparkles through, spawning an ethos of creativity and upliftedness.

We started to collect quotes from private and public social media communications between our Lamas and the worldwide sanghas – but also from teachings recorded and teachings using *Zoom*. Students from around the globe also started to send us quotations and it became apparent that a book could easily be compiled.

Ngak'chang Rinpoche and Khandro Déchen are our root teachers. To us, they are the ultimate example of kindness and awareness – and we may never be able to repay them. In our interactions they have shown us how appreciation for all phenomena can be increased. It is through the Arts that they have given transmission in terms of how to live life as Vajrayana practitioners.

As we both have passion for a range of Art forms, we have always felt connected with the transmission of living life as Artists. Through the years of being disciples of Ngak'chang Rinpoche and Khandro Déchen, we have noticed a development. We notice increasingly, that everyday-chores can be activities of Art. Art is also there when investigating thoughtfully, to find more innovative solutions to everyday living.

This *disciplined stimulation of the senses* brings more quality and joy to life and sustains our lives as practitioners. We feel that Ngak'chang Rinpoche and Khandro Déchen teach this by example. We find it equal to the way that the Mahasiddhas manifested in India. Although this is the Western world and we are a Western audience – the Mahasiddha ambience is alive.

The quotations in this book cover a variety of *Essential Vajrayana* topics such as vajra commitment; the rôle of the Vajra master; and, Dzogchen[1] view. Lamas, as vajra masters, display the entire range of emotions so that we as their students can witness the possibility of our own potential for realisation. This possibility is never addressed when Vajrayana is spoken of from the perspective of Sutrayana – and this is the way that Vajrayana is most commonly presented.

From the explicit perspective of Vajrayana however – if you have no desire, you have no potential for compassion. This is because passion and compassion have the same energy – and this energy is either transformed through Tantra[2] or self-liberated through Dzogchen. We cannot fully manifest without this energy – just as a car cannot run without fuel.

Ngak'chang Rinpoche and Khandro Déchen explain in these quotations how Vajra command actually works. They explain that vajra command is actually the instruction to be totally alive – and to manifest the vajra pride of being an authentic practitioner. When we are in vajra commitment with Lamas and receive suggestions, we are always free to present the limitations of our conditions – and to express perceived difficulties in terms of carrying out our Lamas' suggestions. This is highly beneficial as it means that we, as disciples, are faced with the reality of our condition and conditioning.

1   *rDzogs chen* / ཛོགས་ཆེན་ – utter completeness.
2   *rGyud* / རྒྱུད་

Ngak'chang Rinpoche and Khandro Déchen state extremely clearly that there are precise requirements for students entering into Vajra commitment. It requires a prolonged period of working with the Lama in which students gain a degree of self-transparency. This clarity and transparency produce frustration in terms of encountering our subjective and self-referencing logic head on.

They explain that one should be highly cautious about psychopaths – cult leaders who just inform you that you are in Vajra relationship. There should always be time for exploration beforehand

There are of course rare exceptions. Ngak'chang Rinpoche was ordained by Kyabjé Düd'jom Jig'drèl Yeshé Dorje, more or less at their first meeting.

Extreme examples of 'obedience' are merely a way, in certain quarters, of discrediting vajra commitment through failure to give real examples.

Vajra commitment almost always stays within the remit of what is possible in society. The Vajra master has therefore no need to make use of unkindness, immorality, illegality, or unethical behaviour of any kind. This message clearly shines through in many of the quotes and we deliberately chose them for this reason.

In the topic of Dzogchen view we give several quotations that comment on the practice of the Aro Naljor Zhi – the four Naljors of the Aro gTér. Ngak'chang Rinpoche and Khandro Déchen have written two books, *Roaring Silence*[3] and *Shock Amazement*[4] solely on this topic. In the quotations we give here however, they explain how boredom functions as one of the defence mechanisms of dualism.

3   Ngakpa Chögyam and Khandro Déchen, Shambala Publications, 2002
4   Khandro Déchen and Ngakpa Chögyam, Aro Books worldwide, 2020

They humorously point out that *without going through the experience of boredom* there is no progress to be made toward establishing the basis for approaching Dzogchen. We also learn that we are bound to experience difficulty and obstacles as we engage in this personal experiment. We therefore need a robust sense of humour in order that we are able to smile at failure. At one point, Ngak'chang Rinpoche and Khandro Déchen point out that 'duality has to commit suicide'.

There is a wealth of advice given in a pragmatic earthy manner in terms of what is required in order to arrive at the base of Vajrayana practice. This advice includes: finishing projects we have started; keeping our dwellings clean and tidy; being kind and genuine with others; and, simply being natural.

The quotations are divided into sets for each day of the year. At the beginning of each month there are quotations from His Holiness Trülku Ögyen Dro'dül Thrin-lé Künkyab Rinpoche and Khar-trül Wangchuk Rig'dzin Rinpoche – Bhutanese Lamas who are friends of Ngak'chang Rinpoche and Khandro Déchen. Their styles of communication are different – but equally pithy and direct. One can read the quotes for the day – and let the meaning pervade one's daily activities. One could also read *'Tracts of the Sun'* like a book – or dip into it in a random fashion.

Many of the quotations deal with how we could live as authentic individuals in the world of Vajrayana. Where one begins or ends is therefore less relevant than the inspiration that arises from reading.

The palettes and scales of Buddhist teachings—even within each of the nine vehicles—possesses a multitude of colours and tones. Each colour and texture; each tone and timbre; each teaching style – suits a different person.

Ngak'chang Rinpoche and Khandro Déchen place an emphasis on the Arts. This emphasis comes directly from advice received from Kyabjé Düd'jom Rinpoche Jig'drèl Yeshé Dorje in 1971. He said that Vajrayana, in particular, is linked to the Arts. He stated that Lamas who teach Vajrayana should be *Artists who engage in all the Arts* – and encourage the Arts in terms of how they teach.

In dialogue with Ngak'chang Rinpoche, Kyabjé Düd'jom Rinpoche Jig'drèl Yeshé Dorje explained that the Arts were crucial to Vajrayana – but not simply the religious Arts in terms of thangkas, statues, gTormas, vajra dance, and so forth. The secular Arts—both Tibetan and Western—are also important. It was through the secular Western Arts that Ngak'chang Rinpoche and Khandro Déchen would reach out to people.

"You must—always—music playing. This I see. This important – very important. Always painting. Always poetry writing. Always Art in every part of life. In this way, changchub sem always manifesting. This prediction I am making. Always Art making. Never difference in Vajrayana and Art coming! Always together manifesting. In this way peoples are nature of Vajrayana understanding." [5]

The Arts, as presented by Ngak'chang Rinpoche and Khandro Déchen, include the full range of the sense fields. They present no *hierarchy of Arts* as there would be with the Arts in conventional social terms. They see Craft as not being less than Fine Art. They see the olfactory and gastronomic Arts as being no less than music, painting, sculpture, poetry, theatre, or dance. In addition to the Arts of each sense field, Ngak'chang Rinpoche and Khandro Déchen have encouraged us personally in exploring the *Art of Sartorialism* – and many reflections of this will be found in the quotations we have selected for this book.

5   Ngakpa Chögyam, *Goodbye Forever, miscellaneous memoirs of an English Lama*, Volume One, Aro Books worldwide, 2020

When we first thought of collecting quotations from the teachings that Ngak'chang Rinpoche and Khandro Déchen have given over the last thirty years, we did not realise how often they had discussed the Arts and the many ways there are of living life as Art.

Living life as Art is a teaching on *how to live life as an Artist* – and *being an Artist* is directly connected with being a Vajrayana practitioner. Ngak'chang Rinpoche and Khandro Déchen have always given transmission of Dzogchen – in terms of how the 'mundane' activities of everyday life could become Art. They have always emphasised that *we are all Artists*. As Artists we can fully engage the sense fields in appreciating quotidian reality. In this way, nothing is mundane. Nothing is ordinary. Nothing is tedious.

They have always worked to instil the idea that the activities of everyday life can be harnessed in terms of finding one's authentic individual appreciation, authentic tastes, and authentic predilections. The authentic individual appreciation of phenomena is a crucial aspect of Vajrayana – and, as a Vajrayana practitioner, this is a vital aspect of being in this world. According to Vajrayana the *personality display of the Lama* is a teaching in itself.

As Vajrayana practitioners we should be aware of our Lamas. We should be aware of how they manifest as human beings who interact with the ordinary world of secular appearances.

Ngak'chang Rinpoche and Khandro Déchen are living examples in how they manifest and engage in Sartorialism in everyday life. This becomes apparent in many of the quotations in this book. Not only is their clothing a teaching of how to manifest – but also a teaching on how to value and care for phenomena.

Every day, we need to dress and appear in the world. As Vajrayana practitioners, this can be practised with the help of these salient quotations from Ngak'chang Rinpoche and Khandro Déchen's teachings. Even though there are fundamental differences between the vehicles in terms of base and path – the fruit is the same. They are all within the glorious landscape of Buddhism. The vehicles may contradict each other – but as Buddhism is a religion of method rather than truth, the contradictions are always comprehensible.

From the Sutric viewpoint, one aims towards the experience of emptiness. Emptiness and absence of a fixed self-identity is the goal of Sutra[6]. Once the experience of emptiness has been reached – the landscape of Tantra makes itself available. In Tantra we relate again with form – but the form is empty of fixated self-identity. If we are experiencing ourselves as empty, there is no problem in terms of relating with form – because form and emptiness comingle. Having reached the naked empty state, one can dress, one can don clothing – and the clothes one wears become a compassionate communication with everyone and everything everywhere.

'In this, one ought not to look merely to the most sublime of the Vajra Awareness-holder mantra-holder's clothes – it is an essential teaching that not only these but even regularly-worn clothes and of enjoyment are inseparable from tèn'drèl or interdependent, auspicious connection.[7] Clothing has the auspicious or inter-dependent connection of the yidam[8]. Fasten yourself without impurities or defilements to what possesses magnificence, spontaneous and natural dignity, and brilliant radiance.' [9]

---

6   *mDo /* མདོ

7   *Tèn'drèl (rTen 'brel /* རྟེན་འབྲེལ*) auspicious connection.*

8   *yi dam /* ཡི་དམ */ ishta devata – awareness being, wisdom being, or meditational deity*

9   see Appendix 1

In Dzogchen the emphasis is finding the natural nondual state in which emptiness and form are non-separate. In Dzogchen one engages with the senses. The senses therefore, should be alert and open. If the senses are dull, one should enliven them – opening them out into the phenomenal world. Engaging with the phenomenal world is an active process.

The phenomenal world is rich, colourful, and delicious – and this can be integrated and communicated in terms of appreciation. In this way, life becomes a field of Art. All activities can be Art – and clothing, as an expression of authentic individuality, is the Art of Sartorialism.

The Art of life requires the recognition that authentic personality is *individuated space*. Individuated space requires enthusiastic investment in terms of what manifests from that space, with respect to being natural ornaments of reality.

When it comes to clothing therefore, there are a multitude of choices. What appears on the market is a small fraction of the different choices and possible combinations. Finding what is authentically enjoyable is a highly individual concern – which involves effort and challenge.

Many think they actually like the available fashion – but is this an honest assessment? One could question one's choices with greater criticality. If one were to do so, one might find one's choices have been choices made by others. The fashion industry tells us what we should like and we usually agree. We are influenced by the fact that everyone else wears more-or-less the same clothes. Even where we differ – we are influenced by herd behaviour in terms of the herd to which we wish to belong. To find authentic individuality, energy must be invested in openness to a broader spectrum of possibilities. One needs to be authentically open to choices that are out of the ordinary.

This means stepping out of the referential framework of what we think is acceptable, relaxed, and appropriate to wear. The questioning of choices is an opening process. It is a process of becoming aware of the time-frame in which one lives – and being able to step outside this time-frame. With regard to time, it is valuable to comprehend the patterns of one's temporal milieu. The social current in which one swims is difficult to observe. If one is not skilled in stepping out of the social current it never seems open to question. Through viewing the world in relation to other time-periods, one can understand that current society—and what it views as normal—does not have to be rigidly fixed.

'The tantrika needs to be free to cavort with appearances — without addiction to the referential dictates of sartorial approbation or disapprobation.' [10]

What is normal in our time-frame would be viewed differently from within previous time-frames. How we look today would probably be seen as horrific from a period where there was greater self-respect in terms of appearance.

In the 1940s, high waisted trousers were the custom to wear for women when not wearing a skirt or a dress – but today high-waisted trousers are unfashionable, and they can hardly be found on the market. The tide turns in terms of fashion – but changes in fashion have no intrinsic meaning. Being limited to wearing the current fashion seems foolish when there are multiple choices.

Ngak'chang Rinpoche's life is filled with examples of clothing. He never followed the fashion of the time – but always followed his individual appreciation. Even as a young child, he followed what he liked, and did not pay any attention to the comments and pressure from people to adjust his taste according to the prevailing norm. His taste has also followed him through his life and for many years, did not change.

10 This text is from the sixth Vajrayana root vow, the vow of body.

An example is his appreciation for Levi Strauss 501 Serge de Nîmes trousers which started at the age of 8 years and still continues. His old Levi's have all been recycled and used to re-make new items.

From a Buddhist point of view everything is empty of 'attributed meaning'. If one looks at the changes in fashion throughout history one cannot find 'intrinsic meaning'. There is no governance as to previous fashions belonging solely to previous time frames. There is therefore no reason merely to wear what presents itself as available and 'normal' to wear at the present time. The entire history of clothing styles is there at our disposal.

By enthusiastic investment in finding clothing—valued through authentic appreciation—one will make choices that are linked with authentic personality. One will have found a link between personality and the phenomenal world. This is an individual communication fuelled by simple admiration. The process of finding authentic appreciation in clothing creates sensitivity to one's other senses – and this sensitivity expands and becomes increasingly perceivable to others. The process has an entrancing quality. It promotes further investment in terms of delving deeper to bring a greater variety of forms into existence. It generates rLung rTa[11]: upliftedness – the spirit of enjoyment in everything within reality. rLung rTa is a sense of deliberateness in terms of constantly reminding ourselves to appreciate. This becomes evident in one's care of clothes and in the development of the Art of sartorialism.

---

11 Lung-ta *(rLung rTa / ཀླུང་རྟ)* – wind horse.

'Improper clothes are those which are unattractive and which possess a form displeasing to the eye: they are made of impure materials, they are badly made, they exceed their proper proportions, they have ugly colours, they are rough in texture, and so on. When one wears sumptuous clothing one imagines that one is putting on the Dharma-robes of the body of the yidam which possesses the clear or vivid appearance of the Creation Stage.' [12]

Maybe one might find that a female cyclist's costume from 1880 communicates itself through appreciative fascination. One might then decide to tailor it—or have it tailored—and wear it in one's daily life. One would need to invest time in the selection of fabric – in terms of colours and material that suggest themselves. After having the costume made, one might find one needs to have others made in different colours and materials. There could be one for each season in different materials. There could be one in green tweed that reflects the trees in the nearby park.

There could be one in Serge de Nîmes for manual work situations. There could be one in suede or William Morris upholstery fabric for restaurants and celebrations. It is endless.

During the years, as students of Ngak'chang Rinpoche and Khandro Déchen, we have engaged in several projects in which we have brought pieces of clothing into existence.

One project was the reproduction of the *Farnham Girls' Grammar School* blazer. When Ngak'chang Rinpoche was at Art School in Farnham – one of the prised items of clothing was a Girls' Grammar School blazer. This was due to the fact that they were modelled on boating blazers – and thus bore stripes of vividly contrasting colours. This was, of course, highly desirable in the hippie era, in which colourful dress was particularly appreciated.

12 see Appendix 1

If you look carefully at the book cover of '*an odd boy*' Volume III[13] you will see a photograph of a group of Art students. A lad on the left is wearing a Girls' Grammar School blazer.

The fabric for our Farnham Girls' Grammar School blazers was specially woven for the job. It is extraordinary what one can do with three colours in terms of their balance. We have seen many such blazers in Britain – but none as astonishing as these.

Many students ordered these blazers – and when groups of students wear them in public, there are always enthusiastic comments from the people they meet. The blazers had their design specifications from Ngak'chang Rinpoche and Khandro Déchen – who specified that they should have working cuff buttons, ticket pockets, and that they should be considerably longer that the standard blazer. For the breast pocket they specified a white emblem. It was an embroidered text which is an adaptation of Dante Alighieri that reads: 'Abandon Hope and Fear, All Ye Who Enter Here'[14].

This text in Dante's archaic Italian encircles a capitalized letter A taken from a military artillery motif. The letter A has great importance in Dzogchen, as a symbol of the natural state. We think these blazers will be passed on to a new generation of practitioners, as sartorial treasures.

Another sartorial project came to light when we found an array of fur coats on Swedish eBay. They had fallen out of fashion and the older generation in Sweden were afraid to wear them due to rumours of aggressive behaviour from certain quarters.

---

13 Doc Togden, *an odd boy*, volumes I–IV, Aro Books worldwide.

14 'Lasciate Ogne Speranza e Paura Voi Ch'itrate' is Ngak'chang Rinpoche's re-casting of a line from Dante's Inferno. 'Inferno' is the first part of Italian writer Dante Alighieri's 14th Century epic 'Divine Comedy'. Dante passes through the gate of Hell, which bears an inscription ending with the famous phrase *Lasciate ogne speranza, voi ch'intrate – abandon all hope, ye who enter here.*

Nevertheless, as Vajrayana practitioners, we can wear antique fur coats with a sense of respect for the animals whose hides they once were. Through the practice of awareness and mantra, we can honour these animals and establish a connection with them. Throwing these fur coats in the garbage, as some do, would be to disrespect these animals. Instead, Ngak'chang Rinpoche and Khandro Déchen have encouraged all of their students to care for all leather and fur objects, so that they will last a lifetime or more. We view this as another element of respect to these beings.

Wonderful fur coats of fox, raccoon, wolf, goat, and sheep were found and these were then distributed to both Ngak'chang Rinpoche and Khandro Déchen, as well as to their students. In actuality, all of us who wear these fur clothes, during winter time, were met with positive comments in the streets.

Naljorma Kha'drön is tailoring an on-going series of clothing items for Ngak'chang Rinpoche. One of them is a waistcoat he designed – which she had made up in various different materials. The design originates from a British Rail worker's waistcoat, which Ngak'chang Rinpoche noticed due to its particular features – such as the narrow band of frontage-fabric at the nape of the neck. This adds great strength to the garment without losing the satin back.

The waistcoat has six pockets—three on each side—that have been made in a. thick hardwearing historical re-enactors' woollen fabric – woven by a maker who specialises in fabric in period colours and weaves; b. fabric from Ngak'chang Rinpoche's old Levi Strauß 501 Serge de Nîmes trousers; c. Farnham Girls' Grammar School blazer fabric; d. hand woven traditional fabric from Bhutan.

Naljorma Kha'drön also made a jacket for Ngak'chang Rinpoche in the Golden Lily midnight/green William Morris upholstery fabric. This type of blazer was popular in the 1960s, when several musicians—such as Jimi Hendrix, John Lennon, George Harrison, and Steve Marriott—wore them on stage. The blazer has wide lapels and a longer cut and has two pockets on each side, one ticket pocket and one larger pocket. At the moment the same type of blazer is being made in traditional Bhutanese fabric. An upcoming project is a Union Jacket made from two Union Jacks specifically made from heritage-weave linen – sewn with French seams in order that they lie flat in the garment *(rather than having ridges)*.

The more one appreciates – the more one develops one's sartorial repertoire. The more one appreciates – the more one wants to know the history of items. One wants to know the provenance of the fabric one has chosen. Ripples of appreciation are created which extend outwards to others as the appreciation sparkles through – and appreciative reciprocity is ignited. Appreciation leads to creativity – and creativity to further appreciation. When one makes authentically individual choices—and invests energy in those choices—one is involved with Art.

'Since the dyes and colours are connected with one's feelings towards beings make the oil pigments bright! Since the adornments are linked with the retinue and students, decorate it beautifully! Since the way one wears it is connected with the accomplishment of one's actions, abandon improper behaviour like wearing it crooked, having one side pulled below the other, wearing it inside out or upside down, letting the front sag down or trampling the back of it underfoot, and don it properly!' [15]

15 see Appendix 1

Wearing clothes can be an expression of compassionate activity. Any human being can be beautiful in appearance and their manifested form will be there for others to enjoy. Every day, throughout the year, one can manifest in this world, spreading the wonder of displaying the Art of being alive. The appreciation for what one wears—and the selection based on authentic appreciation—will sparkle for others to enjoy. This expression of compassionate activity is based on empty form. It does not have to be based on wanting to express oneself. It does not have to be based on wanting to be original or unique. It does not have to be based on following any concept of manifesting. The only criterion is following what is authentically appreciated.

Chö *(chos)* – as it is

January

Even if one is never afraid of gods, humans, or anything
– one should be afraid of cause and effect.

Ögyen Dro'dül Thrin-lé Kunkyab Rinpoche
རྒྱལ་བ་ཨོ་རྒྱན་འགྲོ་འདུལ་ཕྲིན་ལས་ཀུན་སྐྱབས་རིན་པོ་ཆེ་

Rice can be cooked in any receptacle, when you have the
positive will – I am amazed!

Khar-trül Wangchuk Rig'dzin Rinpoche
མཁར་སྤྲུལ་དཔལ་གྱི་དབང་ཕྱུག་རིག་འཛིན་རིན་པོ་ཆེ།

The first of January

Nondual emptiness is undivided from nondual form. Therefore, everyone and everything everywhere has the intrinsic nature of nondual awareness – the spontaneously arisen universe of pure qualities. *Kyabjé Düd'jom Rinpoche Jig'drèl Yeshé Dorje*

———— · ————

To *become* calm or composed – simply recognise *what it is* that makes anxiety feel advantageous. To *remain* calm – give up adversarial or self-protective stances. Perils which can be avoided, can usually be avoided. Those that cannot, cannot – and are better faced with composure.

———— · ————

Emotional embroilment is the result of *oceanic Mind* failing to self-recognise – failing to understand that its waves are fundamental to its nature. There is no relaxation in this failure to self-recognise. To be calm is not to become becalmed – nor to imagine there are opportunities to be inventive with the energy that merely prevents relaxation.

———— · ————

Calmness or composure, is called shi-nè If you are composed then, everyone around you will become composed – simply by knowing that you have composure. The more people have composure, the more composed others will become – unless they are determined to be frenetically demented.

———— · ————

Someone said to Ngak'chang Rinpoche *"You're always very composed"* and asked *"What's it like to be so composed?"* Ngak'chang Rinpoche replied *"Like any piece of music."* Then after a moment's pause, he added *"But I'd aspire to a be a 'cello suite by Johann Sebastian Bach – rather than many other things that come to mind."*

The second of January

Anarchy from the perspective of Dzogchen has nothing to do with rebellion or overturning the social order – one simply needs to ignore the rules of cyclic derangement.

———— · ————

It may sound like an oxymoron – but Vajrayanists are anarchist-monarchists. They are anarchist because they are not chained by the regulations of societal indoctrination. They are monarchists because they freely choose to be bound by vows to their chosen Tsawa'i Lama[1].

———— · ————

Everything has to be assessed in the moment, for what it is. There is no absolute rule to follow – and no way to avoid mistakes. One can only do what seems right in the moment. Kindness is more amorphous than the 'rules' of ethics and morality. Dzogchen is nondual anarchy – where anarchy refers to the anarchism of freedom with responsibility. Dzogchen is not merely doing as you please.

———— · ————

To incorporate Vajrayana into everyday life, the essential point is this: wherever you are and whatever you are doing, remember you are a practitioner. Remember—especially when you might wish to speak harshly—you are a Vajrayana practitioner about to speak harshly. This invariably undermines the need to speak harshly. It is an act of anarchy in respect of the laws of knee-jerk responsiveness.

---

1   *(rTsa ba'i bLa ma /* རྩ་བའི་བླ་མ་*)* – root teacher.

The third of January

rLung rTa—Wind Horse[2]—is enjoyment. Enjoyment means *to occasion* or to *engender* joy. Joy is upliftedness – the natural response to phenomena and to being alive.

——— · ———

To raise rLung rTa is to rise above quotidian pedestrianism. Everyday walking can be elevated. It is certainly the equal of flying a jet just above the tree tops – one needs to be vitally present.

——— · ———

rLung rTa is upliftedness – the spirit of enjoyment in everything within reality. rLung rTa contrasts with depression – the feeling of expectations not being met: the mistaken sense of *it being my right to be happy.* Whether I'm happy or not, is entirely dependent on 'me'.

——— · ———

The upliftedness of rLung rTa is possible for anyone. It simply requires being alive to the sensations of being alive. It requires doing nothing half-heartedly. It requires washing in the morning and wearing clean clothes. At the very minimum one could tuck one's shirt into one's trousers. That could be an important beginning.

——— · ———

rLung rTa is connected with Drala[3] – the living quality of phenomena. rLung rTa and Drala are closely related – because they both engender a sense of heightened appreciation of the sense fields and everything they contain. This sense can be cultivated. rLung rTa is a sense of deliberateness in terms of constantly reminding ourselves to appreciate. When walking through the woods, one could ask *"Am I actually hearing the birds?"* We can be actively involved in enjoyment – rather than being passive viewers of phenomena.

2   Lung-ta *(rLung rTa /* རླུང་རྟ་)
3   *sGra bLa /* སྒྲ་བླ་ pertains to the living communicative energy of the natural world.

The fourth of January

One cannot avoid falling in love with one's Lama – but it cannot be romantic, in the *Mills and Boon*[4] sense. It is the love one feels for a benevolent monarch, the noble captain of a ship, or an altruistic hero or heroine. More than this however – it is the love that is inspired by the nature of reality.

———— · ————

However much one needs to replace the love of a mother and father, this is never provided by the Lama – at least not indefinitely. There's no going to sleep on the back seat of the car – because the Lama might have a destination in mind that would not suit average expectations. You might wake up outside Dracula's castle; in the middle of the Sahara Desert; somewhere in the frozen tundra; in a war zone; or even Basingstoke.

———— · ————

We need to be careful that we do not 'fall in love' with the Lama – because whatever is based upon 'falling in love' is lost when we 'fall out of love'. Even love in the romantic sense is stronger and more dependable than most expressions of devotion. Shakespeare in his 116th Sonnet wrote *'Let me not to the marriage of true minds admit impediments. Love is not love which alters when it alteration finds, or bends with the remover to remove: Oh no! It is an ever-fixed mark that looks on tempests and is never shaken. It is the star to every wandering bark, whose worth's unknown, although his height be taken. Love's not Time's fool, though rosy lips and cheeks within his bending sickle's compass come. Love alters not with his brief hours and weeks – but bears it out even to the edge of doom. If this be error and upon me proved, I never writ, nor no man ever loved.'* When love is thus expressed, it would seem clear that true love is perhaps as rare as devotion.

---

4   Mills & Boon is generally described as '1930s escapist fiction for women'. The stories offer a comforting familiarity which meets reader expectations.

The fifth of January

The essential method is to be *free in the nature of chaos*. We always look for *pattern* in order to understand anything – but that kind of understanding is manacled to mundane meaning unless one can allow understanding to be *amorphous, nebulous, unstructured, formless*, or *unformed*.

———— · ————

It can be valuable to see patterns in reality and to see the similarity between phenomena. One needs to remember however, that this form of sense making is fundamentally illusory – and undermines freedom of perception. There is pattern and there is chaos – and they dance with each other as if they were separate.

———— · ————

The main way that we understand anything is as follows. Knowing something to be a red sphere – should another red object appear, one tends to conclude *"This is red, so it must be a sphere."* People understand by comparing – and create patterns from comparisons. The problem however, of concluding that a variety of different objects are red; because they're spheres – is that they may not all be red. They may be entirely different. Bubbles and billiard balls are spherical – but they're not even similar.

———— · ————

If you can only make sense of what is linear—and conforms to known structures—you will not be free to enjoy the greater part of the richness available; Avant-Garde Jazz, Surrealist Art, Critical Mass Poetics, or any of the Arts which leave conventional logic behind. Quite apart from this – you will not be able to relate to the vajra master. The vajra master is the choreographer of chaotic order – so you have to move beyond conservative, orthodox, conformist, predictable parameters if you wish to take the great leap into where you already are.

The sixth of January

There is no sense in which 'vajra command' is anything other than the instruction to be totally alive.

———— · ————

'Vajra command' is being bound by the Lama's instruction. This however, is no more onerous than a suggestion which is taken as transmission.

———— · ————

Dzogchen is not academic. Meditation is not academic. Academic knowledge has value – but that value is limited. When you speak directly from experience – everyone understands. When speaking from academic knowledge – then only academics understand.
Kyabjé Düd'jom Rinpoche Jig'drèl Yeshé Dorje

———— · ————

Vajra commitment is manifesting the vajra pride of an authentic practitioner. When people in vajra commitment receive suggestions from their Lamas, they are always free to present the limitations of their condition. They are always free to express their perceived difficulties in terms of carrying out suggestions. Naturally, in presenting perceived limitations, disciples are faced with the reality of their conditioning.

———— · ————

One is not necessarily trapped by vajra command – because one can always describe the nature of one's inability to follow through with a suggestion. One has to have sufficient integrity however, to know that one is not merely following the desire to sink into 'marshmallow practice'. The definition of 'marshmallow practice' is the cringing, squirming, whingeing cry of *"I can't do it!"* when all that is expected is that one tries.

The seventh of January

Authentic Art is always authentically religious – even though it might not resemble any existing religion.

———— · ————

Authentic Art is not 'the shock of the new' nor is it something that has never been seen before. Authentic Art could be recently composed Baroque music – or a recently written play in iambic pentameter.

———— · ————

Authentic Art is uplifting – but not in the trite sense of the average happiness that alternates with despondency. One can be uplifted both by laughter and tears – by astonishment and serene recognition of that which has never changed.

———— · ————

There are times when movements occur in the Arts – this is natural because of interconnectedness. When this gives rise to legislated stylistics however – authentic Art declines. Art needs to be free of the restraints of fashion or it becomes little more than gimmickry.

———— · ————

The Arts can be social or political statement – but that does not make social or political statement Art. Artists cannot be wedded to social or political statements – or they are no more than unqualified sociologists and politicians.

———— · ————

Authentic Art relies far less on the intellect than on the other sense fields. Even literature and poetry need to transcend linear rationality to some degree. The place of Mind in the Arts is to provide the empty space from which the Arts arise.

The eighth of January

Those who require overt reference points to feel secure, experience the most initial discomfort with shi-nè – but once that discomfort dissolves, they are able to progress more rapidly than those who never experienced discomfort.

———— · ————

We speak of reference points as if they existed. The reality is that they have no existence other than in the imagination. It is the way that one attempts to appropriate phenomena which creates the illusion that reference points exist.

———— · ————

When we say that reference points do not exist – we do not mean that we can function without them. Refence points are valuable in terms of negotiating and navigating phenomenal reality – but we need to bear in mind that they are merely expeditious measures. They exist only in the moment.

———— · ————

Those who require overt reference points find practice easier at a later stage – but their problems begin almost as soon as they sit down. Those who have less need of overt reference points find sitting easier in the beginning – but they tend to run into more problems with subtle clinging at a later point. There is somehow, poetry in that reversal.

———— · ————

It is fashionable to be cynical. It is sometimes fashionable to be naïve. It is not fashionable to sporadically occupy either camp. Neither, however, should be taken as *reference points for one's identity*. If one wishes to impress people with one's intellect one opts for cynicism. If one wishes to impress people with one's spirituality one opts for naïveté. If one has no desire to impress anyone, one opts for *treating both imposters just the same*.

The ninth of January

In 1971, Kyabjé Düd'jom Rinpoche Jig'drèl Yeshé Dorje looked at me—or through me—and said *"O yah – I see one White Khandro. You are seeing since young child."* Time and space simultaneously exploded and imploded. These are the words that made sense of nineteen years of bewilderment.

———— · ————

Kyabjé Künzang Dorje Rinpoche looked at the photograph. It was a hand-coloured monochrome picture taken in Thimphu, Bhutan in the 1940s. The image was of a Lama in a green chuba. The Lama was an albino. Künzang Dorje Rinpoche said *"This is Aro Yeshé."* It was a matter-of-fact statement that transcended time and space.

———— · ————

'Khordong gTérchen Tulku Chhi'mèd Rig'dzin Rinpoche was chanting with his students in Geneva, Switzerland – in the Chapel en Bois. He paused for a moment and said *"When I was Khalden Lingpa you were 'a-Shül Pema Legden – my thangka painter. You left much work unfinished when you ran away from 'Khordong with that young khandro."* He then continued chanting.

———— · ————

Time telescopes in the context of the Nyingma Lineage. Khar-trül Wangchuk Rig'dzin Rinpoche is the incarnation of Kharchen Palgyi Wangchuk – one of the twenty-five disciples of Guru Rinpoche. Knowing this is inspiring. When he told us that he remembered us from that time as Mélong gZa' Rinchen Tso and Aro gZa Druk-tsal Sheldrakma, time dissolved. It went beyond inspiration in being utterly ordinary.

The tenth of January

Study is necessary. The brain is like any muscle or organ – if you don't use it, you lose it. Vajrayana is not a Hollywood setting for 'The Night of the Living Brain-Dead'.

_____ · _____

We study because both practice and study are advocated in all Buddhist schools. There is no school of Buddhism that does not advocate study. It occurs to us that we may have over-emphasised the idea of 'intellectualism as a disease' – because complacent illiteracy is hardly admirable.

_____ · _____

We are not an academic tradition – but we still need to give time to establishing a good knowledge base. There seem to be arguments as to which is superior – the intellectual approach or the experiential approach. Those who gravitate toward either approach seem to need to disparage each other. This is entirely unnecessary and entirely foolish.

_____ · _____

Intellectual imperialism can cripple Buddhism. It can convert it into an academic museum of cerebral contortionism and erudite verbiage. If you do not study however, then it will be impossible to delve deeper into what is available within the tradition. It will be impossible to ask questions about how practice exists in terms of experiences identified within the structure of the six Tantras. It will be impossible to ask questions about the structure of the inner Tantras in terms of the full spectrum of what is available. It will be impossible to develop an understanding of the tradition which will enable full participation in the transformative quality of belonging to a lineage.

The eleventh of January

Engage with the energy of the sense fields. Become authentically involved with the senses. Being alive is being surrounded by colour, sound, fragrance, and texture.

———— · ————

The senses can be explored and enjoyed. *Enjoyment* has breadth of meaning beyond pedestrian pleasure. It is the enjoyment an artist would possess in noticing aspects of the world. Noticing a texture. Noticing disparity – and what arises from that. Enjoyment is innate creativity of being alive.

———— · ————

Everyone is an artist, and so anyone can invest in the Art of how they see – how they hear, fragranciate[5], taste, touch, and ideate. There is always enjoyment to be found in everything – and, whilst finding such pleasure, one can extend it to others. One can bring cheer to others through one's appreciation and innate cheer. That is always there.

———— · ————

The eyes that see are not separate from what is seen. No separation exists between seer and seen – yet multiplicity remains. Buddhist nonduality is not monist. Everything is empty – yet multiplicity manifests. My emptiness and Chögyam's emptiness – are not different. They are the same emptiness – but different forms are shown. Emptiness is emptiness. If there is more than one emptiness; this is not emptiness. Form arises from emptiness and every form is different. Emptiness and form are not divided – but this does not mean 'everything is one'.
Kyabjé Düd'jom Rinpoche Jig'drèl Yeshé Dorje

5   Olfactory sensing.

The twelfth of January

Not following fashion does not have to mean the rejection of everything that is fashionable. It means being free to make choices based on individual perception. If one authentically appreciates something within the realm of fashion – one is not a follower of fashion. If one rejects everything that is fashionable – one simply follows the fashion of rejecting fashion.

———— · ————

There was a time when many people concluded a correspondence: *Yours in the Dharma*. I considered it for a while – but decided to continue writing *Yours Sincerely*. I did not feel it would be *sincere* to pretend I was a Buddhist – when I was only trying hard to be a Buddhist. The other issue, of course, was that it seemed strange to fall in with fashion, especially when the linguistics were so peculiar.

———— · ————

People imagine that fashion applies mainly to clothing and other passing social phenomena – but almost everything is governed by fashion. There are fashions in diet, medicine, relationship, marriage, child rearing, politics, philosophy, psychology, religion – every area of human involvement can be governed by fashion. Vajrayanists are not followers of fashion – even when attempts are made to convert Vajrayana into a fashion.

———— · ————

When I was young it was fashionable to be a Marxist. There *were* some things that I liked about Marxism – but I never bought the package. I never believed it was 'the answer'. I believed that the closest thing to 'the answer' was kindness – and that the further one moved from kindness, the less it looked like 'the answer'. I believed there would be no 'answer' to the social dilemmas of being human as long as human beings remain dualised. Due to this, I would only ever admit to being a Groucho Marxist.

The thirteenth of January

The Lama's anger is a flash in time and space. Then it vaporises into vacuity. There is no escalation. There is no residue. It is merely the moment.

———— · ————

If Lamas never reflected voracity, irritability, desire, suspicion, or remoteness – their students would never witness the possibility of their own potential for realisation.

———— · ————

Lamas, as vajra masters, display the entire range of emotions. If they did *not* do so – they could *not* teach transformation. Lamas, as vajra masters, are *not* conditioned by the emotions they display. If they were – they could *not* teach transformation.

———— · ————

Conspiracy theories are an example of the propensity to make duality more complicated than it has to be. It doesn't seem to be enough that circumstances are bad – there has to be some devious, powerful group involved in making it bad. Conspiracy theorists are avid in their search for someone to blame for whatever the current bad situation happens to be.

———— · ————

The Lama's displays are not entirely different from those of actors. There is however, a crucial difference. A Lama's anger is more dramatic than an actor's anger – but there is no sense in which it is theatrical. The Lama's anger is not *personal* as it would be if experienced from a fellow human being – even though it is personally felt. The Lama's anger has a definitive purpose and lasts only as long as absolutely necessary.

The fourteenth of January

Because words change in meaning, nuance, implication, inference, insinuation, and connotation – Dharma needs to be continually re-expressed.

———— · ————

Dharma never ceases to grow. Wherever there is misunderstanding, Dharma develops to address the new forms which misunderstanding takes.

———— · ————

Dharma continues to be re-expressed, in forms of language that people understand. Dharma is continually re-expressed in terms of how it can best be incorporated into life.

———— · ————

There are no fixed Dharma linguistics – or one book that contains Dharma. If Buddhists were required to swear on Buddhist bibles in courts of law – what would need to be sworn upon would take up the entire courtroom.

———— · ————

The expression of Dharma—*how a teaching is given*—is based on understanding. Expression is based on how people understand. Expression is based on their vocabulary – what words mean in terms of connotations, implications, colour, and texture. This is important to how Lamas work with people.

———— · ————

Vajrayana is indestructible – but those who approach it frivolously are highly destructible. We are not destructible in terms of being destroyed as beings – but the possibility of Vajrayana can be destroyed. We can cut ourselves off from Vajrayana by destroying the vitality of the connection. What is meaningful can become meaningless if we feed our dualistic decadence and convert Dharma into a debauched dalliance.

The fifteenth of January

The *clothing* of vows is only complex if we become estranged from compassionate culture – through taking refuge in self-oriented dementia.

————— · —————

The dance costume of Vajrayana is demanding in terms of personal responsibility, integrity, and honour. One can don the costume and enter the dance – but to sustain the dance throughout one's life requires a degree of familiarity with the pattern of motivation. Life resembles dance – and a piece of advice which Trungpa Rinpoche gave was to 'dance with the situation'.

————— · —————

To wear costume as if it were *natural to wear it* is a matter of acclimatising – and acclimatisation is not merely a matter of duration. One has to wear the meaning and lead the life. This applies to evening tails as much as it does to Vajrayana robes. This, of course, is yet subtler with the clothing of view – the way one comprehends reality.

————— · —————

If one is born into the culture of Vajrayana, the life with which one is clothed is relatively simple. If one is not born into the culture of Vajrayana, the clothing of the religion can become complicated through convoluted ideas of personal identity. Some address this by becoming Vajrayana reenactors and others address it by rejecting Vajrayana. This problem can really only be overcome by falling in love with Vajrayana – in the way that people of different ethnic groups can fall in love with each other.

The sixteenth of January

If you rely on the absence of form: insubstantiality, impermanence, lack of discrete functioning, discontinuity, and lack of definition (or continuous redefinition) then you have a far more reliable situation.

———— · ————

The elements can be referentially appropriated as substantiality, perpetuity, distinctness, correlation, and characterisation. These appropriations will substantiate us for limited periods – but they are unstable and unreliable beyond the moment.

———— · ————

Happiness is a matter of finding security in insecurity. This is because whatever security occurs in life, is temporary. If you can find security in the temporary nature of phenomena, then that makes you permanently secure. That's known as paradox. It's the logic of Vajrayana.

———— · ————

Earth, water, fire, air, and space are reflected in solidity, permanence, separateness, continuity, and definition. These reflections of reality will appear to corroborate one's existence – but only on a temporary basis. Because of this one has to play hopscotch with them, in order to feel real.

———— · ————

We're always betrayed by the form aspects of the elements – because they keep disappearing. We are only betrayed however, because we expect the elements to perform impossible functions. It's as if they occasionally provided financial assistance. That's all well and good – but you can't rely on it. No one is going to bail you out for the rest of your life.

The seventeenth of January

It's a simple choice for any Vajrayanist: you can either become star craving mad or stark raving mad.

———— · ————

The most disturbing aspect of society is that it is relatively tolerant of mild varieties of insanity. There tend to be few definite consequences until one has drifted too far.

———— · ————

Reality does not depend or rely on our acceptance of reality. Reality is not comforted by our approval of reality. Reality has no interest in our personal preferences. That being said, reality is highly supportive to realists.

———— · ————

When you begin to veto reality—in terms of its acceptability—you lay the foundations for what will eventually become your personal private mental hospital. That might not be seem so terrible – but then you would place yourself in the position of having to co-opt friends and relatives as nursing staff.

———— · ————

Whatever is accepted as normal becomes normal. Once any form of behaviour becomes normal, it becomes possible to deviate from that normality into more aberrant behaviour – which then becomes normal. This is healthy for the nascent Mahasiddha – but pathological in almost all others.

The eighteenth of January

In terms of Drala, everything has history and connections. The longer the history the more connections there are. These connections create a fantastically rich texture – a consummately emanating texture. One can tell it when one touches objects, when one sees objects, when one hears sounds. One becomes aware that there's an inherent communication taking place.

———— · ————

With Drala, there's continual communication taking place. One is part of that communication without necessarily making any determined decisive effort to that end. It's more that one becomes sensitive to the nature of this communication in and from objects – in and from scenes and scenarios. One becomes sensitive to pools of time.

———— · ————

The meaning of Drala for farmers, chefs, and artisans in all areas of life – is that we value our tools and implements. That our early 20th century kitchen knives have history, is important. We are connected with that history and to the many people who may have used these knives. The fact that they have all been owned by other people—and that they have all come together at Drala Jong[6]—has its own extremely subtle self-existent significance. These knives also have a future at sGra bLa lJongs – and that will develop in terms of the place and the people who use these knives.

---

6   (*sGra bLa lJongs* /སྒྲ་བླ་ལྗོངས་) – Sparkling Meadow of Primal Iridescence, the Aro gTér retreat centre in Wales, https://www.drala-jong.org/

The nineteenth of January

Authentic power has little to do with *power to* – but rather, *power not to.*

——— · ———

Power is the ability to be significant in one's insignificance and insignificant in one's significance.

——— · ———

Power is the recognition that fear is a sensation which can be greeted with a degree of humour.

——— · ———

Power is allowing the patterning of society to blow through the open window of one's identity.

——— · ———

Power is not a question of developing siddhis or supernormal abilities. Power is a question of being prepared to die in the next moment.

——— · ———

Power is being unafraid of looking like an idiot – of not being personally concerned with what people make of one's innocuously eccentric existence.

——— · ———

Power is not a question of being physically, intellectually, or emotionally strong – but of being open to annihilation. Everything has to matter and not matter – at the same time.

——— · ———

Power is not necessarily concerned with having great capacities – but knowing the limits of one's capacities and being willing to go to the edge.

The twentieth of January

The lower the yana[7], the higher the throne.

———— · ————

Dzogchen is not divided from the quotidian round. Dzogchen teaching is not divided from the flow of ordinary conversation. Dzogchen transmission could take any form.

———— · ————

Dzogchen does not divide sacred and secular. Dzogchen does not segregate spiritual and materialistic. Dzogchen does not separate profound and mundane. Dzogchen does not distinguish rare and commonplace. Dzogchen simply asks *'Look—see—what is the same?'*

———— · ————

In the lower tantras, teaching is formal and far from discursive. With Dzogchen however, the student and Lamas could simply be conversing. There would be no ostensible difference between them – other than the point at which transmission occurs. This might sound ideal – but one would have to be prepared for transmission in every moment.

———— · ————

In terms of Dzogchen the Lama could be anyone at any moment – engaged in any activity. The Lama could be dressed in any style of clothing. The Lama's speech could be refined or vulgar. The Lama's mind could appear concentrated or distorted. It is purposeless to approach Dzogchen as if it could be codified in terms of human appearance.

7   Skt. – Buddhist vehicle; *(theg pa /* ཐེག་པ་*)*

The twenty-first of January

Birth and death are the creative play of existence. They move within the womb of Space. Waking and falling asleep are the mirror image of birth and death.

———— · ————

The play of experience which arises in a mirror is the key to understanding the nature of illusion and reality. Just as waking and sleeping can be a seamless flow of awareness – so can birth and death.

———— · ————

Birth and death are Art – the creative play of existence in which somethingness and nothingness appear to tickle each other.

———— · ————

Birth and death are the nature of every situation. Whatever else we imagine is taking place is simply one of many sub-plots.

———— · ————

Living and dying are not a polarity. Dying is an aspect of living just as birth is an aspect of living. Living is the continuous alternative of birth and death.

———— · ————

To become a child, the infant has to die. To become an adolescent, the child has to die. To become an adult the adolescent has to die. Simultaneously, the infant, child, and adolescent have to become facets of the adult array of possibilities – or the adult will grow elderly through the absence of creative play. We all have to grow old but we do not have to become elderly.

The twenty-second of January

Only through direct experience can we begin to perceive our world differently.

———— · ————

Philosophical speculation and intellectual conjecture which are not experienced directly, will remain abstractions.

———— · ————

Whatever the marvellous idea, if it cannot be incorporated as a fundamental perception of the world – it will gradually cease to have value.

———— · ————

The experience of meditation practice is essential as a means of realising the view. It is only within the development of the meditational experience that we become transparent to ourselves. When we become transparent to ourselves, we can witness the mechanics of stylised perception – and only then can we free ourselves from restriction.

———— · ————

Direct experience is simply the abandonment of filters and compulsive systems of classification. It's all very well to wander through a garden and say *'That's Abelia Pieris, Malus, Gypsophila Kolkwitzia amabilis, Epimedium, Campanula, Arcostaphylos uva-ursi, and Dendranthemum.'* These flower names have value in certain contexts. To know them, however: one also has to be able to see them simply – and inhale their fragrance simply; without conceptual interference.

The twenty-third of January

The good part of following fashion is that it is always possible to laugh at what you once used to wear. If you look back and find your appearance risible however – but cannot laugh at yourself, then there is nothing to be gained from fashion.

———— · ————

There is a subtle difference between emulation and following fashion. Emulation is a sign of genuine appreciation that is free of considerations of status, rank, prestige, importance, eminence, prominence – or fear of ridicule, mockery, scorn, derision, disdain, disparagement, or snobbery. Following fashion is prone to everything previously listed.

———— · ————

The Western Buddhist fashion was once to wear a teng-ar[8] around one's neck. Then it came to be considered gauche. Then the fashion was to become a monk or nun. Now the fashion seems to be to wear a striped yogic shawl sans white robes and uncut hair. First these shawls were difficult to obtain – but now they're available online. We're looking forward to the day when it becomes fashionable to be kind and generous.

———— · ————

When we commenced teaching Vajrayana in the West, Western people imagined that we were untraditional. They imagined we were popularists. However, over the years—incrementally—we have come to be viewed as conservative traditionalists. This is amusing because we have not changed. Everything changes with fashion – apart from the fashion for the necessity of fashions. Maybe—given time—we will be seen as fundamentalist bigots.

---

8 (phreng ba / འཕྲེང་བ་ / bGrang 'phreng / བགྲང་འཕྲེང་ / mala) – Vajrayana 'rosary' or mantra beads.

The twenty-fourth of January

Practice is a pain in the anatman – the inauthentic anatomy of body, speech, and mind.

———— · ————

Practice is frustration. One has to have something greater than oneself in order to keep going through frustration. There has to be an energy that is not primarily self-orientated, self-validating, or self-referencing.

———— · ————

If one is not a practitioner, life is difficult because is outside one's control. If one becomes a practitioner, life is difficult because it is within one's control – but one is aware that one fails to control it. If one gains accomplishment as a practitioner, life is difficult because the final goal is just out of reach. If one attains liberation, life is difficult because it is so sad to witness the difficulties of others and to fail so often in one's attempts to help them. In view of all this difficulty, it's a good idea to have a sense of humour.

———— · ————

Sometimes student couples come to us with their relationship problems. They tell us they want to work on their relationship. We tend to say *"Yes, you—can—work on your relationship – but only as long as you have the energy for it. That is to say: as long as you still love each other. If you don't still love each – how can you resolve your differences? How can you give up territory? How can you be generous with each other – when there is no love to promote selflessness?"* The same applies to Vajrayana practice. To be a Vajrayanist one has to have energy that exists apart from one's inner processes. If one merely deifies one's inner processes, one fails even to be a solitary realiser. One merely becomes an ineffectual, inefficient, incompetent, narcissist.

The twenty-fifth of January

If you actually hear the teachings – they are shocking. Shockingly wonderful and shockingly normal.

———— · ————

Vajrayana simply is as it is. If one allows it, it cuts through to the heart of reality. That could be shocking.

———— · ————

In terms of Dzogchen – the teaching is the central core of existence. The only people who are not fabulously shocked by Dzogchen are those who have already recognised Dzogchen – or those who have no interest in Dzogchen.

———— · ————

Yidams are shocking – shocking possibilities. Arising as the yidam is the utter quintessence of thespianism. Being able to act the part of who you are—at the same time as being superbly serene, sensationally seductive, or searingly savage—is conceptually impossible. Being able to release the tight grip on conceptuality is therefore a jolly good idea.

———— · ————

One can be shocked by almost anything that deviates from the norm – if one is addicted to unalterable conventions. There were times when certain forms of clothing were thought to undermine morality – such as women wearing trousers. It is probably still a cause of anxiety for men to wear skirts, unless the skirts are Scottish kilts – and then, somehow, they are perfectly acceptable. It is useful to examine these causes of outrage and question why one should accept any of them.

The twenty-sixth of January

'khorwa[9] never *will* function – *no matter* what *we do*. The knowledge that 'khorwa is a hoax, is provided by all lineages and the traditions of realisation. They all offer the means of living in the immediacy of the sparkling moment.

——— · ———

A hoax has to be believable – even if it is preposterous. Preposterous hoaxes work because they pretend to offer something. 'khorwa pretends to offer substantiality through the acquisition of physical, intellectual, and emotional territory. 'khorwa pretends to offer effective aggression through the vanquishment of contestants, contenders, competitors, challengers, rivals, and enemies. 'khorwa pretends to offer satisfaction, fulfilment, gratification, and pleasure through the consumption of physical, intellectual, and emotional foci of delight. 'khorwa pretends to offer security and invulnerability through the acquisition of physical, intellectual, and emotional defences, armour, and fortifications. 'khorwa pretends to offer experiential immunity from failure through becoming physically, intellectually, and emotionally inert and insensate. It would seem prudent to be sceptical of such dubious offers.

——— · ———

Everything becomes chö[10] – in the real meaning of the word: *as it is.* This does not mean that we abandon responsibility in our jobs, families, and friendships – but we have to abandon hope of remaining 'part-time Vajrayanists'. This could either be seen as a fearful or fearless step to take. It could be seen as requiring prodigious confidence. This could cause an enormous panic. It could be a statement of hope and utter futility. However – it could also be the recognition of the hoax. The hoax is the idea that 'khorwa is functional.

---

9 *('khor ba / འཁོར་བ་ / samsara)* – the self-defeating cyclic nature of duality.

10 *(chos / ཆོས་ / Dharma)* – as it is.

The twenty-seventh of January

Empowerment[11] is to be gutted like a fish, refurbished with a diamond heart – and set free to swim in the clear stream of lineage.

——— · ———

Empowerment is to be spontaneously immersed in a blazing world of light-play for fractions of a second; or for an eternity.

——— · ———

To receive empowerment is to be struck by lightning in the gentlest possible manner. To be burnt—by searing kindness—into nothing other than what is naturally there.

——— · ———

Empowerment—in essence—is not merely a Vajrayana ritual – a cultural form that will vanish in time. Empowerment is a 'teasing apart' of the *dualistically fixed quality of existence.*

——— · ———

Empowerment is to be perceptually dismembered – and sewn together again with the fabulous threads of commitment. It is to wake up—softly startled—at one vivid moment in time. It is to realise that one has slept – and that suddenly one is both older than the Earth and younger than it is possible to conceive.

——— · ———

With empowerment, the sense fields dissolve into each other. One enters the reality sphere of the Lama. In that dissolution of conventional reality – the power of visionary integration can be so clear one experiences strong sensory shimmering sometimes. Some people faint. The word hallucination might be employed – but this would be a mistaken rationalisation. Both worlds exist at once.

11 *dBang* / དབང་ / *abhisheka* – empowerment through symbol.

The twenty-eighth of January

The *Art that is life* requires enthusiastic investment – if one is to witness authentic sentience in the mirror of creative effulgence.

―――― · ――――

In terms of the *Art that is life, the unique* and *the undifferentiated* compose ephemeral cameos of character – who experience themselves in kaleidoscopic scenarios of life: the charismatic catherine-wheel of birth and death.

―――― · ――――

The *Art that is life* requires the recognition that *personality* is individuated space – within space. Every individuated sentient space allows the birth of the spaces of the five elements. The play of the five elements is a continual performance.

―――― · ――――

Every moment of life is spontaneous choreography. The *stage of life experience* is designed moment by moment by the extemporaneous thespians who move in from the wings – having performed elsewhere in a hall of mirrors where elsewhere is everywhere. There is endless reflection in the mirror of existence. Each reflection is the same – yet each reflection is unique. That is *the Art that is life.*

―――― · ――――

Every point-instant in which the senses engage is Art. There is nothing other than the effulgence of creativity. Each tactile refinement. Each gustatory subtlety; each fragrant distinction; each auditory gradation; each visual trace; each ideational indication – is, in itself, *the Art that is life.*

The twenty-ninth of January

Language ought to communicate meaning – but it is mainly used for the governance of societal herd-conformity.

———— · ————

Cliches are not necessarily bad – but one ought to be aware when one is using them. As a Vajrayana practitioner one ought to use language with care and attention.

———— · ————

Dranpa[12] means *bare attention*. It can also be translated as 'mindfulness'—but mindfulness seems to mean a business syndicate —so *bare attention* is a preferable translation.

———— · ————

When it can take as long to spell out an acronym or letterisation in speech – there is more dignity in using the words the initials represent. A Vajrayana practitioner needs to communicate with dignity – because Mind, Speech, and Body need to be the focus of practice in every arena of life.

———— · ————

Speaking of 'the cushion' when referring to meditation – is indicative of a hackneyed understanding. It is true that Vajrayana can be experienced in twilight language[13] – but twilight language is poetic. 'The cushion' is clichéd, overused, trite, and banal. This and other such trivialisations are not the modern-day equivalent of twilight language. This lack of daylight is merely *'setting sun mentality'* [14].

---

12 *dran pa* / དྲན་པ་ / *smriti*

13 Twilight language (gong-pa'i kèd / *dGongs pa'i sKad* / དགོངས་པའི་སྐད་ / *sandhi bhasa* / *samdhya bhasa*)

14 The 'setting sun mentality' is Chögyam Trungpa Rinpoche's coinage: *"The setting sun is the notion of eternal depression."*

56

The thirtieth of January

When performing gar'cham[15], one moves outside of the tired self-protective rationale into a frame of mind in which dualistic contrivances and excuses are cut away by the enacting of precise movements.

———— · ————

To dance with situations is to relate to situations as one's dance partner. There is both freedom and restriction according to the nature of the dance.

———— · ————

Skilled dance partners do not *dance* each other – there is no domination involved. Dancing with life circumstances can be just like this – whether the nature of the dance is peaceful, joyous, or wrathful.

———— · ————

The living situation is dance – relating through the body in physical situations. Errors provide blunt messages. Knee-jerk responses cause pain. The message is direct if one has direct contact with the living energy of the situation – rather than strategising in attempts to reshuffle the deck. Taking direct messages from life provides innate suggestions and life becomes musical. One can then discover that one can dance with life. One does not need to thrash and injure oneself like a trapped animal. Dancing with life is nonaggressive. This is Gyu rTsal[16] – dance, or dancing with the situation.

———— · ————

Dance is not limited to physical movement – but occurs within each sense field. Conversation is dance when those who converse are conservationists vis-à-vis the value each attribute to the expressions of each other. Dance occurs when talking and listening are symbiotic.

15 *gar 'cham* / གར་འཆམ) – Vajra dance.
16 *sGyu rTsal* / སྒྱུ་རྩལ / *lalita*

57

The thirty-first of January

If silent sitting[17] is separate from the flow of life – it is merely a hobby.

——— · ———

Silent sitting has to be incorporated into life. One actually has to realise that one is practising shi-nè or lha-tong all the time. This awareness has to be present. The more practice develops, the more life reminds us of Vajrayana. If this is not the case, then one is not practising.

——— · ———

Silent sitting is the basis of all practice. If silent sitting does not permeate the chanting of drüpthab, then little will be accomplished – because it will not actually be drüpthab.

——— · ———

Silent sitting should be a noisy affair – noisy because nothing is rejected. Every aspect of the world is there – we simply allow it to perform without attempting to appropriate parts of it to prove we exist.

——— · ———

The 'peace' of shi-nè has nothing to do with finding a peaceful place to sit. The peace of zhi gNas—peacefully remaining—is the non-manipulation of the senses. It is when the senses are not involved in self-validation.

——— · ———

Silent sitting should not become internalised. Silent sitting has nothing to do with going deeply into oneself. Silent sitting has nothing to do with cutting off from the world. Silent sitting has nothing to do with anything other than space – and space abounds limitlessly.

17 Silent sitting pertains to the practice of the Four Naljors (rNal 'byor bzhi / རྣལ་འབྱོར་བཞི) – shi ne (zhi gNas / ཞི་གནས), Lha-tong (lhag mThong / ལྷག་མཐོང), nyi'med (gNyis med / གཉིས་མེད), and lhundrüp (lhun grub / ལྷུན་གྲུབ).

Rigpa *(rig pa)* – intrinsic awareness

February

It is extremely hard to analyse Buddhist philosophy with ordinary consciousness.

HE Ögyen Dro'dül Thrin-lé Kunkyab Rinpoche
རྒྱལ་བ་ཨོ་རྒྱན་འགྲོ་འདུལ་ཕྲིན་ལས་ཀུན་སྐྱབས་རིན་པོ་ཆེ་

The knower knows the known.

Khar-trül Wangchuk Rig'dzin Rinpoche
མཁར་སྤྲུལ་དཔལ་གྱི་དབང་ཕྱུག་རིག་འཛིན་རིན་པོ་ཆེ།

The first of February

Shakyamuni Buddha turned the three cycles of Dharma. They are called cycles because they are whole and complete. The beginning, middle, and end, of each cycle is perfectly positioned at each point in the cycle. They have no beginning or end – just as reality has no beginning or end.

———— · ————

We speak of gTérma[1] cycles because gTér are self-contained. A complete gTérma contains all that it needs to contain to facilitate nondual liberation. There were many in the Himalayan countries who attained liberation solely though the practice of one gTérma.

———— · ————

Every yidam has a *dKyil'khor*.[2] *dKyil* means centre and *'khor* periphery or circumference. The dKyil'khor is the dimension of the yidam and contains every aspect of the yidam – including multiple forms of the yidam according to the five elements.

———— · ————

The circle or sphere is thus of great significance in Vajrayana. When it rains – each drop of water is a sphere. When air bubbles rise through water, they are spheres. The planet and the Solar system demonstrate circularity – and even when orbits are elliptical and waste droplets are distorted, these are merely circumstantial forces in play. The circle or sphere remains the primary shape.

1   *gTer ma* / གཏེར་མ་) – revealed or discovered treasure teaching or practice.
2   *dKyil 'khor* / དཀྱིལ་འཁོར་ / mandala.

The second of February

Someone once asked me to comment on 'the unconscious' and I replied *"I'm a-Freud I'm too Jung to know anything about that."*

———— · ————

'Pride' in terms of *self-obsession, arrogant aloofness, haughty superciliousness,* or *callous misanthropy* is complicated convoluted dishonesty. Simple self-respect on the other hand is quite straightforward

———— · ————

Pride and vanity are only pernicious when they are misanthropic and recidivistically injurious to the happiness or well-being of others.

———— · ————

If we can be ever-so-slightly amused by our pride and vanity – we can be playful. Playfulness—in terms of pride and vanity—leads to kindness towards others, as well as to a relaxed perspective with regard to ourselves.

———— · ————

When vanity is simple and light-hearted it is never too terrible. Everyone has vanity, to some degree, in terms of some quality or skill they possess – and as long as it is not 'mean minded' and unappreciative of others, there is no great harm in it.

———— · ————

There's a tendency to relate 'pride' with 'ego'. 'Ego' however, is Freud's word. It belongs with Freud – but if we consider it in Buddhist terms, we'd say that without a 'healthy ego'—in psychological terms—one cannot begin to undermine the fixation with self-referencing. Self-referencing is the 'me project'.

The third of February

To create a practice appurtenance is to change the world – if only fractionally.

———— · ————

Whatever is brought into being through craft is a miracle in its own right. This is the miracle of the three spheres of being[3]. First there is space. Then there is an idea. Then, through craft – something appears. That is miraculous.

———— · ————

Some see little value in Vajrayana craft work in comparison with meditation. We have noticed that those who take this view seem to gain little benefit from their 'meditation'. Those however, who take on craftwork and develop enthusiasm for it – seem to change and show the beneficial changes one would expect to see in terms of meditation.

———— · ————

To engage in Vajrayana crafts is to become partially immortal – even though one might be forgotten. The Vajrayana appurtenances one creates are handed down over the centuries. Objects made in the present will eventually become priceless antiques – if sufficient love and delight in perfection are involved.

———— · ————

Craft is authentic practice when it is successful. Success necessitates the development of integrity, honesty, scrupulousness, accuracy, authenticity, genuineness, and reverence. These qualities are as important to meditation as they are to craft.

---

3   Cho-ku, long-ku, trülku *(chos sKu / ཆོས་སྐུ / Longs sKu / ལོངས་སྐུ / sPrul sku / སྤྲུལ་སྐུ /* *dharmakaya, sambhogakaya, nirmanakaya)* – sphere of unconditioned potentiality (emptiness), sphere of realised visionary appearances (energy), sphere of realised manifestation (form).

The fourth of February

Self-liberation is simply what happens if one does nothing to prevent it. Doing nothing to prevent it, however, can be extremely difficult. It could take a second or a century.

———— · ————

Self-liberation is simultaneously possible and impossible. It cannot be impossible because nonduality is the natural state. It is not possible because duality is the prevalent condition.

———— · ————

Self-liberation is a snake uncoiling its own knot. What is the knot? The knot is the snake – but the snake is not the knot. What is it that's not the snake and not the knot?

———— · ————

The principle of Dzogchen is rangdröl[4]. Rang means *of-itself* and dröl means *liberation*. Rangdröl is mostly translated as self-liberation – but this is not liberation *of the self, for the self*, or *by the self*. There is no 'self' involved. Self-liberation means *of itself it liberates itself*.

———— · ————

The fruit of Sutra is emptiness, which is the base of Tantra. The fruit of Tantra is the nondual state, which is the base of Dzogchen. With Dzogchen, the base is the nondual state; the path is the nondual state; and, the fruit is the nondual state.

———— · ————

Base, path, and fruit are the same in Dzogchen. Everything is the nondual state – which means it can only be practised by a realised being. Fortunately, as we are all beginninglessly realised – we are all qualified. We're qualified because we're realised beings who don't understand that we're realised.

4 *rang grol* / རང་གྲོལ་

The fifth of February

The phrase *'licking honey from the razor's edge'* is used to describe the painful yet seductive aspect of duality – but the phrase is also employed playfully in terms of having an alarmingly vivid sense of presence.

———— · ————

If one rides a tiger – one cannot dismount. If one dismounted, one would be devoured. This is not a warning against riding tigers – but rather, a playful suggestion in terms of not breaking vows.

———— · ————

Tantra *is* playful – but it is seriously playful. Its playfulness is the searing kindness that is founded on awareness – when the awareness is that which is required to play on a girder, near the clouds, on the Manhattan skyline.

———— · ————

We *do* respect psychotherapy – but our respect is based on its 'relative value', *not* on its parity with Vajrayana. One has to learn to be playful in order see what is of value in terms of different circumstances, situations, and frames of mind.

———— · ————

One can play with fire—or firearms—but one requires presence and attention. Revolvers can be loaded with blanks or live ammunition – but one must be able to distinguish. If one forgets, there can be deadly consequences. If one cannot rely on awareness, then one needs to play in designated arenas where there are strict rules which must be followed. If one cannot abide by the rules – one should not play at all.

The sixth of February

If you cannot be kind, try being kind. Failing that, be kind.

———— · ————

Kindness is not always comfortable in life situations – but the alternative is far more painful.

———— · ————

Kindness is inherently joyful. If this is not obvious—if this is not self-evident—then further and more protracted silent sitting is necessary.

———— · ————

Kindness gives confidence to others. Kindness encourages self-respect and authentic dignity. Tantra is the hot blood of kindness. In essence – vajra commitment is the ultimate acknowledgement of that.

———— · ————

Kindness is inseparable from appreciation and enjoyment. If one likes people, one will be kind in relation to them. One cannot like people without appreciating them – without enjoying their presence.

———— · ————

Compassion—changchub sem—tends to be a term of a highfalutin[5] usage. We use the word kindness[6] – because it's blunt, sincere, honest, candid, frank, direct, unaffected, straightforward, and uncompromising. Grandparents understand the word – as would the next-door neighbour.

---

5   Pompous or pretentious in relation to speech, writing, or ideas.

6   ka trin thugje *(bKa' drin thugs rJe* / བཀའ་དྲིན་ཐུགས་རྗེ) – graceful kindness; nying-jé *(sNying rJe* / སྙིང་རྗེ) – heart mind, empathy and sympathy.

The seventh of February

The Lama is the *terrifyingly compassionate gamester* who reshuffles the deck of one's carefully arranged rationale.

———— · ————

The Lama is the ecstatically serene, placidly wild, and ferociously gentle electrician who short circuits the neat and tidy wiring of one's systems of self-referencing.

———— · ————

The Lama is the only person in one's life who cannot be manipulated. If one imagines one can manipulate one's Lama – one does not have a Lama.

———— · ————

The Lama is both a mother and a father – but not a parent. The Lama may listen to petty sorrows, disappointments, troubles, distresses, anguishes, agonies, miseries – but only in the context of teaching.

———— · ————

The Lama is the invasion of unpredictability one allows into one's life. Predictability is based on patterns – and patterns are based on conceptuality. Conceptuality is based on categorisation – and categorisation is based on maintaining duality.

———— · ————

The Lama is like the monarch of a country – yet both more intimate and more remote. Actually… the Lama is unlike anything that can be described. The Lama is beyond both simile and metaphor. This will only make sense if you are the student of a Lama.

The eighth of February

Birth and death are the creative play of existence. They move within the womb of Space. This is the nature of existence.

————— · —————

Death will always be a cause of fear until it is realised that death happens every second. When that is realised, it will also be realised that birth happens every second.

————— · —————

Death happens. It is not a terrible juncture. It simply happens. Birth simply happens. Birth and death take place magically, within every moment. When one discovers birth and death within every moment, it is no longer possible to live a pallid half-hearted life, haunted by morbid fears of visceral recycling.

————— · —————

Death could be described as emptiness; but when form arises from emptiness, that is the end of emptiness – until the form dies. To comprehend death – one has to experience the nonduality of emptiness and form. As long as they seem separate, birth and death will seem separate.

————— · —————

Life and death are not naturally twinned in Buddhist writings – because life is both birth and death. Life contains birth and death – and they alternate. Every day one passes into sleep. Every day one wakes up. The epochs of one's life arise and dissolve. Birth and death simply happen.

————— · —————

Death happens in forgetfulness. Death happens in absentmindedness, amnesia, vagueness, oblivion, blankness, and obscurity. There are constant reminders of death – unless one screens them out. One could drop the screening process – and the result would not really be so terrible.

The ninth of February

Vajrayana requires that we prioritise promise over process. To make promises malleable according to process is no way to be a mensch – and one needs to be a mensch to practice Vajrayana.

——— · ———

Before one can take damtsig[7]—Vajrayana vows—one needs to develop the ability to keep promises to oneself and to others. To be taken seriously as a human being, one has to be trustworthy, dependable, reliable, constant, faithful, and loyal. One has to be able to keep promises, or one is not a mensch – and not worthy of anyone's friendship. If one is not worthy of anyone's friendship, Vajrayana is out of the question.

——— · ———

Damtsig are the prime method of moving toward the goal. Once one knows where one is going and why one is going – it's best to be a mensch and desist from taking detours.

——— · ———

Vajrayana requires that one is not a 'sensitive insensitive' – being sensitive about yourself but insensitive towards others. The ability to apologise—and have it mean something—right then and there. Not to be emotionally reactive in terms of knee-jerk responses. To be able to keep promises, to keep commitments, and maintain discipline. To commence projects and complete them – rather than talk about it and never carry it out. To keep your house clean and wash: one has to be able to maintain adequate hygiene. Finally, one has to able to laugh at oneself. This describes what it means to be mensch and to be a Vajrayanist.

---

7   *dam tshig* / དམ་ཚིག

The tenth of February

A Lama is someone who has a Lama, belongs to a lineage – and is known by other Lamas. There may be exceptions to this rule – but we have no idea what they might be.

———— · ————

The Lama is both ultimately reliable and relatively unreliable. The Lama is ultimately reliable with respect to Vajrayana – and relatively unreliable with regard to supporting dualistic neuroses.

———— · ————

Dung-sé Thrin-lé Norbu Rinpoche said *"A three-year retreat does not make a Lama. The only thing that makes a Lama, is having students – so you cannot describe yourself as a Lama before there are students who see you are a Lama. Once you have students – no one can say you are not a Lama."* This is a valuable statement in these times.

———— · ————

Lamas are those whose devotion to *their own Lamas* is evident. If Lamas rarely refers to *their own Lamas* – then they are probably not what they present themselves as being. If you look around the shrineroom and see no picture of your Lama's own Tsawa'i Lama— either as a photograph, thangka, or statue—then there is good reason to have doubt about the authenticity of your Lama.

———— · ————

There are many descriptions of the qualifications of an authentic Lama – but not every Lama meets those qualifications. Some Himalayan Lamas had little formal education—some were illiterate —but what made them Lamas was their practice; their maintenance of vows; their devotion to Guru Rinpoche and Yeshé Tsogyel – and, the honour in which they hold their Tsawa'i Lamas.

The eleventh of February

Kyabjé Künzang Dorje Rinpoche wanted me to be natural – less shy and timid with him. The first time he found that I had some pride about being honourable, he was immensely happy. It happened when he challenged me with respect to giving my word. That was the only subject on which I would stand my ground and say *"When I give my word, I keep to my word – and nothing stops me other than death or serious illness."* Künzang Dorje Rinpoche had never seen me that serious before – and he was pleased by it. I think that was when our relationship began. It was my expression of honour, in giving my word.

———— · ————

An Irish mythic-raconteur[8] once explained the real meaning of boasting – as it was in Irish legends. When one boasted that one could do something – one was obliged to do it, or die in the attempt. It was a question of honour. There was no honour in dying. Those who fulfilled their boasts were heroic – those who died in the attempt were merely foolish. It struck me that this is the kind of realism that is required if one wishes to take Vajrayana vows.

———— · ————

Natural pride is a question of never doing the minimum; never leaving work to others; never avoiding responsibility; never making excuses; never forgetting obligations; never taking the easy option; never: rationalising, justifying, vindicating, oneself. One needs to be able to admit fault – and omit the extenuating circumstances which remove all fault. Natural pride means that one stops slipping and sliding like an eel in order to maintain an extremely shabby sense of self-respect.

8   Shivam O'Brien

72

The twelfth of February

Thought can no more examine *thought* than a knife can cut itself.

—— · ——

Thought itself is not a problem. Thought is not the deceiving enemy. I am the deceiving enemy – because I appropriate thought to validate my existence as solid, permanent, separate, continuous, and defined.

—— · ——

If being free of thought was realisation then the brain-dead would be Buddhas. It is being free of the dominion of 'thought' as the arbiter of reality that leads to realisation.

—— · ——

Ideation is one of the sense fields – and central to poetry. Ideation is both more and less than conceptuality. Conceptuality is a portal through which the open dimension of ideation can be pervaded by the other sense fields to create a sensory symphony.

—— · ——

Worry is wonderful. Worry is the perfect indication that one relies on thought when thought fails to accomplish what one wishes it to accomplish. If a tool reportedly failed to work it would be jettisoned. That is all there is to understand in respect of thought as the universal remedy.

—— · ——

There was a song by Jefferson Airplane that ran *'Sitting around thinking / Thinking and a thinking / And it ain't doing me no good. / Well I thunk and I thunk / Couldn't think of anything better / I tried and I tried / Trying ain't doing me no good.'*[9] It seems that other people have come to the same conclusion.

9   Joey Covington, Jefferson Airplane, Thunk, Bark, 1971

73

The thirteenth of February

The nondual stage is thespianism sans: rehearsal; sans script; sans narrative; sans intermission; sans remission; sans intimation of a final scene – and sans the requirement of playing a part.

———— · ————

The eight manifestations of Guru Rinpoche and eight manifestations of Yeshé Tsogyel are vajra actors in the play of nondual liberation. We could each discover ourselves as actors in that play or movie – because it is there, simply waiting. It is self-scripted. The set has already been created by the sense fields.

———— · ————

The Art of the stage or screen although sometimes contraindicated by Sutrayana – is, from the point of view of Vajrayana, possibly the greatest of the Arts in terms of divesting oneself of self-image. The best acting is performed by those who can disappear as themselves and arise as someone else.

———— · ————

The nondual theatrical stage requires our presenting spontaneously in an improvisational drama; on an intermittently vacillating set – whose stage props self-develop as the play proceeds. It requires interacting with a fluctuating cast who improvise their scripts and movements on stage, from unpredictable inspirations.

———— · ————

Theatre or film could be seen as escapism, diversion, or distraction – but for a Vajrayana practitioner, it is an opportunity to move between reality and illusion. If the actors are not really what they are representing themselves to be it is not enjoyable – but if the actors really are the characters they are acting; one has the chance to practise the illusory body, if only marginally. Then one can reflect on the emotions one may have felt in relation to events that were simply the play of light on a screen.

The fourteenth of February

Falling in love—if it is authentic love—betokens the eventual death of the 'me project'.

———— · ————

Romance is a remarkable challenge – but one needs to rise to the challenge by disappearing as a solid, permanent, separate, continuous, and defined entity.

———— · ————

Love is centreless dance: the spontaneous self-reflection of the interpenetrating-interengulfing quality of reality. Love is the poetic turbulence of each moment, in which mutual rhyming manifests without effort or contrivance.

———— · ————

Love is there when the artificial divisions dissolve into the iridescent spectrum of the beginningless nature of individuation. The love which radiates from the primordial state cannot help but sparkle through – no matter how insecure, frightened, isolated, anxious, or bewildered people become.

———— · ————

Falling in love is catching a glimpse of one's self-secret inner dPa'wo[10] or khandro[11] – the hidden male aspect of yoginis and the hidden female aspect of yogis. For Vajrayanists, falling in love is khandro dPa'wo reflection – and if one finds the presence of awareness in that refection, one discoverers rigpa.[12]

10 *dPa' bo* / དཔའ་བོ
11 *mKha' 'gro* / མཁའ་འགྲོ
12 *rig pa* / རིག་པ་

75

The fifteenth of February

One doesn't have to be humile to be unpretentious. Humility and hauteur are both affectations – and best forsaken. It is simpler to describe what one can do and what one cannot do – but only when asked.

———— · ————

The only area in which pretensions are valuable is comedy – where, if one is astute, one might reflect concerning the nature of any pretensions that may still linger in one's persona.

———— · ————

Silent sitting meditation—in terms of shi-nè—allows space to experience emptiness. There is something rather uncompromising about this. The intellect is out of its depth, and one is left either with the experience of emptiness – or without it. There are no half-measures and no pretences.

———— · ————

One could pretend to do or be many things – but one cannot pretend to practice shi-nè. The pretence would be so oppressively boring that one would give up. The alternative would be going to sleep without actually losing consciousness. Those who adopt this alternative find meditation relaxing and 'spiritual'.

———— · ————

One can pretend to be nonmaterialistic or renunciate. One can pretend to have no pride or vanity. One can pretend to be humble and self-effacing. One can pretend to have no 'ego'. One can pretend to have knowledge or wisdom. One can even pretend to be extraordinary or to have special powers. One cannot, however, pretend to be kind.

The sixteenth of February

Authentic individuality and nondual realisation are inseparable –
otherwise Buddhas would be identical and indistinguishable.

——— · ———

Becoming an authentic individual is a journey of discovery in which
one unlearns how to appreciate only those things on the socially
prescribed list – even of minority social sub-sets.

——— · ———

Authentic individuals might easily have no concept of their
individuality. This is largely because they see no advantage in
manipulating the idea of their individuality in terms of reference
points.

——— · ———

Outside the remit of the Five Precepts and the vows one has taken
– there is nothing that need govern one's choices, other than one's
Lama. One is therefore free to ignore socially sanctioned
regulations. It was once said that *blue and green should never be seen
unless there is something in between* – but this is no longer held to be
valid. Whatever the new aesthetic law may be – it too will be
overridden at some point; so, you are free to like what you like
merely because you like it. That is part of what makes you an
individual.

——— · ———

One cannot become an individual by seeking to be an individual –
by looking for alternative approaches, or by actively being different.
That just merely makes a person one of many almost identical
nonconformists. One cannot be a conformist or a nonconformist –
but one can be free to appreciate on the basis of the criteria that
continuously and spontaneously present themselves.

The seventeenth of February

Interdependence and *independence* are nondual. Independence is *emptiness* and interdependence is *form*.

——— · ———

Dad'dun[13]—devotion—tends to be confused with bhaktiyoga – but dad'dun has nothing to do with adoration, adulation, idolisation, or glorification. There is no romance in dad'dun even though, in some ways, one loves one's Lama. That love however is based on study and practice experience.

——— · ———

It requires there to be an 'atman'[14] to imagine one can be 'independent'. From the Buddhist point of view there is no 'atman' – no solid, permanent, separate, continuous, or defined entity. This is why Shakyamuni Buddha spoke of anatman[15]: the absence of atman. One can be *independent* in the moment however – but that moment is empty in the next moment. Because each moment becomes empty each moment there can be no *continuity of independence*. Independence can only exist in respect of interdependence. They are nondual.

——— · ———

Dad'dun must be based on clarity and insight. Love does arise through clarity and insight – but it cannot be fabricated from cloying emotionalism; gaga dependency; inane dreamy-eyed euphoria; asinine infantilist idolatry; sycophantic schmaltz-rapture; and, saccharine sentiments vis-à-vis surrender and submission. Dad'dun is as far removed from cultic surrender as children's toys are removed from the real objects they represent.

---

13   *dad 'dun* / དད་འདུན་ – devotion. Gü-pa kyèpa *(gus pa bsKyed pa* / གུས་པ་བསྐྱེད་པ་) – to inspire devotion.

14   dag *(bDag* / བདག་ / *atman)*

15   dagmé *(bDag 'med* / བདག་འམེད་ / *anatman)*

The eighteenth of February

Moderation is valuable as long as one does not resort to it *too* often. Once moderation becomes a habit – it loses its moderating value.

———— · ————

Nothing lasts for ever. That has two meanings. The first meaning is that *nothing*—nothingness—is *emptiness*. If *emptiness* had a 'beginning' or 'end' it would identifiable – and therefore it would be *form*. The second meaning is that no *thing* lasts forever. The phrase is delightful – if you don't think about it *too* much and ruin the simplicity of it.

———— · ————

'khorwa is unsatisfactory. It cannot be made to work because it is fundamentally faulty – but it doesn't have to be quite as bad as human being are capable of making it. However, as Khandro Déchen always says *"That is the nature of 'khorwa."* I always agree, of course – but I still wish that people would opt for the less horrific possibilities in terms of 'khorwa and not make it *too* horrible for themselves and those around them.

———— · ————

It's valuable to be sensitive – but not too sensitive for humour. It's valuable to be gentle – but not too gentle to be playful. It's valuable to be forgiving – but not so forgiving as to allow abuse. It's valuable to be tolerant – but not so tolerant as to support intolerance. It's valuable to be generous – but not so generous that it becomes too obvious. It's valuable to be open minded – but not so open minded that honour is compromised. It's valuable to be logical – but not so bound by logic that the irrational becomes unknown territory.

The nineteenth of February

Whilst we are enthusiastic about what modern science divulges; nondual realisation is not simply informational knowledge of the universe – no matter how amazing it is.

———— · ————

Nondual realisation is the direct experience of the essential nature of the universe – and without this direct experience, all one can have—in terms of science—are 'samplings' which are constrained by the limits of their particularity.

———— · ————

Whilst it is fascinating to chart the brain waves of meditators – one has to be aware that one is only looking at one consequence. To study brain waves in respect of meditation is rather like examining the fæces of someone who has eaten a meal. The fæces may reveal something about what has been eaten – but the fæces do not resemble the meal.

———— · ————

Because sem nyid[16]—*the nature of Mind*—is not 'the brain' the rhythms detected by an electroencephalogram are fairly meaningless in terms of meditation. A Dzogchen Lama's electroencephalogram result might well be indistinguishable from that of random members of the public – as long as they were of sound mind and not given to anxiety.

———— · ————

One of the most worthwhile findings of science is that there is far greater similarity between the brains of men and women than difference. This means that two men or two women could display greater differences than most men and women. From the Vajrayana perspective gender differences are largely due to societal conditioning and karmic patterning.

16 *sems nyid* / སེམས་ཉིད་

The twentieth of February

Boredom is a sign that: one is not alive to one's senses.

———— · ————

Boredom is being unable to find anything in one's situation that substantiates one's existence as one wishes it to be substantiated.

———— · ————

Boredom could be described as a repeating malfunction of the 'me project'.

———— · ————

Unless you're prepared to accept boredom, there is no future in shi-nè. Boredom is one of the defence mechanisms employed to maintain duality.

———— · ————

Boredom has to be a continuing creative project which has no goal. Strangely enough however, shi-nè is a key to understanding boredom – and, eventually, discovering what life is like without boredom.

———— · ————

Once you develop experience of shi-nè, boredom is no longer boredom – it becomes a rolling wave of energy. So, boredom marks the beginning of realisation. Without boredom there's no discovery.

———— · ————

Death is very sad. Death also very normal. Everyone born must die. Everyone who dies must be reborn. We are all dying. We all take rebirth, countless times. What is important is keeping awareness through bardos – and taking awareness into the next life.
Kyabjé Düd'jom Rinpoche Jig'drèl Yeshé Dorje

The twenty-first of February

The Lama is the living example that the actualisation of Vajrayana is possible – and that this actualisation is possible through the unique perceptual personality of each student.

———— · ————

The Lama has direct knowledge of the nature of Mind – and experiential comprehension of the distorted patterns that evolve to maintain the illusion of duality. Because the Lama has this faculty, direct apprehension of the student's perceptual personality is possible.

———— · ————

Every Vajrayana sangha has a certain personality. There are characteristics and qualities which are evident because they are different from one's own sangha. These sangha personalities are built by Lamas in conjunction with their students – they are mutually co-created. This is what is known as dKyil'khor.

———— · ————

The personality of each student is important – because each student contributes to the creative gestalt of the Lama's dKyil'khor. This contribution does not necessarily comprise only positive qualities. The students' neuroses are also valuable, if they are acknowledged. Knowing one has neuroses—and that every other student has acknowledged neuroses—there is nothing that is not workable. It is the unacknowledged neuroses that will destroy a sangha and the teaching of the Lama.

The twenty-second of February

An artist cannot fail as an Artist. One cannot fail as an artist unless one is slipshod. One cannot fail unless one becomes determinedly and deliberately clichéd. One cannot fail unless one falls prey to 'the shock of the new' – at the expense of what is personally valuable.

———— · ————

One only fails as an Artist if one ceases to create. Whether the world provides accolades or not – is irrelevant. Whether the world howls in execration; sniggers with derision, or yawns with undisguised ennui – is irrelevant. Wisdom eccentrics are subject to the same banality – as is any authentic individual.

———— · ————

As an Artist, I had the great good fortune to be born in Westphalia – after that, any idea of success was out of the question. Whatever the cardinal direction – failure was guaranteed. This has left me free to create without being encumbered by the need to achieve fame.

———— · ————

One may fail to earn a living as an Artist – but that doesn't mean that one fails as an Artist. As a painter, poet, author, sculptor, playwright, songwriter, cordon bleu chef, or sartorialist – one could simply continue. A sartorialist, for example, only has to dress in the morning. One may, of course, have to readjust one's tie or cravat every once in a while.

———— · ————

Bod Dylan said *'There's no success like failure and failure's no success at all.'* I wouldn't argue with that too vociferously – because the only failure is the refusal to try. An Artist has to keep trying. A Vajrayanist has to keep trying. One only fails through being indolent and Artists cannot be indolent. Indolence is the antithesis of Art and Vajrayana.

The twenty-third of February

The vajra master is the one who say *"Do this."* One does it. One understands. Some people need reasons for doing this or doing that – but if you're in a burning building and someone shouts *"Run the other way"* there may not be sufficient time to ask *"Why?"* Of course, one has to know that the person giving the instruction is not a sadistic homicidal psychopath.

———— · ————

The vajra master is a facilitator rather than an educator. The vajra master may supply information – but that does not define the rôle. The vajra master shows what the information actually means in terms of experience. The thousands of shapes that comprise the jigsaw puzzle of Vajrayana have to be arranged before the picture becomes apparent. Without the vajra master the pieces are always separate – and can only be collected.

———— · ————

Speaking of the vajra master in a religious context tends to sound mysterious - but we have a similar experience with a riding instructor. Unbeknownst to Melissa Troupe[17] – both Khandro Déchen and I decided to relate to her as our Vajra Master in terms of horse riding. Whatever she told us to do therefore, we did it. We did it, because we trusted her. We trusted her because we were aware of her high level of experience. She understood us well as riders.

---

17 Melissa Troupe was the riding instructor at Liege Manor Equestrian Centre, Bonvilston, Vale of Glamorgan, Wales, during the period Ngak'chang Rinpoche and Khandro Déchen were taking riding lessons.

The twenty-fourth of February

Shi-nè is the practice of letting go. Whatever arises, one abdicates involvement. When one finds oneself involved, one lets go of involvement. One just continues in that manner. It's simple.

———— · ————

With shi-nè it's important not to become goal oriented – because the desire to see result is self-defeating. It would be like using anxiety to force a state of calm.

———— · ————

Whatever mood it is in which one may be investing – it is always possible to stop investing in it. Just stop. Of course, you may start again – but then you just stop again. One can stop repeatedly.

———— · ————

With shi-nè, it's important not to indulge in feeling frustrated. Attempting to let go of thought has to be repeated, sometimes for years. However long it takes is however long it takes. It's preferable therefore, to have a sense of humour.

———— · ————

Someone once asked Ten'dzin Wang-gyal Rinpoche is there was an equivalent of the ten-step programme in Tibet, He replied *"In Tibet we have a one-step programme. You tell your Lama you have a drinking problem and your Lama says 'Stop drinking' – and that's the end of your drinking problem."* This is a delightful example of how vajra commitment cuts through the necessity for any kind of processing. It cuts through process. One lets go as one would let go of a plate left too long to warm in the oven.

The twenty-fifth of February

To say that Buddhism is not a religion, is to ignore that fact that it looks like a religion in almost every aspect apart from the belief in a *creator God*. How odd then, that many who are embarrassed to describe Buddhism as a religion are also embarrassed by its being atheistic. It reminds me of a piece, by William Ewer[18], *'How odd of God To choose the Jews'*, to which, Ogden Nash[19] is alleged to have responded *'Yet not so odd as those who choose the Jewish God, yet spurn the Jews.'* Leo Rosten[20] purportedly replied *'Not odd of God, The goyim*[21] *annoy 'im.'*

———— · ————

The major difference between a *religion* and a *way of life* is that one can belong to a religion – but no one has ever said *"I belong to a way of life."* It is the *belonging* that is important – because I can only belong to something that is larger than I am. I have no desire to be the most important element in 'my' universe. Who would want to live under such cramped conditions?

———— · ————

Some people like to opine that Buddhism is not a religion – but a way of life. This is because religion has come to have unfavourable implications. Every religion we have seen however, has looked like a way of life. Not all ways of life are wholesome, and if one found that most ways of life were unwholesome, one might be inclined to say Buddhism is not a way of life – it's a religion. We see no problem with Buddhism being described as a religion.

---

18 William Norman Ewer, British journalist, (1885–1976)

19 Frederic Ogden Nash, American poet, (1902–1971)

20 Leo Calvin Rosten, American humourist (1908–1997)

21 *Yiddish term for gentiles – sometimes pejorative. Ngak'chang Rinpoche has sometimes jested with reference to his four-volume work an odd boy—together with his enjoyment of Jewish culture and Hassidic clothing—that he should have named the quadrilogy an odd goy.*

The twenty-sixth of February

Empowerment consists of wang, lung, and tri:[22] empowerment through the enactment of vision – wang; transmission through the auspices of sound – lung; and, oral exposition of the method – tri. It's a natural procedure. If one meets a stranger, one initially appears in the sight of the stranger. One then introduces oneself by name. One then proceeds to provide details concerning one's location, occupation, and predispositions.

———— · ————

Empowerment is an introduction to the way the possible and the impossible reflect each other. Empowerment is an invitation to another dimension – but a dimension that is self-secret contained within the parameters of the utterly ordinary.

———— · ————

Empowerment is an inducement, provocation, incentive, incitement, enticement, and summons – but that could easily be missed, if one were not fully present and free of conceptual constructions. The more one understands Vajrayana symbolism, the more one understands *everyday life* as an empowerment. When that becomes apparent, one's life commences to glimmer with limitlessness.

———— · ————

Empowerment is a context in which Vajrayana speaks in twilight language. Twilight language is the bridge between the known and the unknown. It is poetic in the way that Vajrayana ritual is artistic. Every sense field is a conduit of realised communication.

---

22 *dBang* / དབང་ – empowerment through symbol; *lung* / ལུང་ – oral-aural transmission; *khri* / ཁྲི་ – oral-aural directive explanatory transmission.

87

The twenty-seventh of February

Art is an obligation to a sensory entity. This is even true of objects. What is a fountain pen without a writer?

———— · ————

Art bursts into being when one notices the communication taking places between: colours, shapes, textures, pitch, tonal variations, and rhythm – throughout the sense fields. Where one takes it, is called life—the *Life of an Artist*—which could also be called the beginning of Vajrayana.

———— · ————

Appreciation spawns creativity – because appreciation begets involvement. There's a communication that's constantly taking place — and that communication is necessarily developmental. A multiplicity of ideas emerge – and choices are made on the basis of how phenomena are juxtaposed. This could sound complex – but it is absolutely simple.

———— · ————

First there is space which is free of characterisation. This space however, is womblike – and so infinite appearances emerge as the natural energy of space. This energy then coalesces as the multiplicity of form manifestations. The energetic appearances include ideas – and these ideas conjure with the manifest dimension. That is what is known as Art. It is a natural process that occurs continuously.

———— · ————

Creativity becomes Art when one refuses to make compromises about the nature of creativity. Art is the refusal to accept the shade of colour available – when the colour in one's mind is different. That's where Art begins. As soon as appreciation leads us to make choices—and expend effort in the realisation of those choices— one begins to recognise oneself as an Artist.

The twenty-eighth of February

Self and *other* is the Sutrayana method vis-à-vis understanding *nonduality*. *Subject* and *object* is the Outer Tantric method vis-à-vis *nonduality*. *Existence* and *non-existence* is Inner Tantric method vis-à-vis *nonduality*. *Nonduality* is the is Dzogchen method vis-à-vis *nonduality*.

———— · ————

Language—although there are dictionaries—is not fixed. Even when meaning remains the same, the connotations shift. This is why we use the word *profferment* rather than *offering*; *wish path* rather than *prayer*; *Lama* rather than *guru*; *liberation* or *realisation* rather than *enlightenment*; *monastic* rather than *monk* or *nun*; and, *religion* rather than *spiritual path*. These words will probably also have to change in time – because what is important is conveying the meaning.

———— · ————

We use Tibetan rather than Sanskrit – *because* the Tibetan words are not as well known. This gives people a fresh opportunity to understand what the words mean. Word can too easily become jargon – or sounds that are used without any real understanding. What, for example, is a sentient being? We have met people who used the term but did not know what the word 'sentient' meant – and no one ever asks whether there are *non-sentient beings*.

———— · ————

The importance of learning ultimately applies to any skill area: knitting; sewing; gunsmithing; horse-riding; parachuting; welding, et cetera. Without technical language speech becomes convoluted. This is why we say *yeshé* rather than *nondual primordial awareness*. Without knowing the technical language of a subject one cannot ask questions or understand the structure of a subject.

The twenty-ninth of February – *in a Leap Year*

Thomas Gray opined that *'Since sorrow never comes too late, and happiness too swiftly flies. Thought would destroy their paradise. No more; where ignorance is bliss, 'tis folly to be wise.'*[23] According to Shakespeare however – it would be better to avoid being … *one that converses more with the buttock of the night than with the forehead of the morning.*[24] As the song goes *'Brush up your Shakespeare, Start quoting him now.'*[25]

———— · ————

The vision of Dzogchen sees reality as it actually is. Reality inseparable from the nature of Mind: the natural state, where there are no distinctions, demarcations, or discriminations. This awareness is rigpa: naked presence of awareness in each point-instant.
Kyabjé Düdjom Rinpoche Jig'drèl Yeshé Dorje

———— · ————

People attending Open Teaching Retreats often used to ask *"Why d'you have to use foreign words?"* to which we would reply *"You mean words like bandana, bangle, bungalow, cummerbund, dinghy, dungaree, gymkhana, jodhpurs, juggernaut, jungle, khaki, loot, pyjama, shampoo, toddy, typhoon, and veranda? These words—and a fair few more—come from India. The words: alcohol, alkaline, almanac, algebra, banana, candy, cipher, coffee, cotton, elixir, ghoul, magazine, mattress, nadir, orange, safari, soda, sofa, sugar, zenith, and zero – are all originally Arabic."* In time the Tibetan words which we employ will become just as familiar – and few will think them foreign. The words *Lama, Shangri-la, Sherpa,* and *yak* are already understood by most people. The Sanskrit words *Buddha, Dharma, karma, mantra, tantra,* and *raja* are also understood as if they were English – as are the names of many dishes at Indian and Chinese restaurants; not to forget the French *escargot* or Italian *pizza.*

23 From the 1742 poem 'Ode on a Distant Prospect of Eton College' by Thomas Gray.
24 William Shakespeare, *Coriolanus,* Act II, scene i, 1608
25 From Brush up your Shakespeare' in the musical *Kiss Me Kate* by Bella and Samuel Spewack with music and lyrics by Cole Porter.

Nang tong *(sNang sTong)* – form and emptiness

March

When one sows the seed of an apple, it gives just a fruit of the apple, no other fruits.

HE Ögyen Dro'dül Thrin-lé Kunkyab Rinpoche
རྒྱལ་བ་ཨོ་རྒྱན་འགྲོ་འདུལ་ཕྲིན་ལས་ཀུན་སྐྱབས་རིན་པོ་ཆེ

I am not here to reveal the faults of others. I am here to uncover my own faults.

Khar-trül Wangchuk Rig'dzin Rinpoche
མཁར་སྤྲུལ་དཔལ་གྱི་དབང་ཕྱུག་རིག་འཛིན་རིན་པོ་ཆེ།

The first of March

Vajra commitment means *willingness to enter the charismatic-chaos of nondual kindness*. This has no connection with becoming a cult guru; belonging to a cult; or becoming a cult victim.

———— · ————

To restrict the freedom of beings in order to enforce an artificial equality is to shrink the quality of life – to homogenise the enormous range of sentient potential to fall within legislated parameters. This is a particular brand of pseudo-democracy which lends itself to the evolution of politically correct despotism.

———— · ————

Vajrayana holds that everyone is equal in terms of their intrinsic vajra nature – and that all are equally worthy of compassion. Vajrayana however, does not hold that beings should be restricted— by the politically or spiritually correct—according to the lowest common denominator in terms of their varying degrees of experiential understanding.

———— · ————

Awareness-spells[1] are the natural resonance of awareness-beings. They are the method by which visionary symbols of innate nondual realisation *reverberatively communicate* the power of transformative capacity. This can be called *enchantment* – the method of *singing power into being*. This is the method by which one gives voice to the dynamic of what one actually is. One then vibrates in sympathy with primal creativity. The power of awareness-spell, is well known in many spiritual traditions. The power of the voice is a multi-levelled communication.

---

1 ngak *(sNgags / སྔགས་ / mantra)*

94

The second of March

We cannot express this awareness in words – and there is nothing with which to compare it, in terms of description. It is not the mundane condition of emotional turmoil and conflicted thoughts – but neither is it the emptiness that is the cessation known as nirvana. *Kyabjé Düd'jom Rinpoche Jig'drèl Yeshé Dorje*

———— · ————

Dzogchen is the ultimate teaching of Vajrayana in both Himalayan Buddhism and Bön. Those who attempt to appropriate it as a system that is separate from these religions is culpable of grave disservice to those who are gulled by this popularist stratagem.

———— · ————

When perceiving the mirror of reality, we have to blink the eyes— and the other senses—in order to maintain duality. Conceptuality is the sense that predominantly blinks in order to deliberately ignore what is there. This conceptual blinking is not haphazard however – as the mode of ignoring has to be systematic and purposeful. This particular 'skill' is the method of handling addiction to form as *the only possible focus of security*. This is the main means of recycling sentience within the circus of complicit confusion. Fortunately, the *mirror of existence and non-existence* is also there – reflecting the knowledge of nonduality.

———— · ————

The base from which we approach the nine yanas is that of beginningless liberation. From this perspective, narcissism is self-liberated in its arising. If one fails in allowing the self-liberation of whatever arises, one relies on the vajra master to *instantly correct* dualistic inertia, indolence, or entropy. This is why *hiding out* from the vajra master is not an option.

The third of March

Rigpa cannot be assembled, constructed, or developed. It cannot be interrupted, discontinued, or extinguished. One is never separate from rigpa – nor does dualistic derangement disturb the nondual state. *Kyabjé Düd'jom Rinpoche Jig'drèl Yeshé Dorje*

———— · ————

Those who are only interested in the most advanced teachings and practices are often those for whom they would be the least benefit. It is wonderful to be enthusiastic concerning amazing teachings. They are amazing – but it is important to have a sense of realism beyond the sensation of their being amazing.

———— · ————

In terms of the *Sutrayana primacy of emptiness* – personality and individuality are largely seen as the proclivity of dualistic delusion. Authentic personality and authentic individuality are therefore not ideas that occur within Sutrayana. In terms of Vajrayana however, *authentic personality* and *authentic individuality* should be prevalent. Be that as it may, Vajrayana is mainly presented in terms of visionary practices: the transformational theatre of the drüpthabs. Vajrayana *does* contain a wealth of psychology which relates to gender, the emotions, and to the nature of creativity – but it is implicit rather than explicit. It therefore requires extrapolation – and for that one requires the guidance of a vajra master.

———— · ————

Dzogchen is undivided from everyday life. Everyday life contains the exotic as much as the commonplace. What is regarded as commonplace is only relegated to the status of mundanity because of our failure to apprehend beauty or rarity where these qualities are not societally sanctioned. That a rose is beautiful – but a dandelion is not, is vapid from the perspective of Dzogchen.

The fourth of March

If the quotidian domain is perceived of as mundane, pedestrian, and unexceptional – it ignores the fact that Dzogchen integrates the nondual state with everyday life.

———— · ————

The world is fabulously variegated – and no valid reason exists in terms of Vajrayana, why a non-monastic practitioner should not explore the wealth of possible appearances and endeavours.

———— · ————

Dzogchen dissolves the distinction between sacred and profane; religious and secular; holy and blasphemous; sacrosanct and tainted; hallowed and worldly. Dzogchen has no interest in artificial divisions.

———— · ————

In the West we tend to venerate self-abnegation as definitively spiritual. This could be because moderate *inconspicuousness of mien* and *partially-ascetic neutral camouflage* reflects the anæmic dilution which has occurred in Western religious culture. Whatever the cause of this pallid pusillanimous puritanism – it is adversative to Vajrayana.

———— · ————

There is a tendency to venerate *that which one would not wish to impose upon oneself*. Glamour, panache, and flamboyance—on the other hand—are seen as spiritually antithetical. This is entirely irrational from the perspective of Vajrayana. One only has to look at the images of the Mahasiddhas of India and the Himalayan countries to realise that there are many possible nondual expressions of humanity.

The fifth of March

Ignorance—as a Buddhist term[2]—is misunderstood. It is not lack of knowledge[3] – but *ignor-ance*. *Ignor-ance* is *not wanting to know* – it is *ignoring*, which includes: *disregarding, overlooking, discounting, declining, rebuffing, rejecting, repulsing, spurning,* and *disallowing*.

———— · ————

As long as we cling to dualistic vision, we will always translate *not knowing* as 'confusion' – but not knowing is simply not knowing. It's an intangible space with endless possibilities.

———— · ————

Dislike of *not knowing* derives from anxiety in relation to vague definitions. There is an aversion to being *intangible in the space of unknowing*. Unknowing seems to foster insecurity – but insecurity is, in itself, a practice if we simply accept it. This is *the wisdom of insecurity*.

———— · ————

'Ignorance' in the sense of simply *not knowing*—and recognising the condition of *not knowing*—is an accomplishment. Ignorance in the sense of *ignor-ance*—of actively ignoring—manifests as myopic indifference and disinterest.

———— · ————

If one doesn't know—and *knows* one doesn't know—one can set about finding out. If one *doesn't know* that *one doesn't know* – how and where does one start? One has to be absolutely honest about how much one doesn't know. One requires a certain sense of humour about *the known* and *the unknown*.

---

2 kuntu mong *(kun tu rMongs /* ཀུན་ཏུ་རྨོངས་*)*

3 kuntag kyi marigpa *(kun brTags kyi ma rig pa /* ཀུན་ཏུ་བརྟགས་ཀྱི་མ་རིག་པ་*)*

The sixth of March

Every time you sit should be the first time. Every moment you live should be the last moment.

———— · ————

In terms of rigpa, it is impossible to say that we are existent in the moment – but neither can we say that we are non-existent.
Kyabjé Düd'jom Rinpoche Jig'drèl Yeshé Dorje

———— · ————

Remember to make acquaintance with death; not merely through *thinking about death* – but through experiencing the infinite numbers of microscopic deaths within the flow of your life.

———— · ————

If you allow present definitions of what you are to flow like sand—slipping through your fingers—you will enjoy life to a far greater degree, and eventually lose your fear of death.

———— · ————

Motivation is only a problem when silent sitting is not part of life — so make sitting part of life. Once it becomes part of life, clarity will begin to develop. When clarity begins to develop, there will be stronger motivation to practise. Then the value of practice will be seen. Once the value of practice is seen – there will be the motivation to make further discoveries. After that, maintaining motivation will no longer be a problem.

———— · ————

Practitioners are serene freedom fighters who engage in non-violent guerrilla warfare whenever they sit in silence – and whenever they comprehend or enact essential Vajrayana. That is the nature of peace, calmness, composure, tranquillity, and serenity.

The seventh of March

Only make promises to yourself which you know that you can keep. Otherwise, you'll never have confidence to make promises.

———— · ————

If you have no confidence in yourself – you'll find that you won't be able to make promises to yourself. Being able to make promises to yourself is consequential. It's portentous. It's a way of giving life real direction – and enabling positive phenomena to manifest. This is even more powerful if you link your promises—through your Lama—to the wish for the liberation of everyone and everything everywhere.

———— · ————

The Lama is indispensable. Similarly—although it is not entirely impossible to learn to ride a horse without an instructor—there are few who would be successful without the guidance of an experienced riding teacher. This—like all analogies—is flawed, because human beings are not *primordial equestrians*. The pragmatics of the analogy however, remain sound.

———— · ————

The 'I' cannot be made into a *project*. A project is anything that extends 'I' beyond the moment. That's not to say however, that it's not possible to plan, in the ordinary sense of the word. It is simply not possible to plan as if *this momentary 'I'* were going to be present at some later point. *The 'I' at the time of planning* will no longer exist when the plan comes to fruition. No doubt the 'I' at the point of the culmination of the plan may remember something of the 'I' who made the plan – but the only connection is a series of reactions in time and space.

The eighth of March

Few people doubt the veracity of those whose assertions are the most voluble and widely quoted. This is why trite spiritual clichés and hackneyed spiritual jargon are so popular.

———— · ————

People seek social acceptance and peer approval. When therefore, achievements are commonly esteemed – it is taken as a sign of respectability and success. It is not intellectually challenging to understand that this is a waste of life.

———— · ————

Most people don't question the commonly accepted version of reality into which they're adventitiously indoctrinated. That is often why people find themselves in opposition to each other. Those who question commonly accepted reality tend to be more tolerant.

———— · ————

People tend to conform to standard values. They support one brand of quasi-functional political values against equally quasi-functional political alternatives. Then they need to argue incessantly in order to reassure themselves they made the right choice.

———— · ————

Few question the version of reality presented by the press and social media. This is the case in either wing of politics – and every shade of philosophy, or branch of religion. The development of disbelief therefore, is the first step toward essential Vajrayana. We do not have to develop disbelief in Vajrayana however – because if emptiness is experienced, Vajrayana experientially explains itself.

The ninth of March

Rigpa is neither infinite nor temporary. It cannot be established though specifics such as experiences or activities. It is the original face of nonduality which is beginninglessly pure, all-pervasive, and all-pervaded. *Kyabjé Düd'jom Rinpoche Jig'drèl Yeshé Dorje*

———— · ————

Religion, in its essential function, is that which dynamically links areas *other than religion*, such as: history, geography, philosophy, psychology, logic, mysticism, biology, medicine, and science – *through* the Arts.

———— · ————

Buddhism is not a faith – even though it acknowledges faith as potent method. When—at the age of 18—I was asked what I believed, I answered *"I believe nothing. There's only what I know and what I don't know. The rest is an assemblage of working hypotheses. As working hypotheses go, Vajrayana is pretty wonderful."* Now, however, I know more than I knew then – but I do not advise anyone to have faith in what I know.

———— · ————

Religion has many appearances and each appearance suits different individuals. Most religions function through the idea of God. Buddhism does not – but it is still a religion. Buddhism is an atheist religion – which is why some people do not see it as a religion. The answer to this conundrum involves investigating the essence of religion rather than defining it according to group consensus on the basis of simplistic formulæ.

The tenth of March

The unobstructed luminosity of nonduality – and the entire spectrum of experience—whether deranged or liberated—is as the sun and its rays. *Kyabjé Düd'jom Rinpoche Jig'drèl Yeshé Dorje*

———— · ————

If one has not at least begun to relinquish the sense in which one's personal identity can be protracted beyond the moment then the vajra master and vajra commitment will not begin to make sense. The logic of Vajrayana begins with the experience of emptiness – and until that point is reached this logic will not seem logical.

———— · ————

Lama'i Naljor[4] is the heart of Vajrayana. Nothing can be practised beyond Sutrayana therefore, unless the experience required to relate with a vajra master is present. This experience requires: kindness that is free of artifice; direct appreciation of emptiness; and, the natural desire to facilitate liberation for everyone and everything everywhere.

———— · ————

To practise perfectly is to proceed without force. If the attempt is made to force thought out – the mind rebels. If the attempt is made to force thought to be continuous – the mind rebels. This is why, in the practice of shi-nè, thought is not encouraged – yet neither is it blocked. This is why it is said *'Meditation – isn't. Getting used to – is'*.

———— · ————

Rigpa is naked perception – a naked flame, which burns with or without fuel. It is naked in the same sense that the blade of an unsheathed knife is naked. Rigpa is pure and total presence. Stripped of referential clinging to the illusion of duality, mind is self-divested through bare attention. The essential reality of what exposes itself, is simply *as it is*.

4 (*bLa ma'i rNal 'byor* / བླ་མའི་རྣལ་འབྱོར་ / *guru yoga*) – the practice of experiential identification with the Lama.

The eleventh of March

Nondual emptiness is undivided from nondual form. Therefore, everyone and everything everywhere has the intrinsic nature of nondual awareness – the spontaneously arisen universe of pure qualities. *Kyabjé Düd'jom Rinpoche Jig'drèl Yeshé Dorje*

———— · ————

The appearance of the *Lama as the yidam* is the method. This appearance is the liberated nature of what one actually is. When one becomes that appearance—through letting go of fixated versions of what one misconstrues oneself to be—one opens to endless possibilities.

———— · ————

The *dKyil'khor* of *Lama as yidam* is the ground from which all potentialities arise. This ground is the vital self-luminous seed-bed of creativity. The elements arise as a matrix of creativity; from the empty ground of existence itself – as a display of the limitless qualities of nondual activity.

———— · ————

Being is both: thought and absence of thought; phenomena and emptiness; pattern and chaos. When practising shi-nè however, it becomes evident that this existential definition is not comfortable to a dualistic mindset.

———— · ————

The phenomenal world is perfect, just as it is – but *diffidence, susceptibility, deficiency, mistakenness,* and *alienation* often characterise experience in uncomfortable alternation with *confidence, perspicacity, benevolence, accomplishment,* and *relaxed openness*. These relate with the five elements: earth, water, fire, air, and space.

The twelfth of March

The 'new age' proclivity tends to employ silent sitting as a form of 'tuning out'. This is a spiritualised form of introversion – a soporific withdrawal from life. This has nothing in common with shi-nè – so it is quite possible that many 'new age meditators' merely sit in a state of blankness.

——— · ———

Kyabjé Chag'düd Tulku Rinpoche once said that he'd found that many people who engaged in 'mindfulness' were merely pushing the 'pause button' – as they would with a media player. The problem with that kind of silent sitting is that as soon as the pause button is released – the movie of dualistic neuroses merely continues from where it left off.

——— · ———

We have a 'Crapper' toilet. It has a wonderfully ornate ceramic flush-pull on the end of a Victorian style chain. The ceramic pull bears the motto 'pull and let go'; which is good advice – because we've known people who stood there holding on for hours on end. These are the kind of people who don't get on so well with shi-nè.

——— · ———

We have come across people who use silent sitting to create an impervious shell, in which non-communication and lack of interaction act as a comfort zone. Ideal candidates for shi-nè however, are not refugees from reality. A dull mentality might well find silent sitting to be restful or serene – but shi-nè can be far from serene if one remains present, awake, and alert. One needs to be a bold adventuring explorer to practice shi-nè.

The thirteenth of March

Do I contemplate death? No... dying is the *very last* thing I shall ever do.

——— · ———

Chögyam Trungpa Rinpoche once crashed into a joke shop[5] in Gateshead. I seem to have done that repeatedly in different ways – but maybe to no good effect.

——— · ———

In terms of 'lack of doubt', the Tsig-sum né-dek[6] is the perfect guide to shooting. *Direct introduction; Remaining without doubt; and, Continuing in the state. Direct introduction* is the perfect image of the sights, together with the decisionless decision in which the trigger is squeezed. *Remaining without doubt* is the sense in which there is no distance. There is an absolute intimacy between the sights and the inner ring of the target. *Continues in the state* is where each shot— shot after shot—goes exactly where it is placed.

——— · ———

Reaching out for familiar patterns is the dualistic function which allows thoughts to serve as reference points. Thoughts, ideas, images, feelings, sensations, people, places, and things, however, are not reference points in themselves. They are empty of referential qualities – but phenomena are reduced to reference points through the fear of ceasing to exist. The phenomena of the external world are thereby overlaid with secondary functions – attributed to them for dualistic convenience. The messages that are imagined as being received from the phenomenal world are attributed rather than inherently provided.

---

5   In May 1969 Chögyam Trungpa Rinpoche drove a sports car into a joke shop in Gateshead in North-East England.

6   *tshig gSum gNad brDegs* / ཚིག་གསུམ་གནད་བརྡེགས་) – Hitting the Essence in Three Words / Phrases.

The fourteenth of March

Finding Mind to be a referenceless ocean of space allows the dualistic knot of panic to untie itself. In experiencing this space, a brilliant discovery is made: being referenceless is not death.

———— · ————

We believe in social revolution through appreciation – a revolution through the Arts which facilitates the creation of a humane civilisation.

———— · ————

A peaceful revolution is possible through each person becoming an authentic individual. We don't need to 'overthrow capitalism' by any other demonstration than that of individual appreciation.

———— · ————

If you cease to purchase the products of fashion – the producers of fashion will become unfashionable. The greater the individual appreciation, the less possible it becomes for the mass market to function. The individual appreciation fostered by the Arts, is an entirely peaceful revolution – and one that cannot atrophy.

———— · ————

If what is perceived substantiates personal definitions, *attraction* arises. If personal definitions are threatened, *aversion* manifests. If the phenomena of perception neither substantiates nor threatens personal definitions, there is *indifference*. What cannot be manipulated referentially, is ignored. Phenomena are rarely experienced as they are. Experience is limited according to the need for definitions – and consequently everything is graded as to its suitability as a possible reference point.

The fifteenth of March

Because Vajrayana practitioners receive empowerments into all three categories of yidam it is necessary to have a vital and vigorous appreciation of each form – in whatever colour, gender, body-type, or mode of appearance the yidam displays.

———— · ————

Because devotion to the form of the yidam is crucial to Vajrayana, there can be no negative æsthetic considerations. People cannot be practitioners of Vajrayana if they have prejudice against any style of human manifestation.

———— · ————

Yidams can appear conventionally beautiful or conventionally ugly. They can appear in any colour. Yidams can appear as young or old. Yidams can appear as conventionally well-formed or conventionally misshapen. Yidams can even manifest the appearance of impediment. According to Vajrayana, everyone is a symbol of nonduality. There can therefore be no form of human who is not essentially sacred.

———— · ————

Those people who surround us in our *world-dKyil'khor* are all essentially yidams. Everyone is a potential Buddha – and therefore, their forms are the forms which symbolise Buddhas. To manifest the vajra pride of yidams – practitioners need to recognise that the forms of their yidams are sacred forms. In being sacred forms – the forms of all beings are therefore equally sacred.

The sixteenth of March

To be authentically *unconventional* is the freedom to be conventional in any way which is pleasing to oneself and valuable to others – without any sense of adhering to convention or rejecting convention.

———— · ————

Eccentric is a description which only makes sense in terms of a perimeter. It depends who defines the perimeter as whether one can be described as eccentric.

———— · ————

The present moment is the superior time because from the present moment you can survey the infinite past assemblages of moments in which there were superior phenomena. These superior phenomena are all still available. JS Bach is still alive if you love his music. Everything there ever was is still accessible *as* the present moment.

———— · ————

The word 'eccentric' derives from Medieval Latin *eccentricus* and from the Greek *ekkentros*. It was first recorded in the 1620s, where it applied to behaviour which was prompted by personal tastes, prejudices, and judgements. It was also applied to behaviours which were unaccountable and irregular rather than merely different from the behaviour of ordinary people. In 1817 it was used in *The Itinerant, or Memoirs of an Actor* by SW Ryley, to mean an odd or a whimsical person. In 1985 the term *wisdom-eccentric* was coined by Dung-sé Thrin-lé Norbu Rinpoche to define those who practised essential Vajrayana.

The seventeenth of March

Recognition of the presence of rigpa, as the primordial natural ground of being, gives innate cognisance of the three spheres of being as the intrinsic awareness of the union of luminosity and emptiness. This is the vision of Dzogchen.

Kyabjé Düdjom Rinpoche Jig'drèl Yeshé Dorje

—— · ——

There's nothing wrong with thought – even though some categories of meditation instruction state that this is the case. According to Dzogchen, thought is a natural function of Mind – and, just as the other sense faculties are natural to physical existence, so too is thought. Moreover, thought—according to Buddhism in general—is a sense-faculty, rather than a function which is separate from the senses.

—— · ——

It is said that places of power should be approached in a somewhat indirect and oblique manner, in a different way from how a tourist would visit. It is not the pilgrim's purpose to tick off a list of places, or to collect these sites as badges of holiness – but to visit merely with a sense of openness to behold what is there. The greater the spaciousness of one's approach to a place of power then the more it makes itself available.

—— · ——

The practice of shi-nè eventually develops into further practices in which horizons of experience open into vivid displays of integration. Shi-nè is the gateway to the experiential freedom in which individuation and oceanic experience are not mutually exclusive. The traditional analogy is of a fish within an ocean. When fish and ocean begin to participate in each other – it is realised that many seeming polarities of experience are simply ornaments of the nondual state.

The eighteenth of March

The cowardly believe they can avoid death. The courageous know they are already dead – and it's merely the time of death which is uncertain.

———— · ————

A stone rolling down a hill will reach the bottom. That is predictable. What happens however, if there's a rabbit hole – and the stone is waylaid by it? The same is true of any prediction. This is why one has to endeavour to realise the Lamas' predictions. One has to actively make them manifest. Sometimes there are no rabbit holes and it is fairly simple. At other times the entire hill is a vast warren.

———— · ————

Fear and anger are the ingredients of cowardice. Whenever we experience cowardice, it is anger attempting to pretend that fear is not there. Cowardice seeks to disguise both anger and fear – and, in doing so, creates a deviously disgusting brew. Anger poses as righteous indignation, resentment, and annoyance. Fear poses as sober consideration. Counterposed anger and fear generate a welter of 'explanations' designed to hide the slime trails of avoidance.

———— · ————

Nothing which comes into existence has the qualities of solidity, permanence, separateness, continuity, or definition. These qualities can never be found as fixed features of anything – yet, everything shares these qualities temporarily. Because everything shares these qualities on a temporary basis, it becomes possible to generate illusory versions of reality. These versions of reality however, are simply oscillations of: substantiality and insubstantiality; permanence and impermanence; separateness and indivisibility; continuity and discontinuity; or definition and indefinability. These oscillations, from the nondual perspective, are ornaments of sheer naked presence.

The nineteenth of March

We have bad news for you all. You've just fallen from an incredible height into a bottomless crevasse. However – that's also the good news. It's bottomless, so you're falling into space. Happy landings.

———— · ————

Sanity is probably poised somewhere between rigid conformity to social convention and irresponsible rejection of tradition.

———— · ————

Those who begin to practise Vajrayana and abandon it, are never free of Vajrayana – because it will haunt them until they return. It haunts us because it is what we are.

———— · ————

You don't have to be embarrassed about what to take yourself to be. What we have and what we are is workable just as it is. Your upbringing may be privileged, underprivileged, or deprived – it doesn't actually matter. Whatever we are is fertile for cultivation if one's Lama is a vajra farmer.

———— · ————

One begins with the accidental nature of what is occurring. One accepts that as the nature of one's current reality. Miscellaneous mishaps and menageries of mischance allow gaps to occur – spaces from which phenomena can be perceived with freshness. One begins to evolve and to become authentically involved beyond the obvious parameters of chaos. One begins to expand into what could be called the unoriginated situation.

The twentieth of March

Of all the Arts, music is perhaps somewhat more aligned with meditation – because it begins with a rigorous discipline which eventually gives way to spontaneity. This applies to all the Arts – but music is the most difficult to fake.

———— · ————

Discovering emptiness is a stage in the process of realising the nondual state. So, if we become fixated with resting in Mind without content, it becomes a spiritual cul-de-sac. Mind without thought is a condition which is as unnatural as Mind occluded by thought.

———— · ————

Oceans are referenceless if their boundaries cannot be distinguished. The sun by day—and the moon and stars by night—allow navigation – but there is no intention or design behind these appearances. The ocean of Mind is referenceless – yet the play of Mind-phenomena allows conceptual navigation – yet there is no intention or design beyond the energetic play of that which arises within Mind. Concepts arise in random-order; in arbitrary-pattern – and as Mind-phenomena they are simply an aspect of the vivid displays of primordial compassion.

———— · ————

Examining the nature of *thought*—employing *thought* as a tool— would limit the character of the examination. *Thought* would be examining *thought* with *thought* – which would become incrementally ludicrous. The *thoughts*—with which *thoughts* were examined—would have to be examined. Then, what would examine those *thoughts* apart from *thought*?

The twenty-first of March

Although the spiritual path can be viewed as systematic, linear, and sequential – this only makes sense according to the requirements of those who use roads. For those who take to the open fields, woods, rivers, and untracked mountains – linear sequentiality may make little sense.

———— · ————

Thought cannot ultimately examine itself – it would be a closed system. Thought can no more examine its own nature than a knife cut itself; or an eye, see itself. The only way an eye can see itself is to avail itself of a mirror. The nature of that mirror—in terms of 'thought'—is the natural reflective capacity of Mind, which is beyond thought.

———— · ————

If one employed a wind generator in order to examine a lake, one would merely create more disturbance. One would only learn that waves can become more pronounced. One would gain no idea of the natural reflective capacity of the lake. If one set up a gigantic cauldron which issued up yet more water vapour into an already overcast sky – one would not be likely to get any insight into the nature of the sky, with regard to its capacity to manifest clouds. When involvement with thought is retracted however, the turbulence diminishes – the cloud-cover attenuates. The wind subsides and we begin to see reflections on the surface of the lake. Occasional gusts may ruffle the surface again – but we know that water is not always in motion; sometimes it is still.

The twenty-second of March

Shame, guilt, regret, and remorse are somewhat underrated in contemporary psychotherapeutic culture – but some lives would be vastly improved by a healthy dose of such feelings.

—— · ——

The free *nature of Mind* is neither a flat screen of thought, nor a void in which nothing occurs. Both are partial conditions. Once we have learnt that we can let go of thought however, we can open up to a more fluid, frictionless, non-adhesive relationship with thought. Mind can simply allow the presence of non-referential movement.

—— · ——

Practitioners who simply remain with 'absence of thought' become absence-addicts rather than thought-addicts. It is difficult to remain for long in stabilised shi-nè without drifting into sleepy shi-nè. It is comforting to dwell in the condition of sleepy shi-nè – and from the initial standpoint of never having practised; it could appear to be an accomplishment.

—— · ——

When fish leap into existence from nothingness—exploding the mirror surface of the lake—there are three vital considerations: the still lake; the leaping fish; and, the awareness which is present in both. The still lake is emptiness, or mi-togpa *the absence of namtogs*[7]. There is nothing there but presence. This is the discovery of shi-nè. The leaping fish, or the arising of colour, pattern, texture, sensation, or thought move without referential co-ordinates. This is the discovery of lha-tong.

---

7   *mi rTog pa* / ཨེ་རྟོག་པ་ – non-thought; absence of all mind-movement including ideation.

The twenty-third of March

One has to address one's fear. Fear can be an aspect of compassion in simply being with 'what is there'. One accepts the entire texture of what is felt. One feels it without acting out; lashing out; or, initiating a primitive bid for self-preservation.

———— · ————

One has to trust the texture of what is happening and relax with the rip-tides of what is felt. If there's space, then relaxation becomes possible. It's a ride, however – but if we reject 'the ride'… we get ridden – and the spurs bite deep.

———— · ————

Ocean can never be defined by the waves which roll endlessly as its surface. One could study waves into eternity and come no closer to a definition of ocean. All one can say is that waves occur in the ocean and that they are limitless in their forms. As soon as we relinquish our attempts to define ocean according to its waves – we realise that waves and ocean are indivisible. Ocean requires no definition – yet waves continually ornament the ocean with their temporary definitions.

———— · ————

The sky is vast and beyond limits. Within the unfettered space of the sky there is endless movement. Clouds appear and disappear. They appear from out of the sky and they evaporate back into the sky. The sky is not affected by the clouds which manifest within it – even when it is completely overcast and it appears as if its expansive blueness no longer exists. Whether we see the sky or not – it remains there, unaltered by that which appears to occlude it. We could take the blue sky to be the perfect state, and yet to be without clouds is not the nature of the sky.

The twenty-fourth of March

Wishing one hadn't done something is the thing that helps us not to do it again. One can begin by asking *"Does a practitioner do this?"* One could ask *"What would my Lama think of this?"* One could conjecture *"Could I tell my Lama what I'm about to do?"* Put simply—if you have a Lama, or anyone you respect—don't do anything you'd be ashamed to admit.

———— · ————

In Dzogchen sem-dé[8] we use the word 'namtog'[9] in respect of *finding the presence of awareness in the movement of namtog*. 'Namtog' is a contraction of 'namtog gom du 'char wa'[10], which means 'thought arising as meditation'. So, when we speak of rigpa being the *sameness of taste* in respect of the absence of namtog and the movement of namtog – this relates with empty presence in terms of *thought arising as meditation*.

———— · ————

The answers to *'why?'* mostly seem to generate more *'whys'* – and there is virtually no end to *'why'*. *'How?'* on the other hand, is a practical question. It's an experiential question. It empowers you. *'How?'* gives you direct access to first-hand experience. *'How?'* puts the process of discovery in your hands. If you ask someone, *"Why are you lighting a fire?"* they might answer *"I want to be warm."* You could then ask, *"Why d'you want to be warm?"* to which they might reply *"I don't like being cold."* Asking *"Why don't you like being cold?"* would probably get you no answer, or be admonished *"Please stop asking me questions – I'm trying to light a fire!"* It would perhaps be better to ask *"Can you show me how to light a fire?"*

---

8   *sems sDe* / སེམས་སྡེ) – series of the nature of Mind.

9   *rNam rTog* / རྣམ་རྟོག

10   *rNam rTog bsGom du 'char ba* / རྣམ་རྟོག་བསྒོམ་དུ་འཆར་བ

The twenty-fifth of March

The Lama's job is to cut through the convolutions of interminable psychological and emotional process. Without the Lama one would have to uproot every illusion individually. Without the Lama one would have an extremely long trail to tread.

——— · ———

A helpful hand pushes you out of the æroplane at the end of a count of ten. You fall – at the rate of twenty-two feet *per second / per second*. You accelerate at that rate 'til you hit terminal velocity—120 miles an hour—which is as fast as any un-propelled object can fall. It takes about seventeen seconds. The parachute opens well before terminal velocity – and then it's no longer like falling. It's like being suspended. How is that possible? How is it possible to feel as if you're not falling – when you are falling? You find out by taking a parachute jump. What happens next is that you look down and something visually bizarre happens. It's termed 'ground rush'. The ground looks as if it's coming toward you – rather than you falling onto it. Then you land and conventional logic cuts in. If you were to explain your experience to a hidebound rationalist – you'd find it vexing. You'd have to ask *"How can you take issue with experiences you've never had?"* To which the hidebound rationalist would reply *"You should be able to explain any experience in rational terms."*

——— · ———

Individuality is a quality of human life. It is enjoyed personally and valued in others. Those who are admired for their artistic achievements are valued for the manner in which they manifest in the world. Portraits of modern legends are painted. Documentaries are produced which depict the lives of those who have left legacies of creativity to enrich the world. The idiosyncrasies of the celebrated are not unfailingly saintly – but they are intriguing nonetheless. Where the celebrated are typified by kindness however – their personal proclivities are illuminating when revealed.

The twenty-sixth of March

It's not the nature of existence itself that has the quality of suffering; it's the experience of existence that is characterised as suffering or dukkha.

———— · ————

Animism and shamanism are as much religions, as any of the other more recent developments. Religion—according to common definition—is that which enables people to communicate, cooperate, and coexist in a meaningful manner. A religion has a history, a calendar, and a culture. It has rites of passage for birth and death and the many significant intervals in between. It is something we all need – whatever name is given to it. Without it, societies become antisocial.

———— · ————

What is known as 'deity'[11] is the awareness being – the spontaneously liberated appearance, which is a wisdom-quality of one's nondual nature. What is known as 'mantra' is the spontaneously liberated resonance of the awareness being – the sonic reflex of your enlightened energy. When one integrates that visionary experience with everyday life, one recognises the world as the dimension of the awareness being – radiating from one's visionary nature. The sound quality of the environment is the resonance of that visionary nature in the dimension of sound.

———— · ————

There are terror rides at fun fairs. One does not take a terror ride if one does not trust the apparatus. Sometimes the Lama might represent a terror ride – so confidence needs to be well established before the ride begins. Confidence is not merely bravado however – confidence has to be established though study and practice.

11 *lha* / ཧ / *deva*

The twenty-seventh of March

The basic illness of duality is the same in everyone and everything everywhere – but personalities and capacities differ. There are, therefore, as many different approaches to nonduality as there are differences of nature and capacity.

———— · ————

Buddhist teachings are methods – vehicles leading towards discovery rather than expositions of 'The Truth'. The methods employed at any time by a Lama will be those appropriate for the individual – depending upon experience, and situation. What is appropriate in one setting might be ludicrous in another. Vajrayana is fluid and infinitely adaptable to the actual needs of everyone when transmission is given by a realised master.

———— · ————

Shi-nè is not extraordinary – it's actually the practice of ordinariness. All it requires is letting go of extraordinary elaborations. If we refuse to erect barriers of any kind; if we remain in the existential statement of presence which doesn't indulge in dividing internal and external; if we practice the ordinariness of letting go of extraordinary elaborations – then we will discover that our natural connection with other beings is vividly convivial.

———— · ————

The practice of generating compassion as the basis for realising emptiness doesn't contradict the practice of realising emptiness in order to discover the spontaneous compassion that springs from that realisation. If we generate kindness, we imitate nonduality – and in imitating nonduality we facilitate the realisation of emptiness. If we let go and let be through the practice of the four naljors we discover that kindness is the spontaneous expression that is liberated by that unfolding.

The twenty-eighth of March

Love and compassion as terms appear different in a relative sense –
but love and compassion as aspects of the energy of nonduality are
divisionless.

——— · ———

The wisdom of emptiness and the infinite compassionate activity
that arises from it are not actually divisible. From the dualistic
perspective[12] however, they appear divided. Having divided wisdom
and active-compassion in this way, we devise means of realising
either, through the practice of manifesting the other. This means
that we either manifest wisdom through non-attachment to
referentiality, or we manifest kindness through contemplative
thinking and processes of active-imagination. The realisation of
both practices is that wisdom and active-compassion are indivisible.

——— · ———

In the epoch of the Mahasiddhas, vajra masters worked one-to-one
with students. Even when Vajrayana was taught in Tibet during the
First Spread the student-teacher ratio was often limited to a handful.
Guru Rinpoche had twenty-five disciples. There were thousands
who took Guru Rinpoche and Yeshé Tsogyel as their inspiration –
but they were composed of small groups around individual Lamas.
Both Kyabjé Düd'jom Rinpoche Jig'drèl Yeshé Dorje and Kyabjé
Künzang Dorje Rinpoche advised us to not to take more students
than we could know by name. This, they told us, was the way to
maintain the integrity and authenticity of Vajrayana.

12 *gNyis sNang* / གཉིས་སྣང་ – dualistic perception.

The twenty-ninth of March

It's not possible to experience either love or compassion if one's *sense of oneself* exists separately from the experience of others.

―――― · ――――

The Outer and Inner Tantras are not simply a body of transformative techniques which facilitate the realisation of the nondual state. Seeing Vajrayana merely as a methodology is mechanistic. It ignores the fact that *a practice* does not exist as separate from *a practitioner*. A practice can only exist in the context of one who is practising.

―――― · ――――

Vajrayana practices depend on the motivation and perceptual personality of the practitioner. This means that *Dzogchen practices* performed by those who practise for their personal liberation alone, are actually *Pratyekabuddha practices*. They are divorced from Dzogchen by virtue of failing to function in terms of Mahayana – let alone Tantra. Those who merely read books about Dzogchen— no matter how convinced they are that they are *living the view*—are merely practising Shravakayana.

―――― · ――――

When your pain and pleasure are to some extent my pain and pleasure, that is love. If we extend that outward to encompass all living beings, then we call that changchub sem. Changchub sem is divisionless – and divisionless is nonduality. Both love and changchub sem are free from the inhibitions and constrictions of self-orientation. Selfishness springs from a sense of dividedness, of being separate from the rest of the universe. Selfishness is the distorted sense of hyper-individuation, in which we imagine we can act on behalf of ourselves alone. We don't often seem to connect with the idea that if we love selectively or conditionally, it can all turn sour. For real love to exist, changchub sem needs to pervade perception.

The thirtieth of March

Although the fruit of shi-nè is the profound relaxation of mind, voice, and body, the initial phase cannot be described as relaxation. Relaxation however, is necessary if one is to progress with shi-nè.

———— · ————

Shi-nè is an introduction to the ability to experience relaxation of perception. That of course influences every area of life. Shi-nè is a continuing personal experiment in which one is bound to find difficulties and obstacles. Shi-nè—from the point of view of duality —is definitely to be avoided.

———— · ————

At the level of *gender relativism*, many people become fixated with difference, At the level of *gender ultimatism*, people become fixated with lack of difference. Vajrayana however, regards both these views as restrictive. Both views are equally true and untrue. The reality is a matter of movement – of fluctuation.

———— · ————

When we see the evidence of our own conditioning, we cannot help but learn about reality – in distinction from how our impersonal conditioning is constructed; out of the desire to be, according to implausible criteria. It has to become apparent, what it is that we attempt to gain from remaining locked into a paradigm of impersonal conditioning – in contradistinction to the spontaneous choice of awareness. The further we go in allowing ourselves to confront the sensitive issue of whether we are unique or not, the harder it is to ignore the irrepressible evidence of addiction to self-defeating mannerisms.

The thirty-first of March

The Arts lie behind everything we've ever done. We do not necessarily mean Art in the literal sense. We mean *that which lies beneath the Arts*: the space from which the Arts arise.

———— · ————

The overt and covert aspects of being male or female are a cogently validated mode of seeing. They are based on nondual experience – rather than on the materialistic facts of existential scientific materialist nihilism. The approach of materialist nihilism tends to impose facts on men and women, whether or not they are known experientially.

———— · ————

Vajrayana fact is therefore not objective according to nihilistic criteria – but neither is it subjective. Vajrayana is not constrained or limited by dichotomous definitions such as subjective or objective. Vajrayana goes beyond concepts of 'personal illusion' and 'group illusion', into a space where the effect of entering the dimension of view is more important than whether the view is 'hard wired' in terms of the fundamental biochemical structure of human beings.

———— · ————

Women are overtly wisdom, and covertly compassion. Men are overtly compassion, and covertly wisdom. That represents a Vajrayana fact. A fact of this nature is a statement whose veracity is self-experienced. It is self-experienced by allowing it to burgeon as personal reality – through its own unrestrained influence. This is not 'fact' according to the 'facts' of psychology, psychiatry, or physics – which tend toward nihilist materialism. It is a *fact of view*—a *fact of yogic experience*—and as such, needs to be experienced rather than intellectually validated according to the enervating empiricism of quotidian equations.

A'a'a

April

It doesn't matter whether you are richer or poorer, if you have enough to live that should be sufficient for happiness.

HE Ögyen Dro'dül Thrin-lé Kunkyab Rinpoche
རྒྱལ་བ་ཨོ་རྒྱན་འགྲོ་འདུལ་ཕྲིན་ལས་ཀུན་སྐྱབས་རིན་པོ་ཆེ་

Buddhism is the *way of seeing* in one's life – rather than a *book of rules* to be followed.

Khar-trül Wangchuk Rig'dzin Rinpoche
མཁར་སྤྲུལ་དཔལ་གྱི་དབང་ཕྱུག་རིག་འཛིན་རིན་པོ་ཆེ།

The first of April

To *play the fool* once meant to *play a wild card*. A *wild card* stands for any other card. A wild card is the emptiness of a deck of cards – and a wisdom eccentric[1] is one who throws wild cards into our carefully arranged plans. Perhaps every day is April Fool's Day[2] for wisdom eccentrics.

——— · ———

Humour was a characteristic of all our Lamas – and it has been a vital aspect of the way we teach. It has been said by several Lamas including Kyabjé Künzang Dorje Rinpoche, that one is closest to realisation when sneezing, experiencing orgasm, or laughing. We have no ability to cause the first. Being monogamous we do not instigate the second. We are therefore obliged to employ humour.

——— · ———

The Fool is a commentator who is permitted, by the monarch, to speak the truth. In Shakespeare's play *King Lear* the *Fool* ridicules his monarch. The Fool sees the King's daughters for what they are — and has foresight to know that the Kings' decisions would prove disastrous. In terms of *speaking the truth as a joke* – Chhi'mèd Rig'dzin Rinpoche used to make predictions to people—concerning their lives—couched as jests. Those who were astute and open to guidance, took his jests seriously. There will be those however, who remember the jokes Chhi'mèd Rig'dzin Rinpoche made in the context of their life-decisions. Those who thought he was *just joking* will now regret not having taken his jokes with absolute seriousness.

---

1 Wisdom eccentric: myönpa / myon héruka *(sMyon pa / སྨྱོན་པ་ / sMyon he ru ka / སྨྱོན་ཧེ་རུ་ཀ)*; Crazy Wisdom: yeshé cholwa *(ye shes 'chol ba / ཡེ་ཤེས་འཆོལ་བ)* – primordial wisdom chaos.

2 April Fool's Day—the 1st of April—is the day in several countries where there is a convention of being able to play practical jokes and perpetrate hoaxes without undue censure.

The second of April

We should have a valid contact with the Lama. This requires authentic communication. The Lama must have sufficient understanding of the quality and texture of our lives. We must receive something experientially tangible in terms of transmission. This is crucial.

———— · ————

Tantrikas develop *vajra pride* which—because it is founded on emptiness—allows the possibility of assuming infinite forms of *otherness*: otherness of colour, otherness of shape, otherness of gender; otherness of disposition, and limitless other varieties of *otherness* – in terms of arising as the yidam. Every variant of vajra-otherness is a glorious manifestation of the nondual state, as it sparkles through the appearance of every permutation of our humanity.

———— · ————

Various words seem to have fallen from modern usage: reasonableness, prudence, judiciousness, discretion, civility, seemliness, composure, politeness, consideration, courtesy, dignity, gallantry, chivalry, graciousness, magnanimity, constancy, fidelity, integrity, loyalty, steadfastness, and honour – and… a host of others. Let us look at gyüd-kho'i shé rig common sense. This is the practically based facility required for navigating everyday exigencies without placing oneself in jeopardy; the wherewithal to see through fraudulence; a reasonable knowledge of the world; and, a healthy level of scepticism. A person with common sense will suspect a knave, bounder, braggart, villain, scoundrel, or confidence trickster. A person with common sense will suspect exaggeration, braggadocio, hyperbole, and lies.

The third of April

It is not commonly understood – but thangkas and statues are not merely inspirational. They are not simply there to bring the lineage to life through making historical personages more easily accessible. The real importance of thangkas and statues lies in the visual-tactile dimension of the vajra kyil'khor in which the teachings manifest through transmission.

——— · ———

Myon héruka[3] means 'mad héruka'. It has no connection with the dubious coinage *nyon mong héruka*[4] – which, if it existed, would translate as *defiled héruka* because *mong (klesha)* means *defilement*. There is a difference in spelling. The 'myon' in mad héruka is spelt *sMyon* and the 'mong' in defiled héruka is spelt *mongs*. This may not seem a great difference vis-à-vis spelling – but consider the difference between crow, cow, cowl, and cowp.

——— · ———

Chhi'mèd Rig'dzin Rinpoche's wrath was as non-ordinary as Künzang Dorje Rinpoche's ferocity – and they were both entirely unalike in their expression. Their wrath was incomprehensible. They could not be defined as being personally involved with the wrath they displayed. Their wrath was entirely display. It was transient and insubstantial. Their wrath was certainly powerful – but never brutal in a heavy cumbersome claustrophobic way. It was always precise – and utterly impersonal. They never became angry about anything that would normally make a person angry. There was no sense in which they were reacting to personal affronts, irritation, or impatience.

3   *sMyon he ru ka* / སྨྱོན་ཧེ་རུ་ཀ
4   The dubious term 'nyon mong héruka' *(nyon mongs he ru ka /* ཉོན་མོངས་ཧེ་རུ་ཀ) was used by a scholar at the Conference of Western Buddhist Teachers in McLeod Ganj in 1993 as part of a negative criticism of Crazy Wisdom – as if it were the Tibetan term for Crazy Wisdom. This term however cannot be found in any Tibetan dictionary. Crazy Wisdom is yeshé 'cholwa *(ye shes 'chol ba /* ཡེ་ཤེས་འཆོལ་བ) primordial wisdom chaos.

The fourth of April

Anyone who wants to lead a full and rewarding life should study the fourteen root vows of Vajrayana. Anyone who values freedom, honesty, honour, courage, and the whole gamut of admirable human qualities would be supported by an understanding of these vows. Anyone who sees life as a field of opportunity to be grasped with enthusiasm – either in the Arts, Sciences, or physical endeavours – would find the directives of these vows a wonderful asset.

——— · ———

sMyon héruka applies to Mahayoga Lamas who are beyond conventional religious limitations. There is a long list, including Kong sMyon – *the Mad Yogi of Kongpo*; Khams sMyon Dharma Seng-gé – *the Mad Dharma Lion of Kham*; gTsang sMyon Héruka– *the Mad Traktung of Tsang*; sMyon pa Seng-gé Wangchuk – *the Mad Omnipotent Lion* and Té-kya sMyonpa[5] *the Madman in White*. Then there's *The Multicoloured Madman Who isn't Actually Mad at all—in terms of realisation—just Vaguely Bizarre*[6].

——— · ———

Buddhists have been helping others in an unostentatious manner since the time of King Ashoka[7]. Chö-jé Akong Rinpoche ran a soup kitchen in Glasgow, Scotland in the 1970s – long before the label 'engaged Buddhism' was coined. Akong Rinpoche did not give a label to the activity and few people know about Akong Rinpoche's activities for the benefit of the poor – or 'financially challenged' as the politically correct would probably refer to them.

5 *rTas sKya sMyon pa* / རྟས་སྐྱ་སྨྱོན་པ་ was also known as Chingkar Donyö Dorje.
6 Ngak'chang Rinpoche was referring to himself.
7 273–232 BC

131

sMyon héruka is the style of the Indian Mahasiddhas – the style that emphasises the transcendence of the pure-impure dichotomy. Such masters overturn cultural norms. They reverse aesthetics and conventional tastes. They eat what would be regarded as disgusting or repulsive – such as the five meats and the five nectars[8] of the tsog'khorlo[9].

———— · ————

Yeshé 'cholwa is a Dzogchen manifestation, in which the concept of pure and impure have no meaning. There is no dichotomy to be transcended. Everything is self-liberated in its arising. For this reason, yeshé 'cholwa is better described as whimsicality – a subtle, oblique, tangential mien. Yeshé 'cholwa is not extreme – it simply functions beyond the boundaries of duality.

———— · ————

It is not easy to be a vajra master. It is not easy to make decisions which deal with the potential realisation of individuals. The vajra master needs to accept a great deal in terms of how he or she is perceived. Vajra masters can become the subject of 'demonising' projections – because vajra masters provide the projection possibilities for both canonisation and demonisation. Vajra masters have to accept both with equanimous dignity and a wry sense of humour

---

8 The five meats, sha nga *(sha lNga / ཤ་ལྔ)* are: human flesh *(sha chen / ཤ་ཆེན)*; cow flesh *(nor sha / ནོར་ཤ)*; dog flesh *(khyi sha / ཁྱི་ཤ)*; elephant flesh *(gLang sha / གླང་ཤ)*; and, horse flesh *(rTa sha / རྟ་ཤ)*. The five nectars, düdtsi Na-nga *(bDud rTsi sNa lNga / བདུད་རྩི་སྣ་ལྔ)* are: urine *(gCin / གཅིན)*; excrement *(sKyag / སྐྱག)*; blood *(khrag / ཁྲག)*; semen *(khu / ཁུ)*; and, pus *(chu ser / ཆུ་སེར)*. The five meats and the five nectars are not eaten or imbibed literally within the Buddhist Tantras. In several Hindu Tantric traditions, the five meats and the five nectars are literally to be eaten and imbibed – as well as other substances which cause revulsion such as scorpions, poisonous snakes, and dangerous reptiles etcetera.

9 *tshogs 'khor lo / ཚོགས་འཁོར་ལོ / ganachakra)* – vajra feast.

The sixth of April

Compassion is not merely the desire to give the whole world a coke or a cookie. It is not simply the most profound altruism. *Active Compassion* is only one aspect of Bodhicitta or changchub sem. Each of the six classes of Tantra expresses this *appreciative interactive empathy* according to progressively subtler and increasingly vivid criteria. We begin by cultivating compassion – only to learn that compassion – is none other than the innate energy of the natural state.

———— · ————

The term *crazy wisdom* is not literal. The word 'crazy' in common parlance indicates irregularity, absurdity, and enthusiasm – but when linked with wisdom we find a meaning that probably comes closer to 'artistic intuition'. The literal translation from Tibetan is primordial (ye) knowingness (shes). The word 'cholwa (*'chol ba*) means chaos – but covers a range of ideas including: thrown into chaos; outside categories; unbounded; undefined; wild; scattered; and, disproportionate. The meaning of yeshé 'cholwa therefore concerns primordial wisdom being beyond the remit of taxonomy.

———— · ————

We conform to categories and classifications and understand mainly by comparison – but what if we cease to categorise? How would we manifest if we dwelt in the experience of yeshé? There would be the lattice of normal life and we would move through it like wind or water. A fish may be governed by a net – but air and water simply move through it. Human society has *customs* and *styles of relating* but whoever manifests yeshé 'cholwa blows through these constraints like wind, or flows through them like water. Yeshé 'cholwa doesn't challenge societal norms. Those who follow societal conventions may be affected by those who manifest yeshé 'cholwa – but there is no force involved.

The seventh of April

Enjoyment of existence is the dance of self-liberated materialism.

——— · ———

The logic of Vajrayana is fabulously precise – exactly lyrical. Understanding it however, has to be a spontaneous realisation – in a similar way to learning how to balance. *Trying* has to occur – knowing that there is something to 'understand'. The sense of balance is then simply something that arrives at a certain point. There is no logical approach beyond trying, and continuing to try.'

——— · ———

There is a valuable quality with every age group. An authentic adult is one who is prepared to be childlike – when that childlike quality is required by existence. Children have enthusiasm and excitement which permeate the moment. Children also move on from one fascination to another. Adolescents can be extreme. They can be seekers of intensity – but that can also be altruistic and unreservedly committed to where they are. Adolescents tend to lack circumspection – but in the best cases they are willing to learn from their mistakes. The elderly—in the best cases—have circumspection and the wisdom which comes from knowing that there are few simple answers. But what of adults? For us, adulthood is the phase in which we have access to all qualities – those of childhood, adolescence, and maturity. As adults we should be able to move in and out of differing modes of being according to what is required by human circumstances. An adult is neither a road-kill on the highway of life nor a tediously predictable survivor with secure pension plan.

The eighth of April

The problem with 'entertainment' is that it's seen as a *leisure pastime* – and consequently needs no work. Real entertainment—of whatever kind—requires serious attention.

———— · ————

People do not expect to have to work in order to enjoy – but the effort of involvement is essential to the Arts. I hardly ever work harder than when enjoying a Shakespeare play. I have to concentrate —all the time—simply in order to understand.

———— · ————

With regard to Art, it is not a matter of sitting back and being vicariously titillated, excited, thrilled, or amused. Authentic enjoyment needs to be an authentic experience. The senses need to be fully involved. In terms of Vajrayana, one cannot listlessly languorate as a lethargic sensory dilettante.

———— · ————

Although Art is pleasure, it is also work. When I listen to *Spoonful* on Cream's *Wheels of Fire* album – I need to concentrate in order to follow the contrapuntal baseline that Jack Bruce plays as the second lead instrument. Then it is like listening to JS Bach. Jack Bruce was highly influenced by JS Bach – but it requires attention to hear it.

———— · ————

Art should not be entertainment. The problem with 'entertainment' is that it is mainly for sensory dilettantes. I have never listened to a piece of music in order to be entertained. I have never been to the theatre to be entertained. I have never been to an art gallery in order to be entertained. Entertainment is for those afflicted with existential ennui – people with too much time on their hands. When I seek out Art I have serious intent to witness the universe coming into being.

The ninth of April

The vajra name—received from one's Lama—begins the process of release from the self-abuse of compulsive self-identification. The meaning of the name increases as the fixation on insular misanthropic sociopathy decreases.

——— · ———

Life can be so simple, when one follows trusted advice. It is not always easy to follow advice – but if one trusts the source of the advice and proceeds with confidence; life simply works. This is how Vajrayana works. This does not mean that everything will be perfect —or that sickness old age and death will be overridden—but that the best that can be achieved can be achieved. This is something that every Vajrayana student everywhere needs to bear in mind.

——— · ———

What people fail to understand about the value of monarchy is that it is, or can be, an aspirational altruistic Art – even where it is secular. Where the monarchs and citizens are interdependently and mutually appreciative – something can evolve which is greater than mere mass-consensus. Where the situation works as it should, the people are ennobled by their sovereigns and the sovereigns are commensurately dignified by honour and accountability.

——— · ———

The Vajra Monarchs have no pre-formulated ideas about the fiefdom, monarchy, or empire that is going to come into being – because it is developed by disciples in conjunction with the Vajra Monarchs they have chosen. This is distinctly different from being born in a country and being the subject of a King or Queen. With Vajrayana there is always a choice. In terms of a secular monarch, one can of course move to a different country and accept a different monarch – but that is not often possible.

The tenth of April

I have never been attracted to mindless obedience – even as a hippie, I never toed the party-line. That I chose to be in vajra commitment then, was an extremely serious decision – and one that was made on the basis of a fundamental conviction that there was no choice if my life was to mean anything.

———— · ————

Apart from the vows taken with my Lamas, I see all secular rules as being subject to personal choice and common sense. I do not obey speed limits – I simply drive carefully. Sometimes this means driving slower than allowed – in streets where children may be playing.

———— · ————

Politically I'm an anarchist. Whichever way one votes, a government is elected. This does not mean that I do not vote. I simply vote for what seems the more compassionate alternative. That does not mean I believe in the party for whom I vote. It is an expedient measure.

———— · ————

Some speak disrespectfully of animism as primitive – but those who accept the sentience of rocks and rivers would not have made as bad a mess of the Earth as the religiously civilised, spiritually sophisticated, or philosophically advanced have done. Maybe animism is not as primitive as some have thought it to be.

———— · ————

Laws are for people who cannot govern themselves – and for whom freedom and responsibility are alien. The reason not to steal or murder is not – that *to do so leads to punishment*. If a person is kind— and seeks the happiness and wellbeing of others as a natural response to being alive—then ethics and morality will be intrinsic. One simply has to like beings, people, animals, and the entire spectrum sentient phenomena.

The eleventh of April

The sounds of the vulture's flight are methods of practice. The great white vulture glides effortlessly above the reach and range of concept. Through these movements, Mind discovers itself in the inherently free space of being. The vulture has no fear of terrible heights – because the sky is her natural home.

———— · ————

The word directness—'trü[10]—pertains to sudden and immediate perception. In terms of Dzogchen, the Lama gives transmission through 'trü – but the texture of 'trü cannot be perceived if one has the mind of contradiction[11] or *the mind that sees contradiction in the words of the Lama* – and interprets that as a problem rather than as an indication that something cannot be contained in conventional language.

———— · ————

For 'trü to be functional, there needs to be intimacy[12]. Intimacy with the Lama refers to: harmony, agreeableness, friendliness, appropriate enthusiasm, eagerness, fascination, ebullience, joviality, vigour, and vivacity. These qualities can only arise when practice has developed to the point where one's practice has passed beyond: querulous quotidian stubbornness; querulous quotidian irritation; querulous quotidian preoccupation; querulous quotidian suspicion; and, querulous quotidian dejection.

---

10 *'khrus* / འཁྲུས་

11 *nang 'gal* / ནང་འགལ་

12 thunpa *(mThun pa* / མཐུན་པ་)

The twelfth of April

The Lama encourages situations in which a direct approach is possible in terms of recognising the essential nature. This is because that essential nature is close, accessible, present, and simple. From the perspective of dualistic derangement however – it is *too* close, *too* accessible, *too* present, and *too* simple.

———— · ————

The Lama—as vajra master—sidesteps the sour orthodoxies of quotidian rationality – in order to present transmission: almost when one is not looking. Then—suddenly—it's there. Suddenly it is seen – and, it could manifest through any means and any expression.

———— · ————

Zha-nak[13] is the exorcism of execrable expedients. We trust we can each divest ourselves of the deleterious decorum of dualistic derangement. It would be wonderful if we could overcome 'triple s' – the sulky sullen surly syndrome. There is no purpose in considering oneself to be a Buddhist of any kind whilst in the grips of 'triple s' – especially in its petulant pertinaciously pestiferous mode.

———— · ————

With rangdröl there is no distinction between arising and liberation. This is journey in which destination same as point of departure. You board a bus that takes immediately to where you are. So, when namtogs arise they instantaneously self-liberate. Your do not leave the state of nonduality. The arising of namthogs arising is their liberation. Division no longer exists. Liberation is instantaneous spontaneous effortlessness. *Kyabjé Düd'jom Rinpoche Jig'drèl Yeshé Dorje*

13 *zhwa nag* / ཞྭ་ནག – Black Hat dance.

The thirteenth of April

Understanding naturally manifests under the right circumstances – due to the individual's beginningless realisation. Because we are beginninglessly realised it is possible to realise the nondual state. Explanations can then flash on the innate mirror of awareness – and understanding of the nondual state can arise as spontaneous explanations.

———— · ————

As self-obsessionalists running scared from the emptiness of self – we look to a vanilla-vajrayana to save us from the voracious vector of vacuity. It seems to have all the answers. Vanilla-vajrayana has 're-incarnating Lamas' whose existence proves that 'I too will survive the stainless-steel dishwasher of death.' It has delightfully dainty deities whose compassion enfolds us all and preserves us from our innate non-existence. Vanilla-vajrayana with Neapolitan stripes has passionate deities who offer to buck up our jaded love-lives, and fierce deities who will protect us from the things we find disturbing. It has Lamas who 'absorb our negative karma[14]' – and mysteriously avoid becoming terminally neurotic or psychopathic as a result. It has practices by which we can overcome obstacles – such as 'having to do things we don't particularly want to do'. It would appear to have remedial measures for everything about Sutrayana that we found uncomfortable and bleak – everything that showed us anatman, when we really just wanted Batman.

———— · ————

How does one know that one is psychologically healthy enough to be at the experiential base for Vajrayana practice? One requires flexibility, adaptability, the ability to bounce back after traumatising experiences in a fairly short period of time without post-traumatic stress disorder.

The fourteenth of April

What is the imputed identity to which karma could adhere? What is this entity that has karma? If there is insoluble karma there must be an insoluble entity to whom it belongs. Buddha Shakyamuni explicitly stated that there was no basis for such an entity. This is the meaning of the word dag'mèd[15].

———— · ————

There is no solid, permanent, separate, continuous, or defined aspect to beingness. There are only characteristics which are continually in flux. When imputed identity vanishes – karma vanishes. Both are merely dualistic derangement.

———— · ————

From the societal point of view there is a *problem* when a poet is not *writing poetry* or when a painter is not *painting*. It is called *artistic block*. Vajrayanists however, are not impelled to name it *artistic block* – or see it as anything other than *the emptiness aspect of creativity*. Artistic block is a referential concept. If a poet—by definition—must be *writing poetry* to be a poet – then the times when there are no words will be disturbing. For poets uninformed by Vajrayana, this could give rise to difficult questions. Is a poet a still a poet when asleep? When eating? When defæcating? When shopping for groceries? When making love? When yodelling? When sky-diving? When sewing or knitting? When cooking lasagne? When refuelling a Harley Davidson Low-rider or skipping down the High Street with no skipping rope? Could a poet be considering a rhyme for Saskatchewan when making love? One would hope not. How often does the poet have to write poetry to remain a poet? What constitutes *an unacceptable gap in writing*? In terms of Vajrayana these questions are meaningless as a Vajrayanist is continuously creative throughout the sense fields in whatever they do or perceive.

15 *bDag med* / བདག་མེད་ / *anatman*

The fifteenth of April

'You' and 'I' can only be independent if we are not there. As long as we exist, we are interdependent. So, what is it that is independent?

———— · ————

'ö-Sèl[16] is not light, as it is normally understood. The word 'ö-Sèl is an analogy. Awareness is *self-luminous* inasmuch as its luminosity does not emanate from elsewhere. This is why yidams in thangka paintings have no light source. The awareness is simply there and simply luminous; self-existent; and, uncreated.

———— · ————

A television presenter asked for our views on 'envy' in respect of 'giving up materialism as the Buddhist way of life'. We provided our view. We were not surprised when no interest was shown in our appearing in the programme on Buddhism. The shocking nature of the view we presented was that we do not need to give up 'materialism' to be free of envy. We said that—from the point of view of Vajrayana—people could be materialistic on behalf of all beings. This could be said to be vajra-materialism. We explained that envy arises from a sense of poverty – however much or little we own. *Giving up materialism* therefore might not be helpful. We suggested that 'appreciation' was the key to shedding the disease of envy – because when we awaken appreciation, we become 'rich' in the sense that our enjoyment increases exponentially. We do not have to own phenomena in order to appreciate or enjoy phenomena. When we become 'rich with appreciative enjoyment', we become disinhibited in terms of appreciating the wealth of others. When we appreciate the wealth of others, envy ceases to exist and our appreciation becomes boundless. Our enjoyment of existence becomes the dance of self-liberated materialism.

16 *'od gSal gyi sems nyid* / ༄ོད་གསལ་གྱི་སེམས་ཉིད་ / *prabhasvaracitta* or *abhasvaracitta*.

The sixteenth of April

Buddhists are neither ascetics nor hedonists. If Buddhists appear as ascetics, it is merely because the nature of their practice is temporarily thus characterised. If Buddhists appear as hedonists, it is merely because the nature of their practice is thus momentarily exemplified.

———— · ————

We attempt to have happy relationships – but somehow success in this endeavour is either rare or fleeting. Our artistic history is sculpted and composed of 'love' – lost and found. It speaks a language unchanged by the passage of time. The popular music industry is founded on the 'love' that most of us fall into, are possessed by, and subsequently lose. Passion would seem to be a temporary state of being - a fire that burns itself out through its own desire to burn. 'Love' is a dimension of our lives as human beings. It is an experience that we are always trying to understand – yet no matter how much experience we accumulate, whenever 'love' manifests it is still highly mysterious. Even for yogis and yoginis it is mysterious – but that mystery is experienced as vastness.

———— · ————

Dualism creates a variety of problems with regard to the 'pure' and 'impure' in which it becomes difficult to appreciate the vajra master in yeshé 'cholwa mode. We want to separate the Lama into: *undesirable mundane conversation Lama* and *preferable didactic Lama; undesirable jocular Lama* and *preferable serious Lama; undesirable whimsical Lama* and *preferable ritualist Lama; undesirable critical diatribe Lama* and *preferable serene equitable Lama; undesirable avantgarde Lama* and *preferable gentle conservative Lama; undesirable politically incorrect Lama* and *preferable psychotherapy Lama; undesirable allopathic Lama* and *preferable alternative medicine Lama; undesirable outrageous Lama* and *preferable socially comprehensible Lama; undesirable nondual Lama* and *preferable samsara accommodating Lama; ad nauseum…*

The seventeenth of April

'Spiritual idiocy' should not be confused with 'vajra stupidity'. Vajra stupidity is concerned with a certain bluntness which abdicates the *intelligence of deviousness* with regard to the Lama. The 'spiritual idiot' on the other hand is merely an absentee from real life.

———— · ————

We do not need to give up materialism to be free of envy. From the point of view of Vajrayana one can be materialistic on behalf of all beings. This is full-blooded unwithheld materialism. Envy arises from the sense of poverty – however much or little is owned. Renouncing materialism might not help unless one renounced attachment to being a renunciate.

———— · ————

Appreciation is the key to shedding the disease of envy – because when we awaken appreciation, we become 'rich' in the sense that our enjoyment increases exponentially. We do not have to own phenomena in order to appreciate or enjoy phenomena. When we become 'rich with appreciative enjoyment', we become disinhibited in terms of appreciating the wealth of others. When we appreciate the wealth of others, envy ceases to exist and our appreciation becomes boundless.

———— · ————

The 'spiritual victim' should not be confused with 'vajra anxiety'. Vajra anxiety is related to the powerful creative tension which exists in the presence of the Lama – for one who is aware of the immanence and imminence of transmission. The 'spiritual victim' on the other hand is a narcissistic paranoid who generates self-importance from the ground of fantasy. The fantasy is one of 'ego slaying' in which the spiritual victim feels singled out to experience the entire wrathful weight of the Lama's Buddhakarma of destruction.

The eighteenth of April

Vajra simple-mindedness is being able to take a direct course and not be swayed by the latest ideas about how Buddhism could be improved.

——— · ———

There is a tendency to imagine that Vajrayana is *Sutrayana with 'added magic'* – and that the Lama is some kind of saint with special powers. There seems to be a need for 'enlightened masters' to dwell in an incomprehensible world which necessarily denies us access. In this incomprehensible world the Lama is like the super brain surgeon who puts everything right. We're sorry to have to tell you it's not like that. You have to do it yourself – no matter how inspiring the Lama may be. That applies to Vajrayana as much as it applies to Sutrayana. It's a do-it-yourself religion.

——— · ———

During the celebration of the tsog'khorlo we become the yidams for each other. In this way the tsog'khorlo is an intensification of the practice of pure vision in which we see the gathering as a vajra mandala. Psychotherapists would describe this as pathological. When hearing pure vision discussed they ask: *"What about the shadow? You are evidently practising in denial and that is not healthy."* It is true that sociopaths and narcissists occasionally crop up in all human gatherings and enterprises – but the practice of pure vision does not cause sociopathy or narcissism. It is actually relatively difficult within any authentic sangha to remain long as a sociopath – because there will be an emphasis on interpersonal kindness. We are never impressed by self-righteousness. We are never impressed by people who manipulate others or take advantage of others. We encourage tolerance, integrity, and exculpation with regard to inadvertent misdemeanours on the part of others.

The nineteenth of April

We are sentient space. Within the space of every being, an endless theatre of the elements performs. There is no eternal identity, but epochs in the timelessness of being can be characterised – either for seconds or centuries. We are such stuff as dreams are made on, and our little life is rounded with a sleep[17].

––––– · –––––

Chingkar Donyö Dorje[18] means *Profound Thunderbolt Clad in White Felt*. He was originally a Gélug monk – but he had visions of Guru Rinpoche and Yeshé Tsogyel which indicated he was a gTértön. He was thus expelled from the monastery. He became a wandering practitioner, who married and lived the life of a ngakpa. He was cursed, despised, and accused of being a charlatan. Once however, when Shabkar[19] was teaching in Bè-tsé Do-yön Dzong in Mangyül province, Chingkar Donyö Dorje was sitting in the audience. No one recognised him or paid him attention as he sat with his sangyum and children – until Shabkar suddenly announced: *"There is someone here who is greater than myself."* The monks, shocked by this revelation, could not fathom who the Lama could be. Shabkar then invited Chingkar Donyö Dorje and his family to come and sit with him. Thereafter everyone accepted Chingkar Donyö Dorje as a realised master. Shabkar and Chingkar Donyö Dorje became friends and Lamas to each other – shared transmission of each other's lineages. Chingkar Donyö Dorje took incarnation as Trülshik Rinpoche – one of the great Lamas of the Nyingma Tradition.

---

17 William Shakespeare, *The Tempest*, Act IV, scene i

18 *phying dKar don yod rDo rJe* / ཕྱིང་དཀར་དོན་ཡོད་རྡོ་རྗེ) – also known as Té-kya sMyonpa *(rTas sKya sMyon pa* / ཪྟས་སྐྱ་སྨྱོན་པ་ – Mad Tekya). Té-kya is khandro cypher language and has no translatable meaning in human language.

19 Shabkar Tsogdruk Rangdröl *(zhabs dKar tshogs drug rang grol* / ཞབས་དཀར་ཚོགས་དྲུག་རང་གྲོལ་ / 1781–1851) was a Tibetan yogi and poet from A-mDo. His yogic and poetic talent rivalled that of Milarépa.

The twentieth of April

Science without religion can be nihilistic. Religion without science can be bigotry. Life without pizza and Barolo could be a trifle limited.

———— · ————

Individuality is a quality that is prized in contemporary Western society. What does it signify however, for Buddhists engaged in meditative practice of recognising their empty nature? If there is no bDag—no eternal soul—what value has individuality or personality? The idea of *authentic individuality* and *authentic personality* may even seem an apostate doctrine to those who believe realisation equates to utter cessation. In terms of Vajrayana however – *authentic individuality* and *authentic personality* are simply the efflorescence of compassion on a moment-by-moment basis. If this were not the case Buddhas would be identical.

———— · ————

The antithesis to bDag, is bDag'mèd. bDag'mèd means 'absence of an eternal identity' – so in what sense can one speak of *authentic individuality* and *authentic personality*? Form is emptiness – and emptiness is form. This is the statement of the Heart Sutra. *Form* being *empty*, is the pervasive theme within Buddhism. It is necessary to understand that *form* is *emptiness* because human beings are habituated to defining themselves according to form criteria – where the forms are attemptedly divorced from emptiness. This is the cause of duality. To realise emptiness is crucial therefore, to free oneself from dualism. Beyond the realisation that *form* is *emptiness* however, there is the necessity of realising that *emptiness* is *form*. This is essential – because without realising that *emptiness* is *form*, duality will persist. The Arts are founded on the fact that *emptiness* is *form*. This is central to Vajrayana as the living experience of *authentic individuality* and *authentic personality*.

The twenty-first of April

If *kitsch* is your style—if you know it's *kitsch*—and you know what *kitsch* means; then by all means celebrate your manifestation of *kitsch*.

———— · ————

In terms of Tantra – the Arts are connected with the path. In terms of Dzogchen the Arts are connected with the goal. The goal, however, is not the completion of an Art work – but the recognition of the self-existent manifestation of Art as the efflorescence of phenomenal reality. This does not mean that the creative Arts play no part in Dzogchen – but that they become expressions of chang chub sem in relation to the dKyil'khor of one's adventitious associations.

———— · ————

When performing Phurba dance, we move outside the tired self-protective rationale. The self-protective rationale is one which wishes to blame someone or something else for our own pain and confusion. The self-protective rationale in that which seeks to avoid personal responsibility – and to take refuge in being a lost and confused victim of circumstances beyond his or her control. In the Phurba dance we stab – and when we stab, we stab our own neuroses. We become stronger when we stab, rather than weaker. We are only losing 'that which makes us small'. *That which makes us small* is dishonesty and sneakiness. We should not be sneaky people. We should not devise philosophies which validate our selfishness. We are capable of slaying our own sneakiness and furtive desires to avoid responsibility. We are capable of being Dorje Phurba because we rejoice in the fact that we are trapped by our commitments and therefore forced to be decent people. Our vajra brothers and sisters hold us accountable, and hold themselves accountable – there is no escape, and the Phurba dance celebrates that fact.

The twenty-second of April

Dad'dun—devotion—cannot be manufactured just as people cannot talk themselves into being in love.

———— · ————

Too many people try to develop dad'dun perfunctorily – merely on the basis that it is 'spiritually mandatory'. This is not so different from refraining from killing people because it's illegal. It is good to refrain from violence – but preferable to be devoid of violent intention.

———— · ————

Devotion is direct knowledge built of the development of skill and insight. A professional musician is a better judge of a world-class instrumentalist and someone whose musical skills are rudimentary. It requires experiences of nonduality to suspect that someone is a Buddha – otherwise one can have no idea.

———— · ————

No one can make you feel devotion. There is *spiritual seduction*, certainly – but the seduction that tricks another person into feelings of devotion, is short lived. There are *career gurus*, skilled in *spiritual seduction* – but they tend only to attract the psychologically needy; cult-fodder; social-climbers with a penchant for the esoteric; and, power-seekers who will pay the price to gain ascendency over others. These are people who claim to have devotion – but their devotion is either: immature dysfunctional dependency; lip-service designed to foster a social image; or, the manipulative adoption of an outer form, designed for the approbation of the grand panjandrum.

The twenty-third of April

Meditation is not fundamentally a technique – it is a state of being.

––––––– · –––––––

The purpose of Buddhist meditation—in any tradition—is not concerned with relaxation or stress reduction. Relaxation and stress reduction are merely side effects. The same is true of Baroque, Classical, Blues, or Jazz. One could use these musical traditions for relaxation and stress reduction – but that is not the purpose of music.

––––––– · –––––––

When secular Arts are practised by ngakpas – ngakpas do not become secularised; nor do those Arts remain secular. Secular Arts practised by ngakpas are transforms into Vajrayana. Ngakpas transform everything into dimension of Vajrayana. People should never think *'Vajrayana only for monks and recluses.'* This is wrong thinking. You must always state strongly that this is 'wrong thinking'. *Kyabjé Düd'jom Rinpoche Jig'drèl Yeshé Dorje*

––––––– · –––––––

It's not so much that there is no point in meditation outside a religious context. It is more useful to question what happens when one practises meditation outside a religious context – and how meditation functions outside a religious context. The problem may be easier to understand if one asks questions such as *What happens when attempting to swim outside the context of water? What the happens when one makes love outside the context of a committed loving relationship? What then happens when one eats outside the context of hunger? What happens when one laughs outside the context of humour?*

The twenty-fourth of April

Target practice—with bow, rifle, or hand gun—is a valuable way of taking awareness into the physical dimension. One sees the proof of one's ability to be present and undistracted. It is there in the target.

———— · ————

It seems to upset some people that I enjoy target shooting with a .357 magnum Colt Python. I usually indicate my naked upper limbs and ask them *"Have you never heard of the Buddhist right to bare arms?"*[20]

———— · ————

Everyone's hand wavers when shooting a revolver in target practice. If you hold out your arm with three or four pounds of revolver in your hand – you are not going to be able to remain motionless. No one can. One can certainly train in stillness in order to remain still for longer periods. One can also develop arm strength in terms of getting used to holding one's arm up at an unaccustomed angle. These efforts will help – but all one accomplishes with this training, is to give oneself a better environment in which to find the empty moment – in which the form-moment-explosion could allow an experience of the nondual state.

———— · ————

Why play with something designed to kill? That question is asked of us in respect of firearms – but it's not asked with regard to Tantra because some people do not see themselves as playing. They imagine they are serious. Tantra however, is not a new age playground, where ultimatist techniques add the piquancy of a Tibetan secret society mystique. If kindness is neglected and narcissistic dilettantism is indulged – one may as well take Hitler as one's yidam.

---

20 The right to bear arms is the Second Amendment of the United States Constitution – 15th of December 1791.

The twenty-fifth of April

The spiritual subset of the politically correct would have us believe that: a whale should conform to the vision of plankton; a cheetah crawl at the pace of a sloth; or that, an eagle fly no higher than a sparrow.

——— · ———

Some advocate dependence on 'the collective wisdom of the sangha' as an initiative toward diminishing the rôle of the vajra master. What is this 'collective wisdom'? Can it be said that a hundred thousand dualistic individuals equal one vajra master? We would suggest that this might be faulty arithmetic.

——— · ———

Descartes stated *'I think; therefore I am'*. Be that as it may, Buddhism experientially questions Descartes' assertion. Buddhism—via experience—asks *'I don't think – therefore what? What if there is no thought? What is that experience? What is behind this need to locate reference points which establish my existence?'*

——— · ———

We do not subscribe to the idea that individuality should be abrogated. We are keen on individuality. We encourage individuality. We see the *individual* and the *social context of the individual* as the creative play of emptiness and form. If the social context dominates then not only is the individual damaged but the social context is also damaged – because what else is the social context but the sum of the individuals within it? If the individual does not consider his or her obligations and commitments to the social context, then not only is the social context damaged, but the individual is also damaged – because what else is the individual but the individual manifestation of the social context which is co-created by each individual?

The twenty-sixth of April

Charisma is not always to be trusted – as it is seen in psychopaths perhaps more frequently than it is seen is saints.

———— · ————

There is the charisma that is natural and the charisma that is lent by those who offer adulation. If one believes in one's charisma when it is merely lent – one stands the risk of becoming sociopathic.

———— · ————

Charisma is a dangerous quality to possess – unless one understands that it is meaningless without altruism.

———— · ————

To be handsome or beautiful is not necessarily advantageous. It is better to be loved or admired for one's personality rather than one's pulchritude – and to love and admire from the same perspective.

———— · ————

To become Matramrudra[21]—negative freedom—is an extraordinary accomplishment. We have rarely met anyone who would remotely qualify. Not even the vilest cult leader of recent times has sufficient chutzpah to be the lowliest servant of Matramrudra. Matramrudra was psychopathically fearless and possessed immense strength. Matramrudra had the power to be totally self-oriented and self-obsessed, totally alone, and entirely self-reliant. To become Matramrudra requires endurance that few possess, or would want to possess. From our limited point of view only the highest-ranking Matramrudras are remembered in history – whereas many are remembered even for miniature manifestations of changchub sem. So if you want to go down in history, be nice to people, be generous, be gentle, be tolerant – and, have a sense of humour.

---

21 Matram Rudra *(ma tram ru tra* / མ་ཏྲམ་རུ་ཏྲ) – was originally a Hindu deity, an emanation of Shiva. In Vajrayana, Matram Rudra is the personification of terminally contorted duality – the reverse of nonduality.

The twenty-seventh of April

In respect of changchub sem – Lamas enjoy the dualistic neuroses of the students. If a Lama does not enjoy the neuroses of a student, it signifies lack of connection with the capacity for transformation in that student. Every neurosis is merely the distortion of nondual realisation – and so the Lama must be able to see that reflected in the student.

———·———

When attraction awakens, desire is awakened. Within the romantic/sexual dimension – two things occur simultaneously: we shine, and we perceive the shining quality of our focus of desire. We start to see what it means to 'be in the pink'. The pupils dilate in order to see more of the shining quality. This shining quality is the lustre of the primordial state as it manifests within the dimension of trülku[22]. Nondual realisation is not just Mind – it is also Voice, and Body. This is why compassion and desire cannot be separated – and it begins with appreciation. It then expands to everyone and everything, everywhere.

———·———

Vajrayana is slightly frustrating from the point of view of wanting an answer – or an antidote to pain, which can be followed as a recipe. Vajrayana does not negate the richness of confusion; neither does it negotiate with suffering in order to secure premium transactions according to prevailing circumstances. Vajrayana does not make life neat and tidy. Vajrayana does not make life serene, unless serenity is what is occurring. Vajrayana is not an answer or an antidote – it is an endless process of opening to the nondual texture of existence. It's the coalescence of energy in the rich moment-by-moment frisson of vajra-romance. It is the infinite sequence of fleeting forms which constitute the flow of our lives.

22 *sPrul sKu* / སྤྲུལ་སྐུ་ / *nirmanakaya)* – Sphere of Realised Manifestation.

The twenty-eighth of April

When motivation is mixed, it has 'drag factors'. Wanting to help someone who is in need of help – but, also wanting to be seen as a good, is a drag factor.

———— · ————

Wanting to be appreciated, thanked, and praised, means that one will be of less help than one could have been. One will have complicated a relatively simple situation. Complicating the situation means that it will not run smoothly.

———— · ————

Being distracted from helping, by the desire for recognition sabotages the help one is offering. When motivations conflict there is inertia – and, when there's inertia, goals become far harder to reach.

———— · ————

Vajrayana is only simple inasmuch as it allows complexity to be what it is. Vajrayana is only complex insofar as it allows the simple fact of our condition to dance in and out of existence. Vajrayana reveals the form of emptiness and the emptiness of form. Vajrayana reveals the emptiness of the form of emptiness, and the form of the emptiness of form. Vajrayana reveals an infinite hall of mirrors in which there is no final answer beyond the fleeting answers – shifting endlessly within the empty mirror. Answers can only be understood by allowing emptiness. To allow emptiness requires that we relinquish the need to concretise 'an answer'. Answers are the impermanent manifestations of a permanent emptiness.

The twenty-ninth of April

Every emotion is an open-ended opportunity.

———— · ————

I[23] don't really ideate or ponder in words at that often. There are arisings in Mind – and I express them in words later, if required.

———— · ————

Every feeling or sensation experienced is an expression of nonduality – a manifestation of the spectrum of radiant energies. Emotions however generally manifest as distorted reflections of those energies. These distorted reflections arise as a result of the way in which the 'natural display of the mirror of Mind' is constructed with compulsive intellectual contrivances. No matter to what degree the dualistic hall of mirrors distorts the emotions; a connection with the intrinsic unmanifested nondual condition remains.

———— · ————

There are many opportunities to experience emptiness: exhilaration, fascination, laughter, ecstasy, joy, peace, stillness, absorption, concentration, suspense, thrill, and wonderment. These experiences could be allowed to be what they are, even if only for brief periods of time. Allowing experiences to be what they are—with the inspiration of the Lama—would garner a sensational experience of essential Vajrayana. In similar vein it is possible to pause—even if only for a moment—to taste the indefinable edge of an emotion or an experience which is in transition. The open-ended quality of the ambivalences which exist across the broad range of life situations and relationships could simply be accepted.

---

23 Ngak'chang Rinpoche *(sNgags 'chang Rinpoche* / སྔགས་འཆང་རིན་པོ་ཆེ་).

The thirtieth of April

Duality—in one sense—is the artificial separation of experience into two fields: 'perception' and 'field of perception'. The word 'perception' applies to the act of perceiving – the way in which the presence of the world is registered through the sense faculties. 'Field of perception' is the world that is perceived. Attempting to establish perception and field of perception as independent, causes monstrous confusion. This divisive logic distances us analytically from direct experience.

———— · ————

Relationships between men and women provide a potent array of tender ambivalences – vivid moments in which the sheer radiance of empty potentiality could be glimpsed. Personal freedom can either be attemptedly grasped through consecutive painful attempts to concretise – or, the amorphous quality of laterality that exists within relationships could be acknowledged. Laterality in this sense relates to the fact that the patterns within a relationship rarely move logically or in consistently straight lines. This laterality could be embraced as a dimension of experience in which being in continual process is accepted – without hope or fear of a permanent direction.

———— · ————

Romance roils with astonishment. It seethes with wonder, precipitating unexpected transitions. Loving passion facilitates reflections of emptiness, which sparkle or glimmer through fogs of habitual patterning. Seeking to practise emptiness, as the basis of Vajrayana, necessitates a Vajrayana approach to the emptiness engendered by a lover. This requires the cultivation of impeccable verve, in which the raw texture of intimate interactions with a lover is celebrated. In this vibrant emptiness, an unbridled lust for the entire exactness of our situation could be awakened.

Hung

May

One should not misunderstand the difference between attachment and devotion.

HE Ögyen Dro'dül Thrin-lé Kunkyab Rinpoche

རྒྱལ་བ་ཨོ་རྒྱན་འགྲོ་འདུལ་ཕྲིན་ལས་ཀུན་སྐྱབས་རིན་པོ་ཆེ་

In Buddhism *tongpa-nyid*[1]—empty nature—means 'openness' – it transcends that which is merely 'empty'.

Khar-trül Wangchuk Rig'dzin Rinpoche

མཁར་སྤྲུལ་དཔལ་གྱི་དབང་ཕྱུག་རིག་འཛིན་རིན་པོ་ཆེ།

---

1   *sTong pa nyid* / སྟོང་པ་ཉིད་

159

The first of May

The way to raise rLung rTa—wind horse—is simply to *authentically enjoy* the phenomenal universe *as Art*. Regarding every act as Art however, requires constant attention and precise care. It is not as easy as inauthentic enjoyment – because authentic enjoyment is real involvement.

———— · ————

Raising rLung rTa through cheerful attention to one's appearance is to take responsibility for what other people see. One can bring pleasure to others through the Art of sartorialism. If what you wear causes people to be complimentary – you have given them an opportunity to raise rLung rTa.

———— · ————

Chögyam Trungpa Rinpoche raised rLung rTa through cultural modalities by sometimes wearing a kilt and Scottish costume to honour his marital family connection with Scotland. The nirmanakaya dimension is one in which infinite sartorial expressions become feasible in terms of the compassionate communication of raising rLung rTa. There is no aspect of the phenomenal world which cannot be employed by realised Lamas in terms of providing transmission.

———— · ————

rLung rTa can be raised through many different guises. DoKhyentsé Yeshé Dorje raised rLung rTa as a realised hunter – and Ling Gésar as a realised warrior. Chögyam Trungpa Rinpoche raised rLung rTa through military appearances – probably causing glorious offense to the politically correct. Such appearances pose a fabulous challenge to constricted views of Vajrayana. I do my best by wearing a 1960s emerald, crimson, and gold striped Farnham Girls' Grammar School blazer with a 'Head Girl' badge on the lapel. It also has a white embroidered insignia of the breast pocket which reads *'abandon hope and fear all who enter.'*

The second of May

Danger is a broad concept. What is dangerous for one person is exciting for another.

———— · ————

Emptiness happens. Dangerous territory is wherever the rules do not apply – and that can be anywhere. Rules are *form* – but then *emptiness* happens.

———— · ————

Some people purposely seek out extreme situations in the wilderness. They embark upon adventures which challenge the limits of their capacities at the boundaries of the physical world. They do this in order to experience the power they find in being on the edge. Similarly—through devotion and transmission—we are invited and empowered to put ourselves at risk in exploring the wilderness of experiential space.

———— · ————

Danger is often a question of how rigid one's parameters of safety need to be. One's parameters of safety can be so minutely defined that even the subject matter of a conversation can be threatening. This is often why people feel they need to take offence or retreat from situations. The world can be realistically dangerous – but it can also be far safer than some people imagine.

———— · ————

Some think that 'culture shock' concerns exposure to poverty and sickness – but that is actually something which can be witnessed anywhere; if one is not in denial. The real nature of 'culture shock' is the sense of danger concerning the ways other people organise the rules, regulations, guidelines, and conventions.

The third of May

The play of the elements is actually all there is. It's completely simple – and the vast spectrum of Vajrayana is an extrapolation of that.

———— · ————

The elements are the world in which we live. The elements are what we are – physically, intellectually, emotionally, and subtly in terms of vision. The elements could be described as the subatomic ground of being. They are reality—from one perspective—from geography to particle physics.

———— · ————

In the Dzogchen practices of the elements and sense fields – wherever one finds oneself, at any given moment, opportunities are spontaneously suggested for *finding presence of awareness*. One does not set out to find these opportunities – because they are continuously available. One cannot avoid them. Thus, there is no entrance or exit from practice.

———— · ————

Externally the elements are the five skandhas[2]. Internally, the elements are the five Buddha families. Secretly the elements are the khandros and dPa'wos. Ultimately the elements are the thig-lés. There is nothing to be found other than the five elements.

———— · ————

The Arts are the play of the five elements; in colour, sound, fragrance, taste, texture, and ideation. They display in cinematography; disport in theatre; and divulge in dance. Nothing either arises or dissolves in reality other than the five elements. This is the quotidian reality of vajra masters – and those students who are authentically within their dKyil'khors.

---

2   *phung po* / ཕུང་པོ་ – aggregates.

The fourth of May

Life is short, it makes no sense not to plunge deep. Plunge into whatever it is that makes life worth living.

——— · ———

We should prioritise what we love – and what animates existence. To do less is to be less than half alive. Life sparkles with intrinsic magic that is suddenly and delightfully communicative when you find yourself in love.

——— · ———

With the long list of 'what I want', whatever comes at the head of the list is what you're likely to get. Take great care with what you place at the head of the list.

——— · ———

If you cannot make sacrifices for what you love – you have to admit that you don't love it enough. Lamenting that you cannot have what you love whilst refusing to make the necessary sacrifices is the puerile pastime of 'thom yors[3].

——— · ———

Generally speaking, you can have anything you want – just not everything. This means you have to learn to give up everything you want less, than whatever it is you want more. Maybe it's a reconditioned 1966 Rolls Royce Silver Cloud – or maybe it's the ability to maintain Vajrayana vows. Personally, I'd love a reconditioned 1966 Rolls Royce Silver Cloud – but I'd rather maintain my Vajrayana vows.

---

3   'thom yor / འཐོམ་ཡོར་ – idiot or fool.

The fifth of May

The multifarious Tantric empowerment robes are the formal means of transmission through the power of symbol – but informally, limitless styles of dress can be worn to express the dimension of vision.

——— · ———

The *Art of Sartorialism*—in terms of Vajrayana—originates from the Eight Manifestations of Guru Rinpoche. There are actually many more than eight forms – but the eight are the most well-known. One sees from these appearances how different styles are employed for different purposes in terms of teaching.

——— · ———

Guru Rinpoche exhibited sartorialism within the space of life as the essence of natural dignity and natural heroism. With his example— and with the example of the eight manifestations of Yeshé Tsogyel —many gö kar chang lo Lamas have employed clothing to illustrate themes within Vajrayana and to offer transmission through appearances.

——— · ———

Quentin Crisp said *"Fashion is not style… Fashion is instead of style. Style is an idiom springing spontaneously from personality…"* In clothing or any area of life personal appreciation is something that has to be discovered. One discovers what personal appreciation is when one learns to perceive the language of the sense fields. Phenomena converse with us, as to their nature. This is an aspect of Drala – and it is what makes a person an individual personality. An individual person is not a fixed entity – but a being who knows how to communicate with others in terms of the nature of reality. This is why Lamas are different from each other. Lamas have distinct personalities, in order to communicate directly with those who resonate with them.

The sixth of May

Vajra simple-mindedness, is the power to cut through the unnecessary complications manufactured by attempting to *edit life*, as if it were a film. We need to abandon attempts to re-write Vajrayana in order to splice together a 'dualistically coherent movie'.

———— · ————

We need to acknowledge that attempting to splice spirituality conveniently into the B-movie of our non-practising lives – is non-functional. Nothing will ever work if we try to rehash Vajrayana. We cannot cut 'this' out, and splice 'that' in – saying *"Yes I agree with* this *aspect of Vajrayana—because it fits my socio-political outlook—but this other aspect isn't right for me"* is doomed to failure.

———— · ————

Vajra-simple mindedness is the ability to make a decision and follow it through. This does not mean being chained to an arbitrary course of action—or that changes in direction are not possible—but that one is not at the mercy of the fear that *there is something better somewhere.* There is always another Lama somewhere who has something special. There is always another lineage with something unique. If one merely chases what seems to be special one will never appreciate what is special in any case – because it is most likely that what is special is already there; exactly where you are.

———— · ————

One has to have courage to be simple — because one has to live without itineraries, agendas, policies, strategies, campaigns, crusades, or electioneering. One has to be able to live without self-justifying rationalisations, self-protective initiatives, defensive enterprises, and covert ingenuity. To aspire to vajra-simplicity one has to discover that complexity is not a safety measure.

The seventh of May

To be true to the nature of Vajrayana – all one has to do is receive teaching and apply what is learnt.

——— · ———

Past mind no longer exists. Future mind is not yet present. Whatever arises in the moment is indecipherable because it cannot be translated by thought without turning it into thought.
Kyabjé Düd'jom Rinpoche Jig'drèl Yeshé Dorje

——— · ———

Authentic Vajrayanists are those who are married to Vajrayana. They married Vajrayana because they fell in love with Vajrayana. They do not file for divorce – because they remain in love. That's a simplistic definition – but it functions extremely well in terms of lifelong commitment.

——— · ———

If one applies Vajrayana, one will resemble a Vajrayana practitioner. One will appear cheerful. One will appear cheerful, because one will not moan, whine, whinge, or kvetch about what is unavoidable. Practitioners bear up well under duress. Practitioners do not engage in status rivalry. Practitioners are never affronted, offended, insulted, slighted – or have any other such bogus reaction.

——— · ———

Authentic practitioners are always welcoming to those who are new to the Lamas' dKyil'khor. They exhibit no display of informational-knowledge beyond answering questions, if asked. They expect no deference for being 'old students'. They take no umbrage at the faux pas made merely through new students being uninformed. In short, one acts like the kind of person one would have liked to have met when first attending a retreat – at the time when one knew little or nothing of Vajrayana.

166

The eighth of May

One needs to perceive as if one were immortal – but act as if death was approaching a little too rapidly.

———— · ————

Awareness of death needs to coexist with a joyous appreciation of the enormous value of life.

———— · ————

A love of life that is based on denial of death, is going to be lacking in authentic appreciation because death is an aspect of life. If one screens out death – one screens out more life than one could possibly imagine.

———— · ————

One can still appreciate even as death approaches. Enjoy the time remaining. Invest in it. That is possible. Ordinary people can be heroic if they simply enter the right mindset of *'Why not?'* The Titanic is sinking. You're a member of the orchestra. Why not continue to play? Would it be preferable to cry or scream?

———— · ————

Vajrayana practitioners don't make projects out of their illnesses or approaching deaths. They simply rise to the challenge — and treat it as 'the next thing' in life. When Khandro Déchen's father, Tres, was a few days from death he said *"You know, Chögyam, I thought to myself this morning: Come on Tres, get on with the next thing."* He also asked me to preside over his funeral and make sure that everyone had a good time. I told everyone what Tres had said to me – and everyone found it a powerful statement. Some asked me if he'd become a Buddhist. I replied that he hadn't – at least not as it would be commonly understood.

The ninth of May

To predict anything, one has to know what one is seeing in the
present. It doesn't actually take much in the way of insight to see
that some people are doomed by their own actions. It is far more
difficult to see it in oneself – unless one engages in silent sitting.

———— · ————

Prediction is predicated upon cause and effect in conjunction with
accidental events. There is always probability and randomness;
inevitability and arbitrariness; certitude and improbability. That is
why Mo divination is always the interface of haphazardness and
pattern.

———— · ————

It was predicted by Aro Lingma that if Aro Yeshé was to take a
male incarnation, he would have certain obstacles. At the level of
Mind, he would be chaotic and mercurial. At the level of Speech, he
would be erratic, disjointed, eccentric and given to absurdities.
Those without conventional religious preconceptions however,
would find themselves inspired by him. At the level of Body, he
would engage in a variety of unlikely activities such as the adoption
of idiosyncratic costume and singing of secular songs accompanied
by unusual instruments of his own devising. He would be child-like
and playful as a means of transmission – but in such a way as to
cause doubt as to his credibility in the minds of scholars. He would
delight in the transient aspects of popular, secular culture as
methods of transmission, but in such a way as to undermine his
status with regard to those who were attached to conventional
religious forms. Aro Lingma predicted that these aspects could
either incite him to brilliance or cause him to dwindle into
mediocrity.

The tenth of May

It's useful to remember death. It's a possibility, even if one is not a suicide pilot, mercenary, Russian Roulette gambler, gun slinger, frequent flier, or Himalayan pilgrim.

———— · ————

It is good to make friends with death. Whenever the plane takes off, we recite Yeshé Tsogyel mantra. Whenever the plane lands, we recite Vajra Guru mantra. This is not for protection or a 'thank you' for the protection – but as the recognition that we may continue to see our students, or not.

———— · ————

Kyabjé Düd'jom Rinpoche, in his *History and Fundamentals of the Nyingma*, writes: *'It would seem correct to state that the Nyingmas are somewhat unlucky.'* Through accident and misfortune, however, inspiration and creativity arise in the context of unlikely events and unexpected situations.

———— · ————

We have always considered it to be important for students to witness the fact that our lives are not always easy or straightforward. Life has a way of providing exciting new departures – but like all exciting new departures, they tend to interfere with the ability to *keep all the balls in the air*, as one juggles.

———— · ————

Human situations are changeable. Human beings are often moved to explore the context of being alive in tangential ways. It is not for nothing that Chögyam Trungpa Rinpoche described Nyingma as 'the accident lineage'. The idea of 'accident' however, could be highly positive – because without unpredictability, life would offer fewer creative opportunities.

The eleventh of May

The Lama's display is indestructible simply because it is not constructed. One can only demolish what has been fabricated.

—— · ——

The Lama's display is continually developed on the basis of what is required by students in terms of transmission.

—— · ——

Every Lama from whom one takes empowerment and transmission becomes one's Lama. Sometimes people do not understand this. They find problems in terms of experiencing devotion toward a number of Lamas. It is not adulterous to feel devotion toward more than one Lama. This is never the case. It could not be the case – because *that to which one feels devotion* is the nondual state manifested through the *unique human vajra display* of the Lama.

—— · ——

If one has more than one Lama—and this is often the case—one can experience conflict in terms of receiving contradictory instructions. This is why it is crucial to have one central Lama—or heart Lama—with whom one can clarify contradictions. There are never contradictions in terms of teachings – because they can all be resolved through distinguishing between the vehicles of Buddhism. In terms of practice however it is not so simple – and one needs one authority to make sense of conflicting advice. Clearly there is no middle ground between the advice to be vegetarian and abstemious – and the advice to eat meat and drink alcohol. Both are possible in terms of advice – and so an answer must be sought from a single source.

The twelfth of May

Because people are symbols of nonduality – there can be no one who is not essentially sacred according to the pure vision of Vajrayana.

———— · ————

Wherever we find ourselves—and whatever the situation—*that* is the source or birthplace of Vajrayana. It lies within the fabric of *the infinite purity of the phenomenal world.*

———— · ————

As Lamas we encourage Vajrayana to emerge from the context of ordinary conversation, concerning subjects *other* than Vajrayana. For us Vajrayana is self-display. Vajrayana is unfabricated – and it self-arises from within whatever the context may be.

———— · ————

Every point-instant is Ögyen. When that is known one can sing *Ögyen yul gyi nub chang tsam: Pema ké-sar dong-po la: Ya tsan chö-gi ngö-drüp nyé: Pema Jung-né Shé-su drag: Khordu khandro mang-pö khor: Khyé kyi jé-su dag drüb kyi: Jin gyi lob chir sheg su sol: Guru Pema Siddhi Hung:* In the North-west of the land of Ögyen: On the pistil of the stem of lotus: Endowed with the most marvellous attainments: Renowned as the 'Lotus Born': Surrounded by dKyil'khors of myriad khandros: I follow your example: May I realise your knowledge and be irradiated by your presence. Om A'a: Hung Bendzra Guru Pema Siddhi Hung: Every point-instant is Ögyen.

The thirteenth of May

Individuality cannot fail to manifest – it therefore has no need of construction.

———— · ————

Trying to be an individual is like trying to get wet when you're already in the sea.

———— · ————

Individuality is nothing but emptiness and form dancing in an infinite number of different ways.

———— · ————

Individuality is what manifests when one gives up trying to be *what one feels one needs to be* in order to fulfil the demands of the destinies fabricated by others.

———— · ————

Let thoughts of past, present, and future settle in the present moment — and, in that moment, simply experience what is naturally there. Visual projections appear in meditation if one distracts oneself with here and there or then and when. If it is considered that Mind is nothing, it will become 'the prison of numb emptiness' – and the richness of the nature of Mind cannot self-emerge. *Kyabjé Düd'jom Rinpoche Jig'drèl Yeshé Dorje*

———— · ————

There is a natural fascination in discovering how Leonardo Da Vinci or Thangtong Gyalpo became who they were. They were similar in many respects. Both were inventors, scientists, artists, and engineers. They were both in love with the phenomenal world in terms of reality. They equally studied the efflorescence of existence – and they both inspired many thousands of others in those fields of endeavour. Even more fascinating is the fact that we could all—individually—be just like that.

The fourteenth of May

Buddhism is not Truth. Buddhism is method – an infinite array of methods for realising truth or reality.

——— · ———

The expression of Buddhism is not *truth in itself.* Truth is not 'the words' as they are written. The Buddhist teachings are *sign-posts to truth* – ways of enabling us to see what is true. The essence that is Dharma can never be expressed. Shakyamuni Buddha said *"I manifested in a dreamlike way to dreamlike beings and gave a dreamlike Dharma – but in reality, I never taught and never actually came."*

——— · ———

Dharma is non-existent. This is not some highly profound statement that cannot be understood – but an expression of method. Dharma however, is expressed in words. That is simply a method by which Dharma can be realised

——— · ———

Because Buddhism is a religion of method rather than truth – there are nine different vehicles of Buddhism. That there are contradictions between the vehicles would only be problematic if Buddhism were a religion of truth. Every vehicle has its unique base – and therefore each vehicle has its own methods that are predicated on each base.

——— · ———

Mind can be investigated with the intellect for the duration of one's life – but one would be no closer to realisation. The real meaning of Dzogchen is natural immediacy in which the presence of awareness is without limit. Whatever is perceived is radiantly clear like the changeless blue of the sky. Whatever arises in Mind is inseparable from primordial radiant clarity-awareness. It is unborn and unceasing in splendour – and joyously manifests in every aspect of phenomenal reality. *Kyabjé Düdjom Rinpoche Jig'drèl Yeshé Dorje*

The fifteenth of May

People often feel they need to explain why they *like what they like*—or *love what they love*—but in reality, it's a mystery: the mystery of emptiness and form dancing in myriad modes.

———— · ————

Guru Rinpoche and Yeshé Tsogyel are dimensions of space, nondual vision, and manifest nondual personality. They are conspicuously existent. One can communicate with Guru Rinpoche and Yeshé Tsogyel—here and now—because their streams of awareness never died. When one lives amongst those who find this to be true in terms of their everyday lives – one cannot fail to be impressed by the texture of that reality.

———— · ————

Love is the knowledge of what is lovable. We will never know how profound John Lennon's words were, *'There's nothing you can do that can't be done; Nothing you can sing that can't be sung; Nothing you can say… but you can learn how to be you in time. It's easy – All you need is love.'* Love is the knowledge of what is lovable – be it the early morning cup of tea; the pint of New York Extra-espresso in a Bhutanese bowl; the 'cello suite by Johan Sebastian Bach; the painting by Max Ernst; the sound of the Vajrayana orchestra; or, the sound of Kyabjé Düd'jom Rinpoche Jig'drèl Yeshé Dorje's voice.

———— · ————

To place one's hand in Guru Rinpoche's hand-print on the wall of a cave—and to have no doubt about that fact that it is his handprint —makes the experience of Vajrayana entirely different. Naturally – one cannot enter into such a state of mind on demand – but one certainly can be open to the possibility. Unless one accepts this possibility, Vajrayana remains an intellectual pursuit until the moment of inspiration begins to dawn. The dawning of inspiration is like falling in love. One has to fall in love with Vajrayana, or one merely remains in a loveless 'arranged marriage'.

The sixteenth of May

When one allows the nature of the transmission to manifest, pilgrimage[4] self-manifests as transmission.

———— · ————

Pilgrimage—in terms of Dzogchen—is not concerned with 'obviousness' or with organised spiritual activities; it is concerned with presence. Presence in all things.

———— · ————

A Hidden Land[5] is hidden because it is too close – just as our beginningless nondual nature is too close. There are said to be four obstacles in terms of Dzogchen and recognising *the nature of Mind*: it is also *too* close, *too* accessible, *too* present, and *too* simple. The same is true of the Hidden Land – and this is why pilgrimage is important.

———— · ————

Pilgrimage is life. It's a journey. It's a journey within the journey of life – that can be emblematic of one's future life. How one behaves on pilgrimage is extremely important because it is predictive of what will follow when one returns home. Pilgrimage is also an exploration of the emotional aspect of being a practitioner – and this is more important, in a certain sense, for Western people. Although there is no impetus to become culturally Himalayan – one is faced with the degree to which one is accepted as following the same religion. Of course, there will be differences – but cheese is cheese: it is always made of milk.

4 nèkor *(gNas sKor /* གནས་སྐོར་*)*
5 beyul *(sBas yul /* སྦས་ཡུལ་*)*

The seventeenth of May

The image in the mirror is a moment in a series of moments. The image in the mirror is the dance of emptiness and form. One sees one's face, but it is not one's face. Vanity is only an issue when one does not realise that every face is an expression of realisation according to the physiognomy of infinite yidams.

——— · ———

The Three Terrible Oaths of Dorje Tröllö: Whatever happens – may it happen; Whichever way it goes – may it go that way; There is no purpose. That there is no purpose means that there is no *one purpose*; no *overriding purpose*; no *heavenly directive*; and, no *God-given purpose*. Dorje Tröllö wishes everything to be exactly as it is. Is that not a cause for exultation!

——— · ———

Dorje Tröllö is the master of yeshé 'cholwa. Yeshé means *primordial wisdom* and 'cholwa means chaos. Chögyam Trungpa Rinpoche translated this as Crazy Wisdom because yeshé 'cholwa appears crazy according to the sensible rules of dualism. That is not to say that being sensible is dualistic – but the sense of dualism is often senseless. Being sensible according to dualism often means predictability, regularity, obviousness, uninventiveness, unoriginality, and imitativeness. These have more in common with being safe rather than being sensible. An old lady—a neighbour when I was young—told me how people laughed at her because she wore her fur coat 'inside out'. She explained that it was not 'inside out' but that it had been made like that. It was how the tribespeople in the Karakorum made the coats. The coats were made in this way to be warmer. So, in sub-zero conditions she was being sensible whilst the people laughing at her were shivering but not thinking of themselves as foolish. The old lady was not a yeshé 'cholwa master – but this may cause reflection on what is crazy and what is sane.

The eighteenth of May

There are no higher or lower vehicles – simply higher and lower practitioners for whom the appropriate vehicle will be the highest vehicle

———— · ————

One has to observe oneself in the moment. Sutra, Tantra, and Dzogchen are a continuum in terms of involvement. One practises what is appropriate in terms of how one is in the moment. One has to observe one's condition.

———— · ————

One does not practise Dzogchen and neglect Tantra. One does not practise Tantra and neglect Sutrayana. These would be mistakes. One has to practise in terms of one's experience in the moment. I spend a good part of my life practising renunciation. Having once been 70 lbs heavier, I had to engage in a great deal of renunciation to be a healthy weight – and that has to continue. There's nothing wrong with renunciation. If it needs to be practised, it needs to be practised.

———— · ————

I used to be fat. It occurred to me that I owed it to my family and to my students to look after my health – so I lost weight. In terms of Buddhist vehicles, I found that the weight did not self-liberate – so Dzogchen was not the answer. I found that the weight could not be transformed – so Inner Tantra was not the answer. I found that the weight could not be purified – so Outer Tantra was not the answer. The only answer I found was in Sutrayana – the renunciation for the benefit of others. This is why one has to practice every vehicle as and when it is appropriate.

The nineteenth of May

Fondness, partiality, predilection, appreciation, and enjoyment are important. In order to have compassion, one has to like people. If you don't like people, you cannot help them.

———— · ————

Through kindness, one gains the respect of our vajra brothers and sisters. Through kindness, one becomes honourable. Through kindness, one's word is believed – when it is given. Through kindness, others learn to trust our motivation, and cooperate with us in our endeavour to create a better world.

———— · ————

If there's nothing attractive, interesting, or pleasurable in people — you can be of no real value to them. Appreciation, liking, enjoyment, pleasure, delight, desire, lust – are contiguous expressions of compassion. We can separate them, and we can find them in dictionaries as different words – but they have the same intrinsic compassionate energy.

———— · ————

Chögyam Trungpa Rinpoche spoke of *changchub sem* as active-compassion, rather than compassion – because compassion is form and form is that which moves. *Changchub sem* is not just a feeling, it's a conversation. *Changchub sem* is appreciative intercourse. Where there is appreciation there is always communication, dialogue, discussion, conference, and colloquy. Beyond subject and object – one cannot look at colours without enjoying them and being enjoyed by them. It's a situation of instantaneous reciprocity. Enjoyment is therefore essential to *changchub sem* – as are pleasure, sensuality, delight, joy, desire, and lust. One cannot generate *changchub sem* from an emotionless, impassive, impersonal, detached, disconnected, puritanical, freeze-dried position.

The twentieth of May

Offering personal opinions to others as if they were objective is deceitful – or dubious at best.

———— · ————

'Khordong gTérchen Tulku Chhi'mèd Rig'dzin Rinpoche always said that opinions were pointless. "*Either knowing or not knowing – otherwise, nonsense.*"

———— · ————

One needs to question how one arrives at opinions. One needs to question why one imposes one's subjective opinions on others – and makes judgments on others based on subjectivity.

———— · ————

On controversial topics, it is wise to listen clearly—and to consider what has been said—before responding clearly. To respond clearly one needs to choose one's words as if they were going to be quoted and published – or to state that one lacks the information to give an opinion.

———— · ————

Once, I was asked for my opinion, and I replied "*I have no opinion. I don't know enough about the subject to have an opinion.*" Then someone else in the room gave their opinion – and it transpired that they knew less than I did. One requires evidence even to have a subjective opinion – so some research at least is required.

———— · ————

It's valuable to examine opinions. If you have an opinion—and you've arrived at it through diligent research—then hold that opinion, by all means. Remember however, that such opinions will be subjective – and another person may have an equally well researched opinion which may be diametrically opposite to yours. Both will be subjective – so there is no need to argue, as if objectivity were in any way involved.

The twenty-first of May

'Weirdness' is a label that is often employed to encourage someone to toe the line – in order that no one becomes conscious of fashion slavery.

———— · ————

Derision in respect of someone who is neither a *conscious fashion-slave* nor an *unconscious fashion-slave* is a sign of insecurity and anxiety. Those without undue anxiety are seldom ridden by the need to deride others on the basis that what they wear is different.

———— · ————

Whatever is taken as normal in any decade is normal due to fashion. Then when the fashion changes the previous decade starts to look outré in whatever way. What was once desirable is now laughable. What was once ethical is now uptight. What was once moral is now puritanical. Then, after a while, it drifts back in the other direction – and a new set of normalities appears.

———— · ————

I made a decision at the age of 11 that I was going to wear what I liked even though it didn't please those around me. I was mocked and ridiculed for it – but decided that derision was preferable to being conditioned and programmed by a point of view that had no connection with me. Of course, I tried hard not to see the boys in my class as the *Epsilons* of Aldous Huxley's *Brave New World*.[6] The title *Brave New World* derives from Miranda's speech in *The Tempest*[7] by Shakespeare: *'O wonder! How many goodly creatures are there here! How beauteous mankind is! O brave new world, that has such people in't.'*

---

6 *Brave New World* – a science fiction novel by Aldous Huxley, set in a dystopian World State, where citizens are environmentally engineered in an intelligence-based social hierarchy. 'Epsilons' are the lowest order of the population, bred to have no imagination or appreciation of the countryside. The novel is similar in some respects to George Orwell's '1984'.

7 William Shakespeare, *The Tempest*, Act V, scene i, 1611

The twenty-second of May

Surrealism is my preferred mode in painting and poetry because it takes Artists beyond conventional forms – through the depiction of conventional forms in unconventional juxtaposition and settings. This then points back at conventional reality and causes questioning.

——— · ———

Being that the phenomenal world is an illusion from the perspective of dualistic derangement – it is useful to have whimsical alternatives to such illusions. Surrealism provides such alternative illusions – and prompts us to examine what we take reality to be.

——— · ———

Surrealism—although not realism—incites curiosity as to what *reality* might be. Surrealism plays with the manner in which conceptual mind translates *that which is received by the senses*. When most people *sense the world*, they see what they expect to see – and not what is actually there. Surrealism plays with the phenomenon of expectations – and draws attention to the sensory discrepancies within our existence.

——— · ———

In 1975 Kyabjé Düd'jom Rinpoche Jig'drèl Yeshé Dorje wanted to know why I'd chosen the name *Savage Cabbage* for the Blues Band of which I was the vocalist in the 1960s. I spoke of Surrealism and replied *'Bèd-tsé Ya'mèd[8] is the linking of two ideas which normally have no connection with each other. Although, there—is—the connection of the 'word sounds'—Savage and Cabbage—which makes it seem as if the words belong together."* "Ya-tsan!" Düd'jom Rinpoche laughed *"Western Arts like Yeshé thab-kyi cho'trül[9] becoming!"*

---

8   Bèd-tsé Ya'mèd *(bad tshe ya 'med* / བད་ཚེ་ཡ་མེད་) was Kyabjé Düd'jom Rinpoche's translation of 'Savage Cabbage' – the Savage Cabbage Blues Band of 1966–1970, see *Goodbye Forever* Volume I chapters 11–13, Aro Books worldwide, 2020; and *an odd boy*, Volumes I and II, Aro Books worldwide, 2011 and 2012.

9   *ye shes thabs kyi cho 'phrul* / ཡེ་ཤེས་ཐབས་ཀྱི་ཆོ་འཕྲུལ་ – wisdom-magic of skilful means.

The twenty-third of May

Pottering is sporadically supervised aimlessness. It could even be suggested to have similarities with the activity of those with nondual realisation.

——— · ———

Tidying is an aspect of pottering – but true pottering is more sporadic. It is a haphazard mode which often facilitates discoveries and unexpected creativity.

——— · ———

It can be useful if one lays aside a day on which nothing needs to be done. One can then simply look around and notice whatever needs attention – but allow oneself to be distracted from it into other endeavours. One can then eventually return to the first task en route from another. It's called pottering. Pottering can accomplish a great deal – but one has to surrender all sense of achievement and live in the moment.

——— · ———

Pottering means moving from one thing to another with no fixed overall intention. It might start with tidying a shelf. Whilst tidying the shelf you happen to notice a little box with a broken hinge, so you go to the hardware shop and purchase a hinge. Whilst purchasing the hinge you notice that there is a sale on the beeswax, so you buy a couple of cans of beeswax in order to work on your furniture. You come home, fix the hinge and look for the turpentine to mix with the beeswax. You then notice that the cupboard in which the turpentine is stored needs some attention. So, you clear off all the shelves and rearrange what is on them. Whilst thus engaged you find a strange object that you lost five years ago. And so it goes on. That is called pottering. The most important aspect of it is that there is no pressure to accomplish anything or to be systematic about it, yet one actually accomplishes a great deal.

The twenty-fourth of May

People are often afraid of their emotions. This is sometimes
because of a tight-minded need to have everything under control –
and because at times people have experience of their emotions
getting them into trouble. When instructed therefore to find the
presence of awareness in the dimension of whatever emotion arises
– some sense of fear is experienced *"What if it overwhelmed me?"* Well,
what if 'me' was overwhelmed? What would happen then? That is
simple. There would then be no 'me' — or no 'me' beyond the
moment. There is only something to fear if one wishes to maintain
a solid, permanent, separate, continuous, and defined sense of 'me'.
Being that this 'sense of me' cannot be maintained as solid,
permanent, separate, and continuous — there is nothing to lose.
This 'me' is vanishing and reappearing all the time. It cannot be
concretised. So, if one finds the presence of awareness in the
dimension of an emotion – that is real. That is never at risk of
being anything other than it is.

———— · ————

Ying[10] means 'totality' in terms of 'dimension'. When *the dimension* is
characterised through *taste* – nothing exists outside the dimension of
taste. Once you identify taste as *the dimension* everything occurs
within that dimension. Whatever occurs: the itching knee; the
sensation on the scalp; the temperature of the room; the thought
that passes through mind; the particular fragrance – whatever it is, is
within the dimension of taste. This means one cannot be distracted
from the dimension, by anything. If one is distracted from the
dimension, then one was not in the dimension. This is what is
meant by ying.

The twenty-fifth of May

There are many practices within the three series of Dzogchen—and many supportive practices—but what is utterly essential, is silent sitting.

———— · ————

With Dzogchen, the central practice is silent sitting. One then extends that into life circumstances by: not trying to reify all the time; not concretising situations; not looking for safe ground in a situation; being willing to entertain ambivalence without having to go one way or the other; and being able to rest in the cognitive dissonance of hope and fear.

———— · ————

Emptiness isn't merely the absence of form. Emptiness is an experience which will be reflected quite naturally, in life – by life. Because this is the case, emptiness can also be seen in confusion, bewilderment, personality crisis, or midlife crisis. It can be seen in any situation where one doesn't understand what's going on – where one loses track of the form. It can be seen in incomprehension, bemusement, bafflement, uncertainty, perplexity, incredulousness, disorientation, obliviousness, or lack of understanding.

———— · ————

As the Lineage Holders of the Aro gTér – we are obliged to adopt a Dzogchen mien with regard to *relative informality* with our students. When we use the word 'obliged' we do not mean that there is a law of some kind. It is more that we should be congruent with Dzogchen rather than with the other valuable modes of Dharma. This Dzogchen mien does not mean we are special in any way – it is simply the tradition we follow. It is our inheritance and therefore our duty to maintain it.

The twenty-sixth of May

The Lamas' appreciation of their disciples' neuroses inspires a sense of confidence in their intrinsic nondual nature. It instils a colourful acceptance in which one does not have to be ashamed of one's personal 'khorwa – cyclic neuroses, or samsara.

———— · ————

Personal 'khorwa is also *personal potential* for liberation – but, this remains true *only* whilst we relate authentically to the Lama. Once neuroses are taken seriously, they need to be justified as manifestations of personal integrity. This leads directly to the cesspool of narcissism. This is why Vajrayana is both dangerous and glorious. Through Tantra we can side-step the 'long process' of therapy and the tighter aspects of Sutric discipline. If however, one abuses Vajrayana theory to concretise identity, one projects oneself into the most painful manifestations of one's own insanity – the *burning sewer of 'me'*.

———— · ————

If through dilettantism, Vajrayana appears to fail, one crashes dramatically. One finds oneself in a situation far worse than the point at which one started. Neurotic patterns escalate and hit with unprecedented force. One then projects self-created pain onto the external world   *and* onto those attempting to help. One becomes like a critically sick patient attacking medical staff as if they were enemies.

———— · ————

When the dance of Vajrayana begins, the clothing of 'khorwa begins to fall away – no matter how embarrassed we are with regard to nakedness. This is not to say that we don't attempt to wrap ourselves snugly again – but at least a sequence of moments or minutes has been experienced in which everything is as it is. The huge hoax, of course, is that there were no clothes in the first place. Naked awareness is beginningless.

The twenty-seventh of May

Dzogchen is unique in that it deals with the fundamental experience of being human at the most essential level of perception. The approach taken in explaining Dzogchen, lays bare the problems which arise through our dualistic vision – and creates a sense of wonderment in the immense possibility of each individual.

———— · ————

It has taken us a long time to decipher this – but we have discovered that the primary refuge of the average Western person is 'feelings'. In the West it seems that 'feelings' have primacy over everything else: y'know, I took refuge – but then I felt it wasn't for me; y'know, I borrowed some money – but then I felt it was actually owed to me; y'know, I got married – but then I felt I needed my freedom; y'know, y'know, y'know…

———— · ————

Personal feelings come before everything in contemporary Western society. This tends to be sanctioned by a great deal of modern literature and music. Most people take refuge in Buddha, Dharma, and Sangha because of feelings. The truth of this refuge then, is *'Feelings la kyab-su ché'* – 'I take refuge in my feelings'. Then, as an afterthought: *'Lama la kyab-su ché, Sang-gyé la kyab-su ché, Chö la kyab-su ché, Gendün la kyab-su ché.'* Feelings are the primary refuge for many – but when this is the case, there is no refuge as understood by Buddhism.

———— · ————

There can be conflicting priorities in one's life – and at such times one can rely on one's vows as the basis of one's rationale. If one has the strength of the vows, life becomes simple. 'Simple' however, does not always mean 'easy'. Often, we take refuge in complexity in the hope that it might provide ease – but often, life is either hard or it is hard. Avoiding difficulty doesn't ensure that life will be more comfortable. There is no situation which is actually overwhelming.

The twenty-eighth of May

The elements of our world, our bodies, our intelligence, emotions, and vision – are the nexus of gnostic noetic[11] nascence. This means that we are open to realisation – just as we are.

———— · ————

There is nothing to change before we begin. Where we are, is where we begin. This is not in order to change *how we are* – but simply to release *how we are* into the dimension of actively appreciative empathy.

———— · ————

As a practitioner, one cannot begin from an idealised position – in which one is not greedy, irritable, acquisitive, apprehensive, and prone to denial. If one starts with the assumption that one is free of such 'unworthy tendencies' it will prove impossible to transform them, let alone self-liberate them.

———— · ————

There will always be kinder people. There will always be those who work harder, longer, and more diligently than oneself. There will always be those who are more naturally altruistic, more generous, more intelligent, more honest, and more courageous. There will always be better practitioners. If these people are inspiring, that is good – but if one distorts one's perception by allowing the existence of these people to invalidate oneself as a practitioner; this is idiocy. We are all exactly where we are – and wherever that is, is the perfect starting point.

---

11 Noetic usually pertains to thought, and means intellectual or rational – but in the Vajrayana sense, noetic applies to whatever moves in mind.

The twenty-ninth of May

Essentially, we have always been nondual. Dualistic derangement is merely the fear of that fact – playing itself out in tortuous patterns.

———— · ————

There is nothing more or less to 'what we are' than 'that' which is immediately apparent – but we seem unable to see it.

———— · ————

Liberation is ours to see, hear, touch, smell, taste, and ideate – but all we seem to sense, is the shifting surface of that vastness. We see reflections, but are blind to the nature of the mirror. We see waves, but fail to experience the ocean. We see clouds, but cannot conceive of the sky.

———— · ————

One takes refuge in *complete, open wakefulness* because one knows that there is no other option. It is not worth attempting anything else. This recognition has to be based on exposing the desire to hide out. This understanding must be grounded on: the experience of having contracted into a smaller space; seeing what that was like; and, having realised that hiding out offers no refuge. One has to have that knowledge of having retracted into a small space and realising that this relative refuge is complete constriction. Whether this *small-space* into which one has contracted is a physical space or a concept is irrelevant – one has to wake up and breathe the fresh air that's available outside.

The thirtieth of May

Through cutting addiction to corporeal form as the major reference point of experience; we become free, not only of fear – but of persecutory hope. Hope is often merely fear in disguise – a wretched demon who drives us with the whips and goads in the direction of self-created misery. In gÇod[12] we unmask the false hope in our lives and learn to live joyously – free from both hope and fear.

———— · ————

gÇod is not a particularly friendly, warm, and comforting way of passing an evening. Why would one wish to destroy one's identity? This is an interesting question in terms of the Buddhist refuge, and what refuge really means. From many Western points of view—particularly from the psychotherapeutic point of view—gÇod is definitely not a good idea. A psychotherapist would tell you that gÇod is pathological – that we need to nurture ourselves and take care of that 'little child within us all'. gÇod is more inclined to napalm or machinegun that 'little child within us all'.

———— · ————

The idea of 'reference point' is essential to the understanding of gÇod – because we are basically cutting attachment to any kind of reference point. 'Reference point' is that which interposes a 'therefore' in relation to 'I'. In terms of Descartes' *I think therefore I am* – 'therefore' is dubious, as is 'I am'. It might be more plausible to say 'I think, therefore I think' – because thinking proves nothing more than *thinking is occurring*. One could say *Thinking therefore nothing*. There is no 'I think'. There is merely 'thinking' – and even that is questionable beyond the point instant in which thinking occurs. When 'therefore' is cut – the reference point to 'I' is cut. Through gÇod one slays 'therefore'.

The thirty-first of May

Every state of mind, however distressed or distressing, is dynamically linked to the intrinsic nondual play of the free elements.

———— · ————

All positivist intellectual formulations, are based either on *wishful-thinking* or *naïve idealism* – rather than direct experience. All nihilistic intellectual formulations, are based either on *sterile safety-seeking* and *self-serving cynicism* – rather than direct experience.

———— · ————

Vajrayana methods reveal mind as intrinsically free. This complete openness of mind needs to be personally discovered. It cannot be created. One cannot artificially re-structure oneself according to a spiritually healthy philosophical perspective.

———— · ————

Monism is the belief that *everything is one*. Dualism is the belief that emptiness and form can be divided and that everything can exist separately in perpetuity. Eternalism is the belief the everything has meaning and that nothing is arbitrary or accidental. Nihilism is the belief that nothing has meaning and that everything is arbitrary or accidental. As Buddhists we deny the validity of these beliefs – yet each one reflects an aspect of human experience. Monism is reflected in the fact that everyone's experience of emptiness is the same. If there were difference in this respect, emptiness would not be emptiness – it would be form. Dualism is reflected in the fact that everyone's experience of form is different and we manifest personality. Eternalism is reflected in the fact that meaning arises from chaos to create transient though coherent patterns. Nihilism is reflected in the fact that one cannot rely on apparently consistent paradigms. These are the *emptiness* and *form* aspects of the four denials. They are, of course, nondual.

Drala Jong *(sGra bLa lJongs)*

June

This is the time to invoke Guru Rinpoche, because he is inseparable from the Supreme Healer – the Medicine Buddha.

HE Ögyen Dro'dül Thrin-lé Kunkyab Rinpoche
རྒྱལ་བ་ཨོ་རྒྱན་འགྲོ་འདུལ་ཕྲིན་ལས་ཀུན་སྐྱབས་རིན་པོ་ཆེ་

Life is infested with woeful discomforts and sorrows – it is also brimming with pleasures and joys.

Khar-trül Wangchuk Rig'dzin Rinpoche
མཁར་སྤྲུལ་དཔལ་གྱི་དབང་ཕྱུག་རིག་འཛིན་རིན་པོ་ཆེ།

The first of June

Pattern and disarray—order and chaos—harmony and dissonance are the play of form and emptiness.

———— · ————

People have the unfortunate propensity to become sectarian. We have been teaching now for 40 years and in that time, we have done what we can to undermine sectarianism. It seems however, that no matter how much we talk about the yanas—the vehicles of Buddhism—people seem to forget that each yana has its own logic. Each yana has its own logic because each yana has its own experiential base. Unless one understands how the logic of each yana springs naturally from its base – one will always encounter contradictions as dilemmas in which other people have to be seen as being in error.

———— · ————

Existential utopianism is a philosophical mode in which 'self-fulfilling evolution' is necessarily always possible – as manifest destiny. It states that all that is required are the right components of a positivist human equation. Such 'right components' however, are fundamentally empty—in themselves—of causes for happiness. They are empty because they are based on speculations which are themselves built on speculations. Any attempt to relate with these components outside an experiential understanding of emptiness is therefore doomed. The existential utopian approach has much in common with eternalism – the dualistic misconception that everything is meaningful. This utopian position rejects the random aspect of reality and is therefore merely the flip-side of nihilism – the dualistic misconception that nothing is meaningful.

The second of June

The world and the body *do* prove that 'I' exist – but they also prove the exact opposite. It's merely that we choose to ignore half the evidence.

———— · ————

Vajrayana is not *world negative* or *body negative*. 'Khorwa is not *the body* or *the world*. 'Khorwa—samsara—is how we relate to *body* and *world* in terms of reference points – reference points which attempt to substantiate existence as eternal.

———— · ————

Practitioners of Vajrayana are not renunciates – even though they are free to practise renunciation in terms of skilful means. The Vajrayana renunciation of 'khorwa does not necessarily equate to the Sutrayana practice of renunciation.

———— · ————

Renunciation is the principle of Sutrayana whereas the principle of Vajrayana is transformation – and self-liberation is the principle of Dzogchen. The most common religious trend is towards renunciation – which is why Vajrayana is often so difficult for people to understand.

———— · ————

Most misunderstandings of Vajrayana are due to imagining that it accords with renunciation. Any attempt to comprehend Vajrayana from the Sutrayana point of view of renunciation, will lead to a plethora of oxymorons – and result in tortuous complexity and confusion.

The third of June

We all suffer from cowardice, even if only fractionally. There is always the tendency to imagine life is avoidable. I was fortunate in learning—quite early in life—that this is useless.

———— · ————

We all have to learn to recognise the loathsome face of cowardice – because there are times when we have to act; knowing the outcome is going to be hideous.

———— · ————

Knowing that you're damned if you do and damned if you don't, can come as a relief. Cowardice is the illusion that avoidance is possible. It's the illusion that you can get away with it – and pretend you haven't engaged in avoidance.

———— · ————

Cowardice is the idea that pain and death can be avoided. One cannot live like that. It is not worth being alive if one lives like a coward. It's not just physical pain and death that cowards try to avoid – it's every kind of *little pain* or *little death* in the field of the emotions. Courage is merely the acceptance that nothing is avoidable. Courage is not necessarily free of fear – but courage is not embarrassed by fear. It is intelligent to feel some degree of fear – because some situations are fearful. Courage is the simple acceptance of fear – and the determination not to be compromised by it. No one gets out of this alive. We can go whingeing, whimpering, whining, and kvetching; or we can go yelling with fierce glee – but go, we must.

The fourth of June

When we accept confusion as the rich ground from which clarity can be discovered, we can cease being our own enemies.

———— · ————

Lamas—in order to teach Vajrayana—need to manifest vajra hauteur, vajra rage, vajra obsession, vajra scepticism, and vajra insensitivity. They need to manifest these qualities in order to give living transmission of what is meant by transformation. Lamas thus reflect that we are potent symbols of what we really are.

———— · ————

We do not have to begin by seeking for clarity, because clarity is inherent in every situation. We simply have to begin with that which presents itself. This will include our mistakes and the mistakes of others. It will include errors, omissions, miscalculations, inaccuracies, blunders, appropriations, misappropriations, oversights, faux pas, follies, indiscretions, and peccadilloes. Clarity is a groundless experience – but one that we can only realise when ground and groundlessness are realised as nondual.

———— · ————

Blatancy in revealing the visceral fire of intimate relationship is gauche. When speaking of a lover, discretion is apposite. The knowledge that hovers above and below the surface of mundane expression is best left unspoken. Voluptuous landscapes of feeling should be left to be inferred. It is not intended that anything will be left unwritten – but Vajrayana needs to disrobe according to its own precise passion: perfectly and with fierce grace. It is neither wise nor practical to expose the heart of this reality before creating a conducive atmosphere in which such perspectives can disport themselves with vivid elegance.

The fifth of June

For the present moment to be born—fully born—the previous moment has to die.

———— · ————

Every moment is death. Every moment is birth. Death and birth flicker as cinematographic film flickers – and gives the illusion of continuity.

———— · ————

Life is a terminal illness – a sexually transmitted disease. We have to accept that we're dying. People seem to dislike that idea – but it's not *that* problematic when we come to understand that we're dying all the time.

———— · ————

Those who have no sense of having continually died, have never actually lived – or have never been fully alive. Life is birth and death: the death and birth of each phase of life; of each year; of each month; or each day – and of each moment.

———— · ————

As a Lama, my poetry satirises duality rather more than celebrating nonduality. I write such poetry to warn against what each one of us could become – if we sold our humanity for success or comfort. My satirical poems are often mock-rabid rants which lampoon or harangue caricatures of fascistic spiritual fashion. This guild of parsimonious pusillanimous pretenders warrants comments – even though I wish them thoroughly well.

The sixth of June

Meditation is appreciation without comment and without commentator.

———— · ————

When all there is, is the felt texture of the canvas against the brush and the direct awareness of colour in motion – that is meditation.

———— · ————

Painting is a meditative state – even for those who would not think of themselves as interested in meditation. The word 'meditative' has many different meanings. Meditation can simply consist of the senses being open to the sense-fields.

———— · ————

When you're creative—especially if the creativity is nonconceptual—that is meditation. Simply playing a musical instrument… simply writing… without controlling the process with *self-conscious conceptuality* – that is meditation.

———— · ————

When you hit the note just shy of the flattened 7th—the Blue note —and you forget who is singing it or how long it lasted; when the faces in the audience are happy and you don't need to be self-congratulatory – because the pleasure is a reaction to the band; when it could be a juke joint on Highway 61 or a pub in Camberley; when it could be 1949, 1969, or 2019 and all labels concerning nationality, ethnic group, and gender disappear – that's when one moment melted into *the moment in* 1971. That was when I first sang Blues to Kyabjé Düd'jom Rinpoche Jig'drèl Yeshé Dorje. And now his incarnation Kyabjé Düd'jom Rinpoche Ten'dzin Yeshé Dorje and I have a connection though Blues.

The seventh of June

Allow the sense-fields to be as they are. Allow the senses to dance with the sense-fields. That, in itself, is the meditative state. Every artist will understand that experientially – even if they know nothing of meditation.

———— · ————

When namtogs arise, stare directly into their arising. When namtogs dissolve stare directly into their dissolution. It is the same, in life. With each life-circumstance: whatever is enacted, stare directly into the enactment – with all the senses. Considering this will make you happy. Be of great good cheer. É: Ma: Ho:
Kyabjé Düd'jom Rinpoche Jig'drèl Yeshé Dorje

———— · ————

Sadly, meditation has become over-used and abused as a word. It is used in so many contexts that it has become meaningless unless qualified. We have no huge argument with inner tennis, inner cooking, inner skateboarding, inner jogging, inner philately, or mindful taxidermy – but meditation is not a hobby or a commercial commodity.

———— · ————

Ngöndro[1] means 'before going' or 'preparation'. There are many different styles of ngöndro in Vajrayana – and the Tantric ngöndro is one of them. The Tantric ngöndro however, is not indispensable for approaching Dzogchen – because Dzogchen sem-dé has its own ngöndro, in lineages where Dzogchen sem-dé is extant. Where only Dzogchen men-ngag-dé exists as an extant lineage, then tantric ngöndro is a prerequisite – followed by the generation phase and completion phase practices.

1   *sNgon 'gro* / སྔོན་འགྲོ

The eighth of June

Devotion is advanced appreciation; educated discernment; exceptional perspicacity; and exponentially devolved expertise. Anything less is something other than devotion.

———— · ————

Devotion is misunderstood as being some kind of emotion. There is certainly emotion involved with devotion – just as there is lust involved with romantic love. This however does not make lust the same as love – or rape would be romantic.

———— · ————

Devotion is not so different from training to play a musical instrument – in terms of how a trainee might view an accomplished musician. The further one advances in one's musical skill – the more one can appreciate a world class master. This is devotion.

———— · ————

Devotion has to be based on experience. Simply feeling *quasi-spiritually romantic* toward a *lovely old Himalayan Buddhist Lama*, is not devotion. If this is the nature of one's devotion then as soon as the Lama needs to provide critical feedback one is likely to lose one's devotion.

———— · ————

Devotion is often misunderstood. People often speak about devotion as if you could decide to have it. People speak about faith in the same way. They say *'You must have faith'* but that is not an instruction which can be followed. One can only have devotion or faith on the basis of experience – and that is not a choice. It simply happens in the way in which you recognise the taste of espresso.

The ninth of June

In 1971, Kyabjé Düd'jom Rinpoche Jig'drèl Yeshé Dorje told me
that a ngakpa must be an artist – and explore all the Arts; both as a
means of experiencing the nature of the elements – and as a mode
of teaching. Kyabjé Künzang Dorje Rinpoche said the same – in
fact all my Lamas have encouraged me to continue as an Artist.

———— · ————

Vajrayana and Art are inseparable because the Arts are linked with
the elements and with the fields of the senses. Vajrayana has its
particular iconographic, symbolic, ceremonial, and ritual Arts – but
this does not mean there is no validity in the secular Arts. If one
approaches the *secular Arts* as a Vajrayanist – the *secular Arts* become
sacred. If the Queen were to wear Levi's – she would still be the
Queen, and lend her Levi's great dignity.

———— · ————

To be a Vajrayanist is to be an Artist. There is a subtle difference
however, between being an artist and being a Vajrayanist. Artists *can*
merely be obsessive manipulators in terms of creativity. Artists *can*
fall into the trap of thinking of themselves as special prominent
people. Artists *can* become arrogant, angry, neurotically obsessed,
paranoid, and closed-minded. As such artists are likely to be prone
to depression. Such artists would become depressed because they
cease to be nourished by the *fields of the senses*. The *fields of the senses*
cannot be reliably manipulated for personal prestige. The fields of
the senses are simply there – and can simply be enjoyed. A
Vajrayana Artist can either have fame or not. Self-obsessed artists,
however, need fame for validation – and that truncates the
nourishment of the *fields of the senses*.

The tenth of June

Vajrayana is a powerful catalyst for terminating the 'me project'. It rapidly accelerates the process of disintegration. It instigates the possibility of dancing with death.

———— · ————

Ngak'phang ordination throws a can of gasoline—or petroleum—followed by a match, into the film-splicing room where 'The Movie of Me' is being produced. The film-splicing room is happy to allow itself to self-immolate – because it is not actually there. The entire scenario exposes itself as a gigantic hoax. It becomes embarrassingly plain that the hoax has hoaxed itself into not seeing itself as a hoax.

———— · ————

Psychotherapy can be valuable where there is psychological damage — but beyond that, the *ethos of socially sanctified therapy* is an obstacle to coming to terms with projections. When the Lama repudiates projections, there are two choices: to allow projections to be dismantled, or to reinforce projections as a vindication of the refusal to let go of the fear of death. One has to learn to dance with death in order to annihilate the 'me project'.

———— · ————

To dance with death is central to Vajrayana. One dances naked of protective projections. One dances on the corpse of one's personality restrictions. One dances into commitment – into the broad flowering fields of the lineage. In these glorious fields of commitment, one finds one's personality to have vajra qualities – qualities which open themselves out to others without fearful restraint or timorous anal-retentive anxieties.

The eleventh of June

Vajra pride means identification with the continuum of the nondual state rather than with the continuum of dualistic derangement.

———— · ————

When life experience seems most arduous or difficult, simply remember that *your Mind is of the same nature as Padmasambhava and Yeshé Tsogyel.*

———— · ————

We are not merely our problems and anxieties – because even when we seem totally identified with them, we can remember that their intrinsic nature is the Mind of Guru Rinpoche… their intrinsic nature is the Mind of Yeshé Tsogyel. This is vajra pride.

———— · ————

If one is able to enter the empty state – the complexity of the dKyil'khor replaces the complexity of duality. The convoluted patterns of frustration subside into shimmering iridescence. It is at this brink of experience that one can realise something outlandishly potent: one's personal complexity is merely a distortion of the energy of nonduality. It is then that the appearance of the empowerment dKyil'khor becomes a transformative experience.

———— · ————

Whatever occurs, remember: This is a passing moment. Remember: There will be another moment—in several days, weeks, months, or years—when the *personality of what I seem to be* will be as different as one life is, from another. Remember: Although I *am* this pain, frustration, joy, or contentment – I am also *not* this pain, frustration, joy, or contentment. Remember: Form is emptiness—and— emptiness is form.

The twelfth of June

In order to establish a connection with the tradition and the lineage, a heart sensation for Guru Rinpoche and Yeshé Tsogyel is indispensable – just as form and emptiness are indispensable in our practice.

―――― · ――――

Deliberately name everything which moves you to smiles, laughter, or tears as Guru Rinpoche or Yeshé Tsogyel – because this is precisely what these experiences are.

―――― · ――――

Guru Rinpoche and Yeshé Tsogyel are trülku, longku, and chöku[2]. As trülku they are the form and emptiness of Padmasambhava and Yeshé Tsogyel. As longku they are the vision and empty nature of our inner experience received through transmission or pure vision. As chöku they are rigpa and chö-nyid – pure and total awareness, and the self-luminous ground of being. It is in *this* understanding that the views of Dzogchen and Tantra dissolve into each other and permeate the fabric of experience.

―――― · ――――

As you enter more into the vibrant stream of the tradition, you will learn to associate heart sensation with the symbolic forms of Guru Rinpoche and Yeshé Tsogyel. If this seems difficult, do not worry. You do have the connection, or you would not be reading these words. Simply practise and allow the empowerment to emerge. We all start from different points. We can only start from where we are – from where we happen to find ourselves. We should not feel disheartened about that – or over-confident. To have made a vital connection with the Nyingma Tradition is wonderful – it is a rare opportunity.

---

2   Trülku *(sPrul sKu /* སྤྲུལ་སྐུ */ nirmanakaya)* is form / emanation. Longku *(longs sKu /* ལོངས་སྐུ */ sambhogakaya)* is energy / appearance. Chöku *(chos sKu /* ཆོས་སྐུ */ dhamakaya)* is space / essence.

The thirteenth of June

There have been many amusing scenarios with Chhi'mèd Rig'dzin Rinpoche in which he discussed knowing and not knowing. In all these discussions he emphasised that *not knowing* is honest, unless it is merely anxious and self-protective. *Knowing* is honest unless it is an *artificially assumed knowing*. We need to be clear about the areas in which we are unclear. We need to be frank about what we know and what we do not know. We need to strive to know, yet accept the discomfort of not knowing. We need to strive to retain our 'not knowing', when it would be more comfortable to enter a false sense of 'knowing' for the sake of comfort.

———— · ————

Chhi'mèd Rig'dzin Rinpoche asked me a question in the middle of a discussion he was having with a Swiss gentleman. The discussion concerned the sentience of plants. Rinpoche was espousing the view that plants were not sentient in order to force the Swiss gentleman to defend his belief with more gusto. After a while, he turned to me *"Ngakpa Chögyam, what you say? Plant sentient or not sentient?"* I grinned *"I do not know, Rinpoche."* Rinpoche laughed *"Ah, you one big diplomat… But you Tantric man! Tantric man must know!"* So I replied *"They are sentient, Rinpoche."* He then asked me *"Why you 'sentient' saying?"* I replied *"Plants respond to stimuli."* Chhi'mèd Rig'dzin Rinpoche then said that one could say the same of machines, to which I replied that people made machines – but that no one made plants. I continued this line of reasoning by pointing out *"If plants weren't sentient then it would prove the existence of a creator God as sublime programmer of all organic machinery – and, as you say I'm a Tantric man, I don't believe in a creator God."* Rinpoche eyed me carefully for a moment – and then, roared with laughter. He turned to the Swiss gentleman and said *"Plant sentient."*

The fourteenth of June

From the point of view of Dzogchen, bliss cannot be found by 'doing' anything. Bliss self-existent as the texture of phenomenal reality.

———— · ————

The Arts are a symbolic equivalent to the natural creativity of reality. The origin is space. Space gives rise to energy. Energy coalesces as the phenomenal world. With the Arts, the origin is empty awareness. Empty awareness gives birth to vision. Vision gives birth to creative expression. First there is nothing. Then there is an idea. Then the idea is manifested in terms of the Arts. It is a natural process.

———— · ————

Bliss is the infinite purity of the phenomenal world. Bliss cannot be forced – neither can devotion. Devotion—the authentic causeless cause of bliss—cannot be aroused through methodology. It cannot be engendered through emotional cathartics. It cannot be promulgated through hysterical television evangelism. It cannot be incited through charismatic overtures to unresolved childhood neediness. It cannot be impelled or commanded by intellectual logic. Bliss is as it is. Devotion is as it is. Dharma is as it is.

———— · ————

The desire to push further and to continually challenge current values and aesthetics is not necessarily artistically valid. There should be no cultural obstacle for a contemporary musical composer to create works in the Baroque style – or any style of the past as long such works are not plagiaristic or excessively derivative. The same applies to all the Arts. Being manacled to the modern trend in the Arts is a form of restriction that is fundamentally obstructive to creativity. The scope of the Arts should broaden over the centuries rather than remaining within the tight band of legislated acceptability.

The fifteenth of June

Dzogchen—as it was originally taught and transcribed—was explained in ordinary everyday language rather than the highly sophisticated literary presentation that characterise its later dissemination. There is therefore no need to be ashamed of lack of academic prowess.

———— · ————

The Lama needs to be understood in terms of the yanas. The Lama in terms of Kriyatantra is never seen by students unless he or she is on the throne and teaching. The scenario is elaborate. There's an attendant who makes sure that the shawl is perfectly pleated and everything is exact. Then the students appear for the teaching. That Lama could almost have appeared in a movie theatre. There's a great distance. As one proceeds through the tantras the throne descends in height until one arrives at Dzogchen – where there is no throne. The Lama and student could be in the pasture milking the dri[3].

———— · ————

Dzogchen is invariably too simple for the intellectually gifted – which is why Longchenpa had to write in the way he did. Longchenpa wrote the most amazing treatises in order to convince certain argumentarians that Dzogchen was not a Shaivite heresy. What he wrote was fantastically elaborate. He was a great yogi and a great scholar, who had the capacity to make Sutra, Tantra, and Dzogchen align – but to do so produced a text which read like a transcendental legal document. It covered every argument and every exigency with such alacrity that his position was unassailable. The only problem with this approach is that Longchenpa's texts became so influential that they became the lingua franca of Dzogchen – and the original presentation of Dzogchen dwindled. It is now the case that few people understand Dzogchen and fewer practice it.

3   The female to the yak *('bri / འབྲི)*

The sixteenth of June

One could describe psychotherapy as a ngöndro for Sutrayana. Where preparation is needed – it is always valuable. The ngöndro for taking a shower is to remove one's clothing.

——— · ———

Ngöndro means preparation. Literally, *sNgon* means *before* and *'gro* means *going*. There is the tendency to use to word ngöndro for the Four Tantric Preliminaries – but there are many different ngöndros, each a preparation for a particular body of practice. There is, for example, a ngöndro for Dzogchen Tögal.

——— · ———

People sometimes ask why we do not practise ngöndro in the Aro gTér system, and of course the answer to this question is that we do practise ngöndro – we practise the ngöndro of Dzogchen sem-dé, the Four Naljors. The Four Naljors equate with the fourfold tantric ngöndro as a means of bridging the vehicles. However, whereas the tantric ngöndro includes all the essential Sutric practices within it, the Dzogchen sem-dé ngöndro includes all the essential Sutric and Tantric practices within it.

——— · ———

From the Nyingma point of view – Vajrayana is not limited by Sutrayana. Nyingma Vajrayana is not a vehicle which exists 'under licence' from Sutrayana. Although this is the view in terms of the two yana system— where Vajrayana is classified as 'esoteric Mahayana'—it is not the view in the nine yana system of Nyingma. Sutrayana and Vajrayana are radically different paradigms – and even though there are many profound resemblances, their principles and functions are often contradictory. This is particularly the case in terms of the rôle of the vajra master.

The seventeenth of June

Drüpthab[4] is mainly thought of as a liturgical text – but drüpthab means 'method of accomplishment' and that can comprise any activity suggested by the vajra master. This is evident in the lives of the 84 Mahasiddhas.

————— · —————

With Dzogchen the non-formal aspect of drüpthab can be manifested through the Arts. It can be manifested through anything – because drüpthab means method of accomplishment.

————— · —————

We have had many discussions over the years with different people — and more than a few have asked us why we practice. The best answer we have ever given is *"We sit because we're Nyingmas – and that's what they do. Bulls bellow; pigs snort; frogs croak; dogs bark; cats purr, tigers roar; kangaroos hop; yetis make curious high pitched wailing sounds – and, Nyingmas sit."* It's our religion.

————— · —————

It is in essential drüpthab where the idea of authentic personality and authentic individuality is obvious – but although examples are abundant, almost nothing is stated. Nothing is stated because the examples are self-evident in their meaning in cultures where Vajrayana is socially viable. This was found in the lives of the 84 Mahasiddhas of Ancient India. It was found in the lives of the Mahasiddhas of Tibet such as Düd'jom Lingpa, Düd'jom Jig'drèl Yeshé Dorje, and Kyabjé Künzang Dorje Rinpoche. It was found in the lives of the Mahasiddhas who taught in the West – such as Dung-sé Thrin-lé Norbu Rinpoche, Chhi'mèd Rig'dzin Rinpoche, and Chögyam Trungpa Rinpoche. There will be other Mahasiddhas who are not as well known – and some, who are secret mahasiddhas. They are always there.

4   (*grub thabs* / གྲུབ་ཐབས་

The eighteenth of June

Buddhas such as Guru Rinpoche and Yeshé Tsogyel are capable of consorting with infinite partners without adulteration of their tralam-mé[5].

——— · ———

Buddhas are capable of benefiting beings through sexuality – but for run-of-the-mill, commonplace, undistinguished, mediocre, lacklustre Lamas such as ourselves, it is not possible.

——— · ———

Realised beings are not limited with regard to having multiple partners – but not every Lama is realised to that degree. We are merely the convivial vicars of Vajrayana. You will therefore find us at garden parties with cucumber sandwiches; holding cups of tea with extended little fingers – rather than at bacchanalias, saturnalias, carousals, debauches, or orgies.

——— · ———

Mahasiddhas such as Trungpa Rinpoche and Drukpa Künlegs were capable of such extraordinary activity and have benefited countless beings through sexual encounter. We however, remain within the limits of our capacities. We do not have the realisation required and are therefore entirely and unreservedly monogamous.

——— · ———

We cannot transform alcohol in the manner of the Mahasiddhas; therefore, we limit our intake. We cannot manifest wrathful teaching methods in the manner of Kyabjé Künzang Dorje Rinpoche and 'Khordong gTérchen Tulku Chhi'mèd Rig'dzin Rinpoche; therefore, we almost never raise our voices. We can laugh however. We do so frequently – but hopefully not in the manner of grinagogs[6].

---

5   *(khra lam me* / ཁྲ་ལམ་མེ་*)* – poetic turbulence; literally, atmospheric phenomena; also, glaring vividness.

6   Grinagog – one who giggles incessantly or laughs vapidly after making statements or relating events which contain no humour. Also, of persons who grin unnecessarily.

The nineteenth of June

With respect to vajra command, it is not so much a question of what one *does* or *doesn't do* – it's a matter of whether one is prepared to let go of dearly cherished concepts.

———— · ————

The rôle of the vajra master is to make vajra suggestions. These are mostly called vajra commands – but the sense of 'command' is how they are *taken* rather than how they are *given*.

———— · ————

One has to have the confidence in one's Lama to trust that he or she will accommodate one's relative existence in a caring yet creative manner. So, it is not a question of *having to implement suggestions* – but having the *willingness* to implement them.

———— · ————

The vajra suggestions of the vajra master are not rigid. In terms of one's personal situation and limitations, one can always put one's personal situation to the Lama for consideration. The Lama will always take account of that situation. One can express one's perceived incapacity to follow a 'vajra suggestion' and expect one's perception to be taken into consideration.

———— · ————

There has to be a sense of excitement involved. The Lama might say *"Hey try eating this squid pan-seared with lemon juice and garlic. / You'd look exemplary in these boots. / You could wear a moustache with perfect dignity. / Maybe you should get a regular job and lead an ordinary life."* Vajra command has to be seen as an adventure – a magical mystery tour. It could also be an extremely ordinary and tedious Greyhound bus ride to somewhere obscure in Ohio – but that could actually lead anywhere at all in terms of transmission.

The twentieth of June

When we're speaking of *chang-chub sem*—from the perspective of Vajrayana—it is inseparable from desire. Kyabjé Künzang Dorje Rinpoche said *"If you have no desire, you can't have compassion."* The two go together because they're part of the same energy. You can't extricate them.

———— · ————

Desire is not necessarily a problem. It depends on one's orientation. In terms of Vajrayana, the base is the experience of emptiness. When desire is experienced in the context of emptiness it is not referential. The experience of desire from the perspective of emptiness is that one is not defined by it.

———— · ————

With Vajrayana, desire is not a debility. One is free to move. One is not dragged hither and thither by the senses in respect of objects of desire. Desire doesn't have to define you. So, whether you get it, or whether you don't get it – can be vaguely irrelevant. You could smile at it or laugh about it. That's a different perspective.

———— · ————

Everyone has their history in terms of Dharma – from whatever they've heard or read. The prevalent presentation of Vajrayana is explained in the language of Sutra. This is valid. One can speak of any of the yanas from the position of any of the other yanas. More rarely however Sutrayana can be explained from the perspective of Tantra or from the perspective of Dzogchen. That is also possible.

The twenty-first of June

You might not achieve what you expect to achieve from Dzogchen practice. If you are not at the experiential base of Dzogchen it will only be possible to imitate the outer appearance of Dzogchen.

———— · ————

Dzogchen practices, even when one lacks experience of the nondual base – are still extremely valuable even in terms of embracing the emotions as the path.

———— · ————

When you let the intellectual scaffolding fall away – the emotional pain changes. It doesn't dissipate – but changes. It moves in terms of the five elements either into clarity, or into appreciative empathy – which is another word for compassion.

———— · ————

One can simply sit with emotions and just let them be as they are. That is not the usual inclination – but when you do that, you discover that there's a vast dimension of energy there. When that energy is free of intellectual scaffolding it becomes—of itself—something else. It's emotional pain only as long as the intellectual scaffolding remains.

———— · ————

In terms of Dzogchen practice, one requires experience of the nondual state as the base in order to practice. We have found however, that the practices of Dzogchen are functional whether you're at the base or not. They function in different ways according to your levels of experience. You just have to be cognisant of whether you are practising Dzogchen or practising a simulacrum.

The twenty-second of June

The vajra master has to reflect the neuroses of their students – because the Lama and students are partaking in the same energy.

——— · ———

The vajra master enjoys our neuroses – because they are simply a distortion of the nondual state. The vajra master recognises that – and that recognition is known as enjoyment.

——— · ———

The Sutrayana teacher is not obliged to enjoy our neuroses. That's not part of the deal at all. The vajra master however has to enjoy our neuroses. Some similarity can be found with counsellors or therapists – they have to like their clients. Vajra masters have to enjoy the neuroses of their students because without enjoying them, there's no relationship. What is enjoyed is the potential of these neuroses to be transformed into realisation. So, the enjoyment of neuroses is the vajra master's personal connection with students.

——— · ———

Ideally, Vajrayana Lamas are not celibate. They are not 'worldly' as such — but live in the world. They appear to inhabit the same experiential domain as their students. This changed in the Himalayan countries over the course of history. During the first spread of Vajrayana, the pattern was that monasticism was often simply the precursor to the practice of Vajrayana. There are different variations in terms of depictions of the 25 disciples of Guru Rinpoche. In some, most are monastics – but in some they are all gö kar chang lo[7] practitioners. This is because many started as monastics and become ngak'phang practitioners when they entered the practice of Vajrayana. Yeshé Tsogyel was a nun at first. The pattern was that monastic training was where you began – then you took Vajrayana vows and entered into the practice of Vajrayana.

---

7   *gos dKar lCang lo'i sDe* / གོས་དཀར་ལྕང་ལོའི་སྡེ་ – the community of non-monastic practitioners.

The twenty-third of June

Abandoning conditioning doesn't mean one cannot retain one's air-conditioning, or have a mild penchant for a re-conditioned 1966 Silver Cloud Rolls Royce.

———— · ————

People often fail to question the commonly accepted version of reality into which they are indoctrinated. It's not necessarily a deliberate process of indoctrination – it merely happens as part of the way human society functions.

———— · ————

The tendency is to conform to standard values: supporting one brand of quasi-functional political values against another equally quasi-functional alternative. Social acceptance, peer approval, and commonly esteemed achievements are taken as respectability and success. Most people therefore experience the phenomenal world and their minds as limited according to the current preordained criteria.

———— · ————

Those who do not tend towards nihilist materialism incline towards eternalism or theism. Those who do not tend towards monism, lean towards dualist separatism. Few people doubt the veracity of those whose assertions are the most voluble and widely quoted. Few question the reality with which they are presented by the press and social media, on either side of the political spectrum – unless it is a branch of the press which opposes their political beliefs. The development of disbelief however, is the first step on the path of Vajrayana. We need to disbelieve the party-political promises of 'khorwa.

The twenty-fourth of June

We can never be free – if 'freedom' is an obsession.

———— · ————

Vajrayana works best when Lamas know all their students by name – and are able to describe their personalities. When this is not feasible it is possible that Vajrayana may have become institutionalised.

———— · ————

Vajrayana does not function as it should when sanghas become too large. We will not put a figure on 'too large' – but it can probably be identified in terms of the existence of political manoeuvring and Machiavellian intrigues.

———— · ————

There is no guarantee that any conventional point of view can create a compassionate society. Obsession with individual freedom at the expense of others is the death of compassion. Obsession with neurotic parental concern at the expense of the personal liberty of others is the death of wisdom

———— · ————

The Vajra master conforms neither to the parameters of democracy nor totalitarianism. Neither offer real freedom. We imagine we have democracy – but we have merely replaced feudal lords with the international conglomerates who govern our movements. Dictators are no freer than those whom they dominate because they are imprisoned by the nature of what they are. Theft of individual freedom has been perpetrated by representatives of the broad spectrum of political philosophies since the inception of societies.

The twenty-fifth of June

The self-defining vector of dualistic derangement has the capacity
to convert religion according to its own purposes.

———— · ————

Mechanisms of dualised identity appropriate meditative techniques
in order to describe the nature of ownership of the meditative
technique. The more meditative techniques which can be owned the
more solid the mechanism feels.

———— · ————

In terms of the mechanism of dualistic derangement – all that can
be established are areas of *faux experience* which seem similar to the
way in which nonduality has been described. That is then labelled
'spiritual'. Once that has been labelled 'spiritual', access to
spirituality is curtailed.

———— · ————

The mechanism of dualistic derangement translates everything in
terms of self-definition – and develops a sense of accomplishment
in so doing. The mechanism seems to create a tangible confirmation
of insulated isolated self-referencing. If practitioners are successful
in maintaining self-definition through religious techniques, then
genuine development becomes impossible.

———— · ————

When the mechanism of dualistic derangement has learned all the
mannerisms and aphorisms of meditation, it attempts to imitate
religion. Because authentic involvement requires the complete
abandonment of self-definition, the last thing the mechanism wants
to do is to give up its mechanistic mode. The experience that is
imitated cannot be the actual experience – it can only be an
imitation of the experience.

The twenty-sixth of June

The most receptive audience for Vajrayana *should* be Artists – but unfortunately Artists don't often seem attracted to Vajrayana because they see it as 'religion' and 'religion' tends to have a reputation for repression of individuality. Whilst this tends to be true of institutionalised religion – it bears no similarity to essential Vajrayana.

———— · ————

Those artists who become interested in Buddhism often imagine that they have to depict Buddhism quite literally in terms of their Art – but that is entirely unnecessary. Insinuating Buddhist motifs into western painting tends to be kitsch. Using rolmo in Minimalist music tends to be ungainly. Combining gar'cham dance movement with ballet would seem vaguely absurd. These efforts although well intentioned are no service to Art or Buddhism. Imagine the Gyütö monks inserting a section of Händel's *Hallelujah Chorus* or Leonard Cohen's *Hallelujah* into a Dorje Shinjèd drüpthab.

———— · ————

The underlying functional parameter of Critical Mass Poetics relates to Buddhism in terms of nonduality as the inseparability of emptiness and form. In terms of poetry, form equates to linear sense; no matter how metaphorical that it becomes. This is then partnered with emptiness in terms of laterality or the collapse of sense-making. With regard to Buddhism form is seen as arising out of emptiness and dissolving into emptiness again – and in this way linear motifs arise out of directionless language or the apparent absence of comprehensibility.

The twenty-seventh of June

Love touches people through Art: not simply through the Arts of music, painting, sculpture, poetry, literature, and drama – but through the constantly performing theatre of existence. Art and the nature of the senses continually imitate, intimate, and initiate each other.

———— · ————

Love is artistic openness: the responsiveness to whatever presents itself – the capacity for tears to well up in response to the poignance of human creativity. It is the way a 'cello is bowed – the way in which an exquisite cadence is given life by the voice.

———— · ————

Falling in love occurs through the exotic ordinariness of coincidence. It is always expressed as falling in love – never as climbing. Such mountains are never conquered, even though the heights of riotous glory are scaled. Love is the discovery of what has always been there, and—when it is found—it is simultaneously known that all that can be achieved is to return.

———— · ————

If boundaries are allowed to blur, lovers become endless flurries of provocative movement – gestures which express love: in the way in which a whale surfaces or a shark discovers its depth; the way in which surf roils in swells of the ocean and waves crash into bright shingle; the way a gull cries; an owl feels night beneath her wings; the wind blows; snow falls; thunder rolls; ice melts; frost glitters; or the sun and moon blaze through the unknown swathe of time.

The twenty-eighth of June

We tend to assume that we *individually appreciate* the clothes we wear, the food that we eat, the books we read and the music to which we listen – but it is mainly dictated by fashion and group consensus. Very few people are free to be individual and authentically appreciate anything.

———— · ————

Fashion in the Arts is no different from fashion in clothing, hairstyles, home décor – or any aspect of life which falls victim to the dictates of fashion. There is no opprobrium that is necessarily attached to *what is new* – unless the demand for *what is new* becomes a barrier to individual creative endeavour. *The shock of the old* could be as interesting, or more interesting, than *the shock of the new*. There is no qualitative difference—in terms of Art—vis-à-vis ancient and modern, other than what may lie in the wish to address a contemporary audience in terms of common experience.

———— · ————

The current fashion in the Art world is for concept – and anything which lacks a thesis tends to be deemed unworthy. Even therefore, in the realm of elite Art, fashion holds sway – and when this occurs, quality dwindles just as it dwindles in the popular market. This becomes evident when it's clear that a painter lacks drawing skills – but is able to obfuscate that paucity in visual abstraction or semantic camouflage. There is nothing wrong with abstraction – but it should be a choice rather than a default based on lack of skill. It is clear to anyone who has seen Picasso's life drawings that his Cubist paintings cannot stem from his inability to draw.

The twenty-ninth of June

Because openness is our natural condition, it constantly nudges us.

———— · ————

Practising silent sitting, encourages openness to the natural state. Shi-nè is the method for *getting used to* emptiness. With sustained practice of shi-nè it is impossible to avoid making a certain discovery – duality has to commit suicide at some point. This is an odd sensation, because it was duality—at least in part—that talked us into practice in the first place.

———— · ————

The drive to continually supersede existing structures and strictures is not creatively defensible. There should be no critical societal impediment for contemporary Fine Artists in terms of producing Renaissance style paintings – or any style of the past as long such work is not unimaginatively imitative. The same applies to music, poetry, and any of the Arts. Manacling oneself to the modern mode is an Artistic moratorium. The compass of the Arts should include the entire history of the Arts rather than immuring itself in the prison of obedience to modernism.

———— · ————

Authentic enjoyment is simply the natural experience of being alive. When there is no referential strategy, policy, tactic, scheme, plan, or manipulative manœuvring – enjoyment simply occurs and cannot be curtailed. Enjoyment cannot be curtailed because: there is no strategy to be uncovered; there is no tactic which might fail; there is no scheme which may prove useless; there is no plan which might go awry; and, there is no manipulative manœuvring which could be exposed.

The thirtieth of June

The ultimate tsam[8] is where the parameters exclude the past and future in order to leave only the present moment.

——— · ———

It tends towards the case that phrases intended to indicate the state beyond concepts – eventually become concepts which merely indicate concepts.

——— · ———

Vajrayana is the proclivity of those who have courage of heart and subtlety of mind. It is for those who have audacity of determination and outrageous endurance in the face of nihilist materialism.

——— · ———

Genuine cheerfulness is choosing the disquiet of seeing the nature of dualistic derangement rather than being unconsciously governed by it.

——— · ———

Renunciation has nothing to do with sacrificing anything. From the point of view of Sutrayana—the vehicle of renunciation—there is nothing that solidly exists. From that point of view all that you renounce is the vague act of identification.

——— · ———

The weight of three million years of human history is massive. To stage a personal rebellion on behalf of everyone and everything, everywhere is a challenge that few would wish to accept – if it were not for the inspiration of those before us, who have accepted the challenge with colossal integrity. These are our heroes and heroines – the authentic Lamas who hold the lineages of essential Vajrayana.

---

8 *(mTshams /* མཚམས་*)* boundaries or parameters. *(sKu mTshams bCad pa /* སྐུ་མཚམས་བཅད་པ་*)* – to draw the boundaries.

Ying *(dByings)* – dimension

July

It is essential to take advantage of pure devotion to realise emptiness.

HE Ögyen Dro'dül Thrin-lé Kunkyab Rinpoche

རྒྱལ་བ་ཨོ་རྒྱན་འགྲོ་འདུལ་ཕྲིན་ལས་ཀུན་སྐྱབས་རིན་པོ་ཆེ་

Although the world is the *self-reflection* of one's mind – it is also actually interconnected with the real world.

Khar-trül Wangchuk Rig'dzin Rinpoche

མཁར་སྤྲུལ་དཔལ་གྱི་དབང་ཕྱུག་རིག་འཛིན་རིན་པོ་ཆེ།

The first of July

Sitting on the ground is the most ancient way of sitting. It links us to the dawn of human history. When you sit on the ground you are linked to the most ancient of all lineages.

———— · ————

Nothing replaces silent sitting, especially for those who are new to Buddhist meditation. As an adjunct to silent sitting however, it would seem that archery and hand-gun target shooting are valuable. Any form of hand-eye coordination is valuable in terms of integrating meditation with everyday activity.

———— · ————

There's something fundamental and solid about direct contact with the earth. Even if you're sitting in a skyscraper apartment – the floor level is always the earth in the dimension of experience. Sitting on the ground has a special quality about it. This is personal. You have to experience what it means for yourself – it's your experiment.

———— · ————

Drüpthab means method of accomplishment. The drüpthab may be the chanting of a text — and such texts are known as drüpthab. One's drüpthab may also be silent sitting — because that is a method of accomplishment. It is worth bearing in mind that chanted drüpthab is dependent on silent sitting — but silent sitting is not dependent on chanted drüpthab. If one's Lama gives the instruction to: wash and iron one's clothes more regularly; cook one's own meals with fresh ingredients; pay attention to diction and correct word usage; or behave with greater circumspection, dignity, and decorum — this, is also drüpthab. It is crucial to understand this if one is to have a realistic relationship with one's Lama.

The second of July

Duality is a condition in which every reference substantiates some other reference. Without the Lama, there is no way out of this experience of infinite cross-referencing.

———— · ————

Self-referencing references evolve elaborate patterns – which relate to other elaborate patterns, which always appear to be different. No matter how differently we experience our various explorations in the internalised world of 'sense-making' – they always add up to the same thing: justification of the need to maintain the illusion of duality.

———— · ————

The empty aspects of the elements: insubstantiality, impermanence, non-separateness, discontinuity, and lack of definition – can also be described as insecurity, evanescence, inextricability, perpetual disjuncture, and serial re-definition. They can also be described as diffidence, transience, indissolubility, disconnectedness, and consecutive re-classification. There are many words here – but they all reflect emptiness.

———— · ————

Maintaining the illusion of duality is a process in which we have to prove that we exist. In order to do this, we have to rely on existence having certain qualities: solidity, permanence, separateness, continuity, and definition. These are simply the form qualities of emptiness; which are only half the story. The other half of the story are the emptiness qualities of form; with which we seem uncomfortable: insubstantiality, impermanence, non-separateness, discontinuity, and lack of definition. These are the aspects of existence which we fear; and, we react to them through endlessly complicated systems of attempting to reference form.

The third of July

If life is not *a work in progress*, it's not going to be as interesting as it could be.

———— · ————

When mind is identified with sky – the circus of meteorology is perceived as transient display.

———— · ————

You've got to be prepared for work in terms of what you love. The harder you work at what you love, the more it feeds you.

———— · ————

Life is far richer when inquisitiveness is more powerful than anxiety – when curiosity is more powerful than fear.

———— · ————

This is your life. It's happening now. We hope you like it. If not, you may need to engage in silent sitting. That won't make your circumstances any better – but at least you'll start to find them amusing.

———— · ————

Being congruent as an artist is never accepting second best. It is not compromising. Not compromising aesthetically results in not being conflicted. It's that simple. That is exciting rather than conflicted. It's challenging. It's hard work – but then so is life.

———— · ————

Happiness—as an artist—comes from not compromising in terms of quality. It comes from being congruent with one's immediate perceptions. It's the natural love of phenomenal reality. A great deal of enthusiasm—joy for others—comes from this. It's always joyful because it's naturally and spontaneously shared with others.

The fourth of July

Tantrikas are heroic. Vajrayana is not for the timid – but it is not for 'thom-yors[1] either.

———— · ————

Being a 'thom yor is bad enough – but that we should invest in being 'thom yors, or justify the condition is a matter for grief.

———— · ————

Being a 'thom yor is not a terrible problem as long as one knows that one is a 'thom yor. It's when one doesn't know that one is a 'thom yor that the trouble starts. As the 'Brothers Twp' remarked in *The Englishman Who Went Up a Hill but Came Down a Mountain.*[2]

———— · ————

There are chest-beating 'thom yors who imagine they are not timid – but only because they come equipped with physical assurance. Heroes and heroines can be physically weak and limited – so, it is not a question of being an archetypal athlete. Heroism is simply the will to move into the unknown – outside the realm of security no matter the size of your physical prowess.

---

1   *'thom yor* / འཐོམ་ཡོར་ – idiot or fool.

2   *The Englishman Who Went Up a Hill but Came Down a Mountain* Film produced by Miramax Films and Parallax Pictures in 1995. The film is based on a story heard by Christopher Monger from his grandfather about the village of Taff's Well and neighbouring Garth Hill in Glamorgan. 20th Century urbanisation led to the film being made in Llanrhaeadr-ym-Mochnant and Llansilin, Powys. Twp is Welsh meaning 'foolish'. Thomas Twp Too *"This is my brother, Thomas Twp, and I am Thomas Twp Too."* Thomas Twp *"We've no learning, and most people say we're twp – but we're not so twp as to not know that we're twp."*

The fifth of July

We cannot be responsible for many things – but we are all responsible for how we feel about what happens. To embrace emotions as the path, one must take responsibility for the style of one's responses.

———— · ————

The key to understanding everything within Dharma, is the Heart Sutra. If one understands how emptiness and form are nondual – then there is nothing that cannot be understood. Every aspect of Dharma is a refraction of the play of emptiness and form. Every aspect of Buddhism is simply practising with emptiness and form in endless ways.

———— · ————

Being natural is not 'natural' to those committed to the illusion of duality – and therefore some encouragement is needed in terms of inspiring practitioners to enter into the felt meaning of the view. This is why essential life-advice is given in terms of mere indication. This method exists in terms of guidelines which undermine the complex contrivances of attempting to maintain dualism. They are invaluable teachings in terms of authentic evolution.

———— · ————

The development of clarity arises from a growing awareness of the natural spaciousness of being. With growing clarity, life problems cease to manifest as painfully. One no longer adds to the intensity of pain as an automatic reflex. Ultimately, our lives are our own responsibility. One's problems are one's own – so there is no use in blaming anybody else. Whatever my father or mother may have done or not done is not the cause of my state of mind. I am solely to blame for how I am – but knowing that is what makes me happy. It means that I can also be responsible for experiencing joy.

The sixth of July

We would go so far as to say that it would probably be quite rare for the vajra master to make suggestions which proved physically difficult – unless, of course, you think you're Naropa or Milarépa.

———— · ————

A tantrika requires a certain degree of chutzpah. But that's not to say that Vajrayana can't help you short-circuit insecurity, fear, loneliness, anxiety, and depression. This may sound like a complete contradiction – but there is an escape clause: devotion. One can short-circuit all neurotic sensitivities if one has complete confidence in the Lama and the practice. But that confidence has to be real – it cannot be adopted. It cannot be brainless bovine braggadocio or rhodomontade.

———— · ————

Rather than continually re-building towers until his back was an entire running sore – the vajra master would be far more likely to take Ngakpa Chögyam to a Country & Western line dancing evening and make him wear sneakers and 'other brand jeans' for the occasion. The vajra master is much more likely to ask Khandro Déchen to sit through a couple of Benny Hill videos drinking sweet white wine and eating boiled sweets. So – let us remain at the level of concrete reality in terms of the vajra master's rôle.

———— · ————

Whenever the vajra master is mentioned by Western Buddhist critics of the rôle – they tend to speak of being ordered to jump off a cliff. What is never explained is what the benefit is supposed to be. We would not say that there could be no benefit in jumping off a cliff – because as long as there is sufficient depth of sea at the base of the cliff; there is nothing to fear but fear. If the purpose of the vajra command is to encourage a student to overcome fear, then leaping from a cliff and descending into a good depth of ocean, could be a highly valuable experience.

The seventh of July

Unless we have a relationship with the 'emotive colour' of Guru Rinpoche and Yeshé Tsogyel, as multidimensional realities who are both personally and universally available – we will miss what the Nyingma Tradition has to offer.

———— · ————

When we look at the idea of communicating with Guru Rinpoche and Yeshé Tsogyel, it could seem that *the manner of communication* might be one which is only open to advanced practitioners. This however, does not preclude any of us from being *open to all possibilities*. We are all beginninglessly realised – and therefore the living connection with Guru Rinpoche and Yeshé Tsogyel is there for all of us.

———— · ————

Chögyam Trungpa Rinpoche described Guru Rinpoche as a 'cosmic principle' – and such he is. He is however, also available as a personal friend – someone who is actually there, and can become increasingly there, according to the evolution of one's emotive / emotional practice. For the scientific and rationalistic all this is probably hocus-pocus – but that is a great pity. The Western world has often looked to Buddhism as a logical religion which abjures faith, and at some level this is not entirely untrue. Logic plays a great part in Buddhism – particularly within the Sutras. But Buddhism also has a strong emotional / intuitive dimension which is found more particularly within the Tantras and within Dzogchen. We have often said that Vajrayana—*in terms of understanding and expression and the presentation of commentaries*—has more in common with the Arts than with the linear logical approach of science. This is nowhere truer than when faced with the meaning of Guru Rinpoche and Yeshé Tsogyel.

The eighth of July

Those who require either excitement or the imposition of external discipline belong elsewhere. We are both unqualified and unwilling to provide either. Those who have the sense that they can be responsible for themselves and their practice will find that they function quite naturally with us.

———— · ————

Someone once commented that our sangha had a *'thin dharma atmosphere'*. We replied that this was not surprising, as our students all lived at high altitude. Untrue, of course, because some live at sea level. Sometimes however, humour is preferable to a purposeless rebuttal.

———— · ————

We are not given to confrontational relationships with people. It does not suit us. We never joined encounter groups when they were de rigueur. We have no interest in interpersonally aggressive forums – we prefer cordiality and decorum by far. We prefer to promote adulthood. The teachings are as they are – and need no special atmosphere other than that of wakefulness and genuine interest.

———— · ————

There is noticeably less discipline within our sangha. This is because —from a Dzogchen point of view—we are disinterested in *imposing* discipline. Some people feel that this is good – but they would be misguided. Some people may feel that this is as we wish it to be – but they would also be misguided. We do not admire lack of discipline – we are merely antithetical to disciplinarianism. We would prefer students to be adult and recognise the value of discipline in terms of its principle and function.

The ninth of July

The state of no-thought is a method. It creates space to see what happens when something arises. Through the practice of meditation, one discovers direct contact with the unconditioned essence of a spectrum of liberated energy. One can embrace emotions and realise the unending vividness of what is naturally there.

——— · ———

When Kyabjé Künzang Dorje Rinpoche addressed the subjects of 'idiots' – the word he used was 'thom-yor. He often said that the world was full of suffering – but that there would be far less suffering without 'thom-yors to make it worse. His definition of 'thom-yor was not simply someone in the dualistic condition. He did not regard the standard dualistic condition as idiocy. For him idiocy was something worse – a 'thom-yor was someone who conspired to make their dualistic state far more ludicrous than it had to be – and in doing so caused other people a great deal of unnecessary nuisance, irritation, hardship, or pain.

——— · ———

Kyabjé Künzang Dorje Rinpoche said *"The world is full of 'thom-yors. There are many kinds of 'thom-yor: foolish harmless 'thom-yors; shy emotionally vulnerable 'thom-yors; oversensitive 'thom-yors; ridiculous pious 'thom-yors; comfort-seeking 'thom-yors; mundane conformist 'thom-yors; tight-minded conservative 'thom-yors; unconventional exhibitionist 'thom-yors; puritanical 'thom-yors; pompous spiritual 'thom-yors; self-righteous hypocritical 'thom-yors; self-satisfied sanctimonious 'thom-yors; academic scholarly 'thom-yors; pseudo-tantric misogynistic 'thom yors; tedious self-centred 'thom-yors; clever scheming 'thom-yors; power-seeking 'thom-yors; arrogant bigoted 'thom-yors; cruel avaricious 'thom-yors; dangerous vicious 'thom-yors . . . I have no time for 'thom-yors."* Of course… for a while, I was one of those 'thom-yors. I hope I am now more-or-less cured.

The tenth of July

Being genuinely in love with phenomenal reality is infinite—in the moment—on a moment-by-moment basis.

———— · ————

In discovering experiential space one can abandon the emotional investment one puts into planning the perfect future. Life becomes easier when one allows oneself to play in situations, rather than having to take them deadly seriously. The lightness of this approach is a manifestation of developing clarity.

———— · ————

When you have it and continue to desire it – that is appreciation. Authentic appreciation is always active – never passive. The 'empty passive aspect' is the space in which one's senses remain active. The senses should not become passive through meditation. When the senses become passive one does not really see, hear, fragrance, taste, feel, or ideate. Everything becomes partial. If there is only partial sensating then authentic appreciation cannot exist.

———— · ————

The fluctuations of fashion can be a valuable barometer of authentic appreciation. If there was ever any item of clothing which you wore and loved, which you now ridicule *(along with yourself for ever having worn it)* – one thing is certain: you never authentically appreciated it; you were merely seduced by fashion into imagining you loved it. If one loves a thing – why should one ever stop loving it? It's not that one cannot change—change is the nature of life—but when there is no connection left between the item loved and the item ridiculed, the authenticity of one's appreciation is in question. This creates a more general question which covers all our ideas and convictions – as to what is authentically personal and what is merely the result of indoctrination.

The eleventh of July

Because Vajrayana is constantly performing itself—in us; through us; and around us—we can either acknowledge it, by taking hold of the bare electric cables of existence and non-existence, or: try to pretend it is not happening. Whether we like it or not – Vajrayana is what is happening. Vajrayana is the warp and weft of reality.

———— · ————

Ecstatic appreciation of every moment of experience is simply what happens when one abandons attempts to create reality according to the banal dictates of security. That the texture of whatever happens is, in itself, the implicit meaning of every Mind-moment – is to say that each Mind-moment is, *in its nakedness*, the nondual state.

———— · ————

Tantrikas remain always in ecstatic embrace with the khandro or dPa'wo aspects of each moment in time. In romantic relationship, Tantrikas refrain from subverting the sexual dimension of being in the attempt to avoid authentic relationship with the khandro or dPa'wo. They avoid obfuscating the inner dPa'wo or inner khandro by objectifying women or men according to sexually distorted or degraded stereotypes.

———— · ————

Tantrikas avoid taking anything that is not freely offered – which means that they avoid freeloading as a way of life. They do not leave others to carry out work which they have been allotted. They do not avoid work and allow others to carry a greater share. They do not fail to volunteer when help is needed. They abstain from asking excessive favours of others, or expecting to be 'carried' in life. They avoid abusing hospitality or taking advantage of the time and generosity of others. They do not steal the time of other practitioners by the refusal to be real, or by engaging in the adoption of an 'artificial buddhist personality'.

The twelfth of July

Pure appropriateness is an invisible dance in which one is transparent in terms of what is taking place. There is an effortlessness that is not even named or differentiated from effort.

———— · ————

Creating conducive circumstances involves planning and making efforts, This, in many respects, tends to be a risky adventure. Plans are made and fall apart – but that is no reason not to make plans. The failure and success of plans simply gives us an opportunity to experience failure and success as the ornaments of equanimity. If one has a sense of space – one finds it amusing rather than dispiriting.

———— · ————

A kind act is an act of pure appropriateness. Therefore, whenever we are kind—whenever we emphasise concern for others—our lives will be infused with the dynamism of appropriateness. Life will seem infused with vivacity. There will seem fewer obstructions and obscurations. Kindness simplifies situations. Acts of kindness enable us to side-step our attachment to past and future. Kindness is a period of remission from 'me-centred concerns', and as such can be lived moment by moment.

———— · ————

Unless one lives in permanent retreat, one has to engage with the richness of the dualistic condition in all its complexity: *monochromatic boredom and technicolour excitement; joy and sorrow; decisions and dilemmas; set-backs and exultations; misfortunes and rewards.* It is a fantastically fertile field of learning – but one has to find the experiential space in which one can pursue plans very lightly. One requires a pronounced sense of humour for such an endeavour. Of course, one still has to engage in short term retreats in order to access that richness in a realistic manner.

The thirteenth of July

Mere indication means that something is suggested – and, in that moment, there is an entire nondual gestalt.

———— · ————

Mere indication in terms of transmission, means that one simply hears directly. One's stream of awareness is 'seeded' with *mere indication* – and there is no more to think. It is perfect in that moment. Then, all one has to do is allow that moment to remember itself.

———— · ————

Vajrayana is not just another hippie hobby. It's not an 'alternative'. This is why we encourage people to make pilgrimages to Bhutan. Vajrayana is simply ordinary life in Bhutan. It's not exotic. These Bhutanese people are not alternative types. They're not hippies. This is their real everyday life. That experience grounds people. It pulls the rug away. It undercuts the false stance of hobbyist-vajrayana. It undermines the idea of creating something personally rarefied. This is important in order to begin dismantling the 'me project'.

———— · ————

Knowledge of Vajrayana is intrinsic to human beings. This is not in the sense of complex symbolism and elaborate colourful mystical motifs – but in the sense of what is essential and transcultural. Vajrayana is our condition, in the sense that it is the thread of continuity which runs through every aspect of what we are. In this sense Vajrayana may be invisible – but it is also sharply and poignantly perceptible. The rôle of the Lama is to purvey this reality.

The fourteenth of July

Life is an existential kaleidoscope in which meaning is only found in the moment. If one tries to extend meaning beyond the moment – meaning often becomes increasingly meaningless.

————— · —————

A kyil'khor is created from coloured chalk dust. Unexpectedly the wind blows. The pattern is no longer what it was. One can grieve the lost pattern – or enjoy the mingling of colours and the strange shapes created by the staggered disintegration. It doesn't have to be a Kyil'khor that is blown away – it could be the best laid plans of mice and men.

————— · —————

Love is a mystery which provokes antithetical sensations: lightness and heaviness; joy and sorrow; pleasure and pain; relief and tension; ease and intensity. It is a mystery which elicits conflicting motivations: sincerity and deceit; gentleness and cruelty; trust and suspicion; openness and manipulation. Attempting to discover what attracts us to others can be bewildering from most perspectives – other than nonduality.

————— · —————

What exists for those who are drawn to the pursuit of realisation – but who remain unattracted by the option of detaching from ordinary everyday society? What exists for those who experience spiritual value in their interaction with the world? The answer is that Vajrayana exists – not necessarily the Vajrayana of liturgical recitation, but the essential Vajrayana, which expounds the dance of emptiness and form within every nuance of experience.

The fifteenth of July

The Lama's personality display discloses evidence that our elemental neuroses are open to transformation.

——— · ———

The elemental neuroses do not have to be obliviated – they could remain as an apparitional array. They could manifest as vajra appetite, vajra alertness, vajra appreciation, vajra cynicism, and vajra composure.

——— · ———

The Lama's personality display is a natural educational phenomenon – and as such corelates can be found within secular culture. Where a musician is admired on the basis of virtuosity – there is a natural interest in the life-style of the musician. This extends to the musician's sartorial sense; cuisine preferences; literary and film partialities; and other cultural predilections. These build a picture of the ethos of the musician – which expands one's enjoyment of the music. This is not equivalent to the Lama's personality display – but it is a reflection and as such conveys the fact that this is something that is natural to the human condition.

——— · ———

In terms of personality display, the Lama can employ voracity, resentment, yearning, doubt, and indifference as skilful means. The Lama can employ excess, antipathy, nostalgia, distrust, and unresponsiveness as skilful means. The Lama can employ surfeit, antagonism, wistfulness, scepticism, and impassiveness as skilful means. The Lama can employ dominance, hostility, lust, uncertainty, and insensitivity as skilful means. The listings are endless – and impossibly subtle in their complexity. The Lama paints continually arising pictures of the manner in which the neuroses can be transformed into transparent manifestations of the nondual state.

The sixteenth of July

Dad'dun—devotion—is knowledge and skill coupled with direct experiential understanding[3]. Anything else is suspect. Anything else will change and eventually be replaced. Anything else will fail.

——— · ———

I always tell people that devotion is not a 'bolt from the blue'. It's not like 'love at first sight'. Devotion is based on developed meditative experience. That, of course, is rank hypocrisy, because as soon as I met Kyabjé Düd'jom Rinpoche Jig'drèl Yeshé Dorje – there was no question. Devotion *was* like a bolt from the blue. It *was* love at first sight. Devotion *was* there in an instant – without significant preparation. The fact that I was outrageously outlandishly lucky however, does not mean that anyone else will be quite *that* lucky.

——— · ———

The development of dad'dun is the development of spiritual experience. The same phenomenon exists in the world of the Arts. Anyone, other than an abject philistine, can appreciate world-class music – but only a highly proficient musician can begin to comprehend the worth of a world-class musician. The greater the musical ability the more astonishing a master-musician becomes. Mozart is a composer of extremely pretty melodies – until you learn enough about music to understand his compositions. JS Bach is a composer of marvellously intricate sonic adventures – until you learn something about contrapuntal composition. If one lacks experience – one cannot judge a Lama's worth or have authentic dad'dun.

---

3 Ngön-sum gyi togpa (*mNgon sum gyi rTogs pa* / མངོན་སུམ་གྱི་རྟོགས་པ་) – direct understanding.

The seventeenth of July

Love is there when the artificial divisions between us dissolve into the iridescent spectrum of our beginningless nature.

———— · ————

The love which radiates from our primordial state cannot help but sparkle through – no matter how insecure, frightened, isolated, anxious, or bewildered we become.

———— · ————

What is considered to be Mind, is not what it is imagined to be. It is purposeless to attempt to understand Mind with thought. It is better simply to allow Mind to see itself – for there is no difference between Mind and seeing. *Kyabjé Düd'jom Rinpoche Jig'drèl Yeshé Dorje*

———— · ————

In order to comprehend vastness, we have to let go of the experiential agoraphobia which cripples the free dimension of being. There is no dipping your toes in to see if the temperature is comfortable – because, for duality, the temperature is never quite right. There is no shallow end in which to linger tentatively. Vastness demands immediate and total immersion.

———— · ————

How can one be open to romance when one is tied up in limitations which govern how it can occur? Basically, we need as few limitations as possible. Body type is a limitation which causes people to restrict themselves too much – especially at this point in history. People have been surprised to hear us say that a yogi or yogini should be attracted to all body types: peaceful, joyous, and wrathful. That is to say: thin, sensuous, and large. One cannot entertain concepts of being a tantrika if there are body types to which one could feel no attraction.

The eighteenth of July

A wingless bird cannot fly. A bird with one wing also cannot fly. One requires both wisdom and method.

——— · ———

A wingless bird cannot fly. Bird-less wings are also bereft of that ability. A wingless bird is someone who lacks wisdom and method. Bird-less wings are usually found in academia. Wisdom and method can be acquired through the Lama – but where there is no bird, there is no one to take the Lama's teaching.

——— · ———

When target shooting, one cannot engage in thought-stories *and* maintain one's aim with a revolver. There is a certain empty point at which the trigger is squeezed – and one has to know when that moment has arrived. One has to know it without knowing it – which means one has to know it *without thought*. Once the thought of recognition is there – it is too late. The squeeze of the trigger has to occur with the bare recognition. That is where one has to begin. That is when it becomes meditation.

——— · ———

Mind is misunderstood as a patchwork or a pastiche of interlocking, overlapping thought. It is as if one were looking at the surface of a lake ruffled by the wind, or the sky churning with clouds. From these impressions, no one would evolve the notion that the surface of the lake could be like a mirror perfectly reflecting the sky. No one would have any idea that behind the clouds lay the infinity in which the sun shone or the moon and stars glittered within the vastness of space.

The nineteenth of July

Emptiness could simply be a moment of delightful directionlessness.

––––– · –––––

Emptiness could be like the first moment one tastes Gjetost[4] – and not knowing whether it's cheese or fudge.

––––– · –––––

Emptiness must be realised experientially as the ground of being from which form arises, before we can relate directly to the magical arising of phenomena which is characteristic of Vajrayana.

––––– · –––––

It is not easy to understand emptiness as the source of endless manifestations. It tends to be especially difficult for emptiness to be a *lived experience* – outside the emptiness discovered within the practice of silent sitting meditation. It is possible however. One can begin by accepting the felt texture of confusion and resisting the need for panic in terms of resolving situations. The same applies to confusion, misperception, perplexity, uncertainty, disorder, disarray, turmoil, havoc, chaos, disorientation, bafflement, puzzlement, or bewilderment. This does not mean we cannot look for solutions to situations – but that we do not need to feel too much desperation about it.

4   Gjetost is a brown Norwegian caramelised cheese made from goat's milk and cow's cream.

The twentieth of July

Every 'democratic society' would appear to be ruled by powerful influential factors which attempt to remain discreet. Within every democracy we find dictatorship manifesting under the guise of consensus.

———— · ————

Some who are critical of Tibetan culture speak as if we in the West no longer live in feudal societies. This is an illusion. We have merely exchanged feudal barons for the multinational conglomerates who control our elected politicians.

———— · ————

Relationship with the vajra master is not democratic. This may appear shocking – but our relationship with reality is not democratic either. There is no tribunal to which we can appeal when our lovers leave us, or when the weather becomes unseasonably hot.

———— · ————

Vajra commitment and vajra relationship cannot be crudely compared with political totalitarianism. Even if one were to make such a spurious comparison, one could not go on to say that the problems of political totalitarianism are absent within democracies. Vajrayana has no need of democratisation. Even if democracy were such a wonderful phenomenon – where do we authentically find democracy in the world? Even in Ancient Greece—where democracy began—the equality in Athens was supported by slavery in silver mines at the other end of the country. The situation has not changed a great deal.

The twenty-first of July

Nothing we see, is as it seems – nor is otherwise. One could simply relax with that.

———— · ————

Nondual awareness sparkles through the filter of conditioning – whether we like it or not.

———— · ————

Thamal-gyi shépa[5] means instantaneous ordinariness: the extraordinary dimension of the ordinary moment. This is discovered through practising the gYowa bardo[6] – the bardo of the changing moment. The nature of time is transcended through the indivisibility of continuity and discontinuity.

———— · ————

In terms of what we see in the mirror of mind – we employ *the blinking of the senses* to avoid seeing *that which reflects*. Glimpsing *that which reflects* is beginningless realisation. Unfortunately, the conceptual sense predominates – and deliberately ignores *what is there*. It is, however, not a haphazard process. Conceptuality ignores the mirror in a systematically intentional manner. This is a particular 'skill' in terms of handling *addiction to form*, as the only possible focus of security. This is our primary method of remaining in the dualised condition. This conveniently appalling delusion permits us to continually recycle ourselves within a circus of complicit confusion. Whatever we do however—and wherever we look—the mirror of existence and non-existence is there – reflecting the knowledge of our nondual condition.

5   *tha mal gyi shes pa* / ཐ་མལ་གྱི་ཤེས་པ་ – in terms of Dzogchen this means 'instantaneous ordinariness' and is one of the nine bardos. In terms of Mahamudra (cha gyür chenpo *(phyag rgya chen po* / ཕྱག་རྒྱ་ཆེན་པོ་) it means 'ordinary mind' – a phrase describing the nondual essence: the natural basic state in respect of thamal gyi shé-pa jènpa la *(tha mal gyi shes pa rJen pa la* / ཐ་མལ་གྱི་ཤེས་པ་རྗེན་པ་ལ་) in the nakedness of ordinary mind.

6   *g.Yo ba bar do* / གཡོ་བ་བར་དོ་

The twenty-second of July

We are not here to champion Buddhism as the best religion – we are here to champion religion per se.

———— · ————

Where we abandon authentic religion – we abandon the self-existent structure which enables the Arts to be meaningful. When religion loses authenticity, the Arts become sanctimoniously soporific. When religion is seen to be inauthentic, people reject religion – and the Arts either become political jargon or nihilistic self-indulgence.

———— · ————

Buddhism is only the best religion when it is practised faithfully – but the same could be said of the other religions. The same could be said of shamanism and animism. Human beings need metaphysical codes in order to maintain sanity – and to be generous, perceptive, kind, creative, and open-minded.

———— · ————

Religion is tainted by human behaviour – so some people find fault with religion. Food however is also tainted by the fact that some people become morbidly obese – and alcohol is tainted by that fact that some people become alcoholic. Religion—in the true sense—is the food and wine of a glorious banquet at which we raises toasts to the health, creativity, and happiness of everyone and everything everywhere.

———— · ————

Vajrayana prompts the need to question the patterns of the world, according to a nondual context. This is vital – because continually evolving new patterns on the basis of previous patterns—when all patterns are questionable by virtue of their unavoidable restrictiveness—is not an option for anyone who wishes to touch the heart of vajra-romance.

The twenty-third of July

Being honest is far simpler than lying. Successful lying requires intelligence equivalent to genius. Fortunately, I have an IQ of 66 and a memory to match[7].

———— · ————

Being honest is the heart of the matter. It is vital to be honest with ourselves, as Vajrayana practitioners. That is central and fundamental. Anything else is a waste of time and effort. If one pours coffee into a pipe as if it were a cup – one would never be able to drink it.

———— · ————

Being honest comes into play continually in the realm of practice. Wanting to be involved with Vajrayana without practising, means you have to become managerial or political. You have to engage with something associated with Vajrayana that is *not Vajrayana*. This leads to manipulation and endless problems. Those who actually practise do not become involved with politics. Those who are honest—and who prioritise practice—don't manipulate or involve themselves with status-issues.

———— · ————

Even vegan and vegetarian parents have to deal with their childrens' head lice. One cannot give headlice tickets for holidays on the Costa Brava – but one can recite mantra for them when one applies the system of removal. Even vegans and vegetarians may require vaccination against viruses – and every virus was once one's parent.

7   Ngak'chang Rinpoche *(sNgags 'chang Rinpoche /* སྔགས་འཆང་རིན་པོ་ཆེ *)*.

The twenty-fourth of July

We want our experiences to be buttoned-up and laced-down tight – squeezed into predictable perceptual pantyhose. Be that as it may, however much we try to constrict ourselves – primordial wisdom sparkles through.

———— · ————

To be completely pretentious – one has to have an extremely low opinion of oneself. One has to present a false front because one feels there is nothing behind it. This could almost be described as humility. Conversely, humility could be the most ignominious form of pretension.

———— · ————

No matter what stiff collar and tightly-knotted blood-drip tie[8] is worn—despite the belt, braces, or girdle—there's always something coming undone. Measures of control are impermanent. The experiential seams unravel – and the perceptual zips come unfastened. Whatever kind of elastic, it eventually loses its ability to constrain and disguise. Primordial knowingness sparkles through as a matter of course – as the wisdom-dance of existence.

———— · ————

John Lennon sang *'You can shine your shoes and wear a suit / You can comb your hair and look quite cute / You can hide your face behind a smile / One thing you can't hide / Is when you're crippled inside.'*[9] And my father used to say *'Handsome is who handsome does'*. The world's cultures probably contain many such examples – so it's not as if it's any great revelation. We all make ourselves beautiful or ugly by being exactly what we intend. Kindliness will make anyone beautiful.

---

8   Blood-drip ties were narrow ties that were popular in the 1950s.
9   John Lennon, *Crippled Inside*, Imagine, 1971

The twenty-fifth of July

The only way out of this mess is to rely on someone who knows the mess – and has experienced the absence of mess.

———— · ————

Taking a vajra master has to be a conscious decision. It needs to be a formal decision, made between the student and Lama. This point is only reached on the culmination of years of study and practice during which time students come to entertain the possibility of going beyond their rationale. During a prolonged period of working with a Lama, students gain a degree of self-transparency which causes them frustration with their own systems of subjective, self-referencing logic. It is only at this point one should consider entering vajra relationship. Having said that, I have to admit that is not what I did. I plunged straight in.

———— · ————

Someone, sometime, somewhere might have suggested heading South as the way to assuage all ills. If you're lost however—and there's no sun in the sky to indicate East or West—the fact that you're heading in the wrong direction will only become apparent through a variety of differences: increasing cold; shortening of days as winter approaches; and lengthening days as summer approaches. This is a simple picture – but mountains will cause confusion in terms of recognising these factors. By the time you arrive in the Arctic you will have travelled far from the temperate climate you sought. Fortunately, cloud-cover is not perpetual. The nondual state sparkles through the fabric of conditioning – and the Lama can be recognised as the one who gives reliable directions. It may be however, that the Lama simply gives you advice about how to live as an esquimaux. Every climatic area has its modes and requirements – you just have to know where you are.

The twenty-sixth of July

If there was no natural passionately responsive appreciation – it could not arise in response to the Lama, as devotion. If appearances were not intrinsic to emptiness – they could not express themselves, as phenomena. If emptiness was not innate – there could be no display of the dissolution of phenomena.

———— · ————

The Khamba and Golok Lamas I've met in the United States have invariably commented on the similarity they see between the culture of Kham and Golok and the culture of the Old West. Once—when invited to lunch with Tulku Thubten Rinpoche—he noticed the Western boots beneath my white shamthab. His eyes lit up and he whispered conspiratorially *"... I have like this..."* He then reached up onto a shelf and brought down a box emblazoned with the name *Tony Lama*. He opened the box and pulled out the cherished boots. I inspected them and he inspected mine. Then he showed his Stetson hat. Then he brought out a photograph of himself riding a bull.

———— · ————

Künzang Dorje Rinpoche was beyond *anything* I'd *ever* known. He *was* kind—extremely kind—but in a manner that was initially incomprehensible. He was also majestically—if not vividly— ruthless. Somehow, I knew he liked me – but whether he liked me as a father might like his son, or as a tiger might like a gazelle, was not easy to distinguish. He was dazzlingly wild—magnificently ferocious —and *he* knew the answer to *the nature of existence*. He read it like a book. He read it in everything he saw, heard, tasted, or otherwise sensated.

The twenty-seventh of July

The word 'suffering' is not the best translation of *dukkha*[10]. Dukkha is perhaps better translated as unsatisfactoriness. Of course, unsatisfactoriness ranges between the most extreme suffering and the very mildest irritation.

—— · ——

One requires a sense of humour about *dukkha* – and, that sense of humour is only made possible by emptiness. Emptiness is a key factor here in terms of the practice of Vajrayana. Without that base in emptiness, *dukkha* can be horribly misunderstood.

—— · ——

Dukkha is not the world or the body and we do not escape dukkha by escaping the world and leaving the body. Dukkha is our dualistic derangement which seeks to make everything other than it naturally is.

—— · ——

Dukkha cannot be escaped by ceasing to exist – because we can only cease to exist periodically on a temporary basis. It's called death and re-birth. The cycle of death and re-birth is only dukkha when we struggle to be solid, separate, permanent, continuous, and defined.

—— · ——

Ta'i Situ Rinpoche said "*I guarantee, that for every bowl of rice you eat there is an equal sized bowl of dead insects killed in producing that rice.*" The previous Kalu Rinpoche said "*You cannot live without killing: drinking water; walking; washing your body; all these destroy thousands of lives. It is what you do with the rest of your life that matters.*" We would add that every time you drive your car in Summer months, the windscreen becomes a charnel ground for insects — and every time you takes a course of antibiotics, genocide occurs.

10 *(sDug bsNgal / སྡུག་བསྔལ་)*

252

The twenty-eighth of July

It is far more interesting to have absolutely uncontrollable lust for *everyone everywhere* to get *everything* they want. When lust is contracted into just being *me* and what *I* want – it's a rather sad, sorry, sterile affair.

———— · ————

'Compassion' is not such a good translation of changchub sem. Chögyam Trungpa Rinpoche used to translate it as 'active compassion' because it's related with form and wisdom is related with emptiness. Form is active and changchub sem needs to be active.

———— · ————

Changchub sem is not just a feeling – it's an involvement. The two wings of Dharma are wisdom and active changchub sem. There is the tendency to consider changchub sem as equating more to the category of wisdom in terms of it being a feeling. Changchub sem however, is form – and form moves. That is the nature of form.

———— · ————

In terms of Vajrayana desire and compassion are inextricable. There has to be energy. Compassion is the energy of desire when it is non-centralised. Desire does not have to be centred on me. Desire can be beyond centre and periphery.

———— · ————

With changchub sem, something has to happen. If nothing happens – if I simply sit here and wish you well—and nothing happens—that is not changchub sem. I actually have to do something. I have to have some kind of real physical involvement. I can't merely sit there and wish that all sentient beings had a cookie and a glass of milk.

The twenty-ninth of July

The gö kar chang lo'i dé are not *holy* in the regular sense of the word. Words such as devout, reverent, worshipful, and pious do not adequately describe them. They are religious – but religious in the style of artists, musicians, and poets; explorers, inventors, and scientists.

———— · ————

The gö kar chang lo'i dé are not lay tantrikas. The word 'lay' means 'unprofessional' and 'not of the clergy'. This is the meaning given in over 30 languages. A Lama such as Kyabjé Düd'jom Rinpoche Jig'drèl Yeshé Dorje could therefore not be described as a lay tantrika.

———— · ————

The gö kar chang lo'i dé have been described as renunciates who nonetheless live in the world. This is an error. Renunciation is the principle of Sutrayana. Vajrayana is based on transformation – and whilst the gö kar chang lo'i dé are free to practise renunciation they are not obliged to do so according to their vows.

———— · ————

The gö kar chang lo'i dé are not renunciates per se. They certainly *renounce* obsession with referentiality – but they are not renunciates as monastics are renunciates. The gö kar chang lo'i dé are at liberty to live in a style which could seem indistinguishable from the average lay person. The gö kar chang lo'i dé however, are as different from the laity as renunciate monastics. The gö kar chang lo vows are all internal, apart from the vow never to cut scalp hair – and even that vow is not common to all lineages. Dung-sé Thrin-lé Norbu Rinpoche was a Lama of this category – as is his son Kyabjé Garab Dorje Rinpoche and other gö kar chang lo Lamas of the Düd'jom gTér lineage such as Dung-sé Namgay Dawa Rinpoche.

The thirtieth of July

The only difference we make in the world is through *how we are*, not *what we say* and *what we try to impose*.

———— · ————

One can speak and write a great deal about compassion—some people do—but if one is not actually compassionate; it doesn't impress anybody. What impresses anyone about anyone is how they actually live and relate with others on a day-to-day basis.

———— · ————

One doesn't have to be parental as a Lama. Our students' lives are their responsibility – and we don't need to police them. We don't have to judge them for their everyday choices. Involvement in what's good for people and what's not good for people is very much part of our culture. It's how we think in the West. As Lamas however, we don't have to involve ourselves in that kind of parentalism. We are simply concerned with Nyingma practice.

———— · ————

Lamas can be many things to many people – on an individual basis. Lamas are not parents, doctors, nurses, psychotherapists, counsellors, life-coaches, social workers, marriage guidance consultants, arbitrators, negotiators, conciliators, intermediaries, intercessors, referees, or judges – but they can fulfil any of these rôles if it is of religious benefit to an individual. As Lamas, we have listened in counselling mode – but we find it a limited rôle and do not like to encourage students to rely on us in that way. The counselling mode is highly time consuming and of far less benefit than providing the insight of Vajrayana.

The thirty-first of July

Demanding respect of others is the surest way to lose it.

———— · ————

If the nature of 'deserving' was *this equals that* – who'd want, or even understand what they deserved?

———— · ————

Whatever you do – have good intention. This doesn't mean that you're not going to make mistakes. You can only have good intention and act on that good intention. There's no rulebook or recipe book.

———— · ————

Chögyam Trungpa Rinpoche described the Nyingma's as 'the accident lineage' – and we're sure proof of that. Accidents are not a problem in themselves – it is what one does in respect of accidents. One has to take full responsibility even if one is not personally responsible – because, as Rang-rig Dorje used to say *"Everyone gets what they deserve whether they deserve it or not."*

———— · ————

Lamas are not infallible – or at least, we're not infallible. This is why we're never *that* keen on giving life-advice with respect to decisions which students need to make. We can't have absolute confidence that what we advise is going to work out. We can only do our best – so are always tentative in relation to advice. In being tentative with advice we are more likely to see what might go wrong. If we were addicted to our 'rightness' this would not be possible.

Gom *(sGom)* – meditation

August

One's present negative thoughts and actions can only bear the fruit of negativity.

HE Ögyen Dro'dül Thrin-lé Kunkyab Rinpoche
རྒྱལ་བ་ཨོ་རྒྱན་འགྲོ་འདུལ་ཕྲིན་ལས་ཀུན་སྐྱབས་རིན་པོ་ཆེ་

One must know how to cool the fire of hatred, in order to live in peace and harmony within humanity.

Khar-trül Wangchuk Rig'dzin Rinpoche
མཁར་སྤྲུལ་དཔལ་གྱི་དབང་ཕྱུག་རིག་འཛིན་རིན་པོ་ཆེ།

The first of August

Humility and arrogance can often be two sides of the same bogus coin.

———— · ————

Overstating one's humility is the surest way to arouse suspicion that one is actually arrogant.

———— · ————

It wouldn't be a pleasant choice to make – but I'd rather spend eternity with a braggart than with someone addicted to purveying a *humile* mien.

———— · ————

It's the fashion amongst Buddhists to be humble. This doesn't mean that humility has no value. It means that *the fashion of humility* has no value.

———— · ————

Fashion has a pernicious rôle in human existence. It dictates what we wear – what we eat; drink, believe; and what we disbelieve. It dictates what we like in the way of music and the Arts. It dictates how we vote and how we make choices about our lives. This is why social media indicates what is 'trending'. We are 'herd animals' and follow the designated herd. The working class follows the working-class herd. The middle class follows the middle-class herd. The upper-middle class follows the upper-middle class herd. The aristocracy class follows the aristocratic herd. Each class may have sub-herds – and these give us the illusion of freedom of choice. The reality however, is that individuality is rare.

The second of August

Healthy humour is being able to laugh at oneself – unhealthy humour is laughing at others.

——— · ———

Humour can be a response to the expression of truth. Somebody says something that is so completely and utterly true, that we recognise it – and burst out laughing.

——— · ———

Valid humour is seeing difference and responding to difference. It is responding to contradiction and situations that don't make sense. Corrupt humour is laughing at difference from a position of being superior. This is usually typified by racism, sexism, xenophobia, homophobia, or the rest of the huge ugly catalogue of prejudices.

——— · ———

Being able to laugh at oneself is crucial. One has to see one's contradictions and find them amusing. Once the contradictions are amusing, they're workable. They're workable because one is not taking oneself entirely seriously. This depends on space – on the emptiness of silent sitting.

——— · ———

Humour requires space. In order to see contradiction, there has to be the space to see contradiction. There are homonyms which give rise to humour – but space is required to realise that there are two or three possible meanings to a word-sound. One needs the space to see that – and to entertain it. If there's no space, nothing is amusing – so there has to be space. This is a good reason for silent sitting.

The third of August

Most people, when they say *"I need space"* actually mean *"I need insulation in which my neuroses can fester."*

———— · ————

Space is important in how you see any situation. Simply being able to refrain from activity for a moment – and not act impetuously. Simply being able to decide *'I'm going to wait a moment.'* Simply looking at the situation without being impelled by knee-jerk responses.

———— · ————

Once one begins to experience space in silent sitting, one can begin to observe one's knee-jerk responses – as *the knee* begins to *jerk*. That's how one ceases to be a jerk. The potential for knee-jerk responses may remain for some time – but one no longer has to act on them.

———— · ————

Those who are not practitioners, have senses like wolverines. Wolverines eat everything including teeth. Practitioners—on the other hand—have senses like wolverines – but they observe their rapacity and question its nature.

———— · ————

Let thoughts of past and future settle in the present moment – and, in that moment, simply experience what is naturally there. Visual projections appear in meditation if one distracts oneself with 'here and there' or 'then and when'. If however, it is considered that Mind is nothing – it will become 'the prison of numb emptiness', in which the richness of the nature of Mind will not self-emerge.
Kyabjé Düd'jom Rinpoche Jig'drèl Yeshé Dorje

The fourth of August

The experience of spaciousness can arise through entertaining uncertainty – and by failing to feel threatened.

———— · ————

Whenever one allows anything simply to be as it is, there's space. With whatever is allowed – it suddenly has space. This doesn't mean allowing yourself to be abused in any way. We're not talking about the ambivalence about whether some foul felon is really going to stab me with a knife or not. We're looking at relative innocuous quotidian events.

———— · ————

One perceives the nondual nature sparkling through – and, because one is form-grasping, one perceives nonduality as emptiness. One therefore rejects emptiness. The emptiness of the fire element—for example—is isolation, so one's coping strategy is to curtail the isolation by reaching out for phenomena with which to unify. The phenomena can be situations, ideas, things, people, whatever. Whatever it is from which one feels separated. It's out there, one is separated from it – and therefore it is extremely appealing. So, one reaches out. One feels less isolated the closer one gets. This is due to anticipation of unification. As soon as one obtains, however – it's gone. It's gone because one's obtained it – and one is therefore isolated again. The most beautiful moment is when one's hand is closing on 'it' – because it's not actually possessed yet. It's just about to be possessed. But when it's possessed, the energy begins to dwindle. Because it's possessed – one is no longer self-defined as reaching for it.

The fifth of August

The aspect of mind which is conscious of *something*, is a discontinuous consciousness – whereas *awareness* is continuous.

———— · ————

As long as the nature of *what arises in mind* and the nature of *that which observes* are seen as separate – one can never realise rigpa.

———— · ————

If—when engaged in silent sitting—you become distracted; that does not have to be seen as failure. Distraction simply happens. What is more significant is being able to stare into the space in which one is distracted from *this* by *that*.

———— · ————

If one focuses on anything – that focus exists as a momentary ripple. The momentary ripple subsides and another momentary ripple arises. If one continues in the attempt to remain with a ripple —however profound or trivial—one will become frustrated by failure. It is valuable to practice concentration – but in the end one has to abandon it. It is valuable to realise at this point, that consciousness is discontinuous. If one wishes to have continuous inexorable clarity – it is preferable to allow awareness to awaken of itself. Expecting consciousness to become awareness is futile. *Consciousness of*—or object consciousness—is an aspect of awareness. Awareness is like the sky. Consciousness is like a bird in sky. Birds fly into sight and out of sight. If one concentrates on the movement of birds, one will lose concentration repeatedly. If one's meditation is based in *consciousness of* – distraction is unavoidable. It's integral to *consciousness of* – so no matter how long one endeavours to turn *consciousness of* into awareness – it won't happen. A ripple will never turn into a stream or a wave into an ocean.

The sixth of August

What you see is what you get – so it is a question of *how we see* rather than *what we see*.

———— · ————

Karma is perception and response. The cause is the perception and the effect is how you respond to the perception. The idea in which *if I steal your piece of pizza* – that *someday someone will steal my piece of pizza* is somewhat primitively mechanistic. What happens is that if I steal your piece of pizza—get away with it undetected—and feel pleased about it; then I pattern myself. What results from this is that any unguarded piece of pizza becomes an object ripe for theft. The karmic result is that I become *a pizza thief* and have to endure other people talking about how pizza thieves are the lowest of the low. The only way out of this is to become a pizza benefactor who supplies pizzas to those too poor to acquire them. This is somewhat farcical — but it gives you an idea.

———— · ————

My brother Græham had an argument with my father. It concerned karma – although my brother didn't know it at the time. It concerned an attempted murder which was reported on the radio news. Someone had attempted to shoot somebody – but the gun failed to function. Græham pointed out, intelligently *"Well, he's just as guilty as if he'd killed the man – because it was his intention."* My father disagreed *"The man didn't die – so the other man is not guilty."* True, the assailant was not legally guilty – but he was intentionally guilty. In Buddhist terms, he was a murderer even though no murder was committed. If you pull the trigger, and nothing happens – you're a murderer. With Buddhism, it's one's intention that creates karma. This is what one can change. One can change one's intention.

The seventh of August

It is a monistic-eternalistic mistake to imagine that Vajrayana is concordant with the entire range of 'wellness' systems. The six vehicles of Vajrayana each have their own function – just as aspirin and diamorphine have. One would not inject diamorphine for a headache on the basis that it had an application in the sphere of medicine.

———— · ————

We do our best to relate the teachings with 'everyday life' in terms of analogies and applications – but it would be a mistake to take this as the only level at which teaching is workable. There are some teachings—such as Dzogchen men-ngag-dé—which are completely outside the range of quotidian analogies and applications – such as *'How would this function with my boss in the office?'* One may as well ask *'How would this advice on horse riding function at the bottom of The Mariana Trench[1] or the peak of Everest.'*

———— · ————

In many cases we take responsibility for encouraging questioning at the pragmatic level – but we also take responsibility for pointing out that this approach is unworkable in terms of Dzogchen. The attempt to relate Dzogchen long-dé or Dzogchen men-ngag-dé to interpersonal problems with work colleagues is not merely futile but highly incongruous. Dzogchen is not in the same category as psychotherapy, affirmations, self-help programmes, or rehabilitation.

---

1   The Mariana Trench is in the Pacific, 120 miles east of the Mariana Islands. It is the deepest oceanic floor on the Earth.

The eighth of August

Nothing makes us happier than witnessing someone falling in love with an aspect of the purity of the phenomenal world. It's an indication that this love could expand to include everyone and everything everywhere.

———— · ————

We enjoy the exchange of information with regard to the Arts, that proceeds in an organic and chaotic manner. The Arts and history and the Artists who have inhabited our history are fascinating. We—all of us—could also be fascinating. All we need is authentic appreciation in order to become authentic individuals.

———— · ————

The world is alive and everything within the world is intercommunicative. This is far more apparent with old objects which have seen a great deal of use. This is particularly the case with musical instruments. Any musician knows this. This is why Stradivarius violins are so valuable. This is why a new guitar has to learn how to become a guitar through being played. This is even true of an electric guitar. It is true of anything that vibrates – and, of course, everything vibrates.

———— · ————

Kyabjé Düd'jom Rinpoche Jig'drèl Yeshé Dorje in his 'Drinking Song' proposed many toasts: first to his Lamas – and finally to the infinite purity of the phenomenal world. The phenomenal world must not be mistaken for 'khorwa – nor must the body which he describes as a sang-gyé 'kyil-khor. Realisation is not the abandonment of the phenomenal world – because the phenomenal world is a treasury of endless wonder. Realisation is waking up—in the entire spectrum of one's senses—to the startling wealth that is simply there is to be enjoyed – and to help other enjoy.

The ninth of August

Emptiness and form are not simply metaphysical abstracts. One has to look for emptiness in life in terms of everything that is not fixed – confusion, ambivalence, uncertainty, chaos, non-understanding.

———— · ————

The nondual state is when emptiness and form are experienced as undivided. That doesn't mean that form disappears into emptiness; after which there is nothing but emptiness – because it is the nature of emptiness that form arises from it and dissolves into it.

———— · ————

Generosity is the space which allows freedom. When phenomena are free, there's no instability because nothing has to be controlled. Likewise with patience – there's no neurotic hurry. Arising and dissolving simply perform. With vitality there is the sparkle of being present – it's not merely a lethargic, stupefied, phlegmatic acceptance. Patience, exertion, and generosity equate with wisdom, energy, and compassion – the three important factors within practice. In terms of Dzogchen, patience, vitality, and generosity are the three spheres of being: emptiness, energy, and form. There's no choice; flashes simply begin to occur.

———— · ————

Like *Classical Music* and *Tibetan Buddhism* – *enlightenment* is an unfortunate term. *Classical Music* refers to one period which was preceded by *Baroque* and followed by *Romantic*. *Tibetan Buddhism* would be better termed *Himalayan Buddhism* – because it does not belong to one country. Highly similar traditions are found in Bhutan, Sikkim, Nepal, Mongolia, Russia, and China. *Enlightenment* is not the translation of a Buddhist term. There are many terms dependent on the method of approach: *tharpa*[2] – liberation; *rigpa* – instantaneous presence; and *nyi-mèd* – nonduality. 'ö-Sel is the closest word to enlightenment – but no one speaks of *the Buddha's 'ö-Sel*.

2   *thar pa* / ཐར་པ་

268

The tenth of August

In times past – there were subjects which were impolite to discuss around the dinner table: politics, sex, and religion. To these we would add: gossip, sport, health, dietary fads, and conspiracy theories.

———— · ————

When one is young and healthy – there is no purpose in endlessly discussing health. When one is old and has health problems there is no purpose discussing them either – as they are short lived, by definition.

———— · ————

People should try to avoid making suggestions to each other in terms of health, or anything else for that matter. We're an old-fashioned English couple. We believe in courtesy – and it is discourteous to offer opinions when no one has solicited them.

———— · ————

Karl Marx is quoted as stating *'Religion is the opium of the masses.'* This statement was the German *'Die Religion… ist das Opium des Volkes'*. The full quotation runs 'Religion is the sigh of the oppressed creature, the heart of a heartless world, and the soul of soulless conditions. It is the opium of the people.' Today *the opium of the masses* is social media, sport, and the tabloids. Maybe religion deserves a reprieve – apart from instances where it is treated like sport, read like tabloids, and argued about on social media.

The eleventh of August

There is nothing to see other than *what is there*. We simply need to see that.

———— · ————

As one dissolves the habit of aggression in one's mind, one begins to experience less aggression in the external world.

———— · ————

When observing others, it is unwise to mistake silence for consent, equability for lack of discernment, tolerance for ignorance, serenity for acquiescence, or kindness for weakness.

———— · ————

It is unwise to take popularity as a yardstick of either quality or lack thereof. Quality can only be individually measured unless practicalities are being assessed – such as durability, stability, resilience, buoyancy et cetera. Where practicalities play no part the question of quality tends to be subjective – and there fashion tends to ascribe quality. Where fashion ascribes quality—and sufficient people accept the ascription—most people accept it as *de rigueur*, until such time as fashion deems it *démodé*.

———— · ————

Vajrayana celebrity is not attributed to those credited with 'celebrity-as-status' due to popular public acclaim. *Celebrity*, in the Vajrayana sense, pertains to celebrating others as well as to being celebrated by others. Being a Vajrayana celebrity requires authentic appreciation of others and of the phenomenal world. Being a celebrity in the common sense – merely requires fame or infamy and either can be obtained or lost according to the dictates of fashion. Fashions are either commercially driven or arise through adventitious coincidence. Sometimes quality is involved and popularity is achieved because of real worth. Sometimes real worth is ignored – and dross is favoured.

The twelfth of August

Art is life and life is Art. Unless this is understood neither is either.

_____ · _____

Because I have drawn, painted, sung, and written poetry since the age of five – I have never divided appearances in sound, texture, imagination, or meaning from other aspects of life.

_____ · _____

I have never seen clothing as any different from painting or poetry. Sartorial creativity is therefore simply another branch of Art which combines dance and sculpture with colour and the poetry of history. It is therefore not easy for me to relate to the normal meanings associated with how one is clad.

_____ · _____

In the north of England there is a couple who are office workers – who, when they return to their home dress, eat, drink, and live as Vikings. Similarly, there is a couple in California who live and dress in late 18th Century costume – without electricity or any 21st Century amenities. This would not be our choice – but we are extremely glad that such people exist. It gives us hope for humanity.

_____ · _____

Why be involved in anything that's not the best that life has to offer? We don't mean by that: the most expensive or rarest. It is not _what it is_ or _who it is_ – because ultimately, it's all equal. No partner is more or less attractive than any other partner. It's simply choice that makes a person special. We need to value the choices we make. One could wear cotton socks or silk socks – it doesn't matter. It's simply a matter of appreciation and having a sense of honour in what we choose. We do not need to check conventional criteria for what is good and what is not so good. That is nonsense. We simply need to value our lives and our time – and through that sense of value, to value the lives and time of others.

The thirteenth of August

In order to be real and to dance ecstatically in the dimension of our own individual experience, we need to welcome the raw texture of whatever we may feel.

———— · ————

What is meant by the word dimension? The dimension, however it is characterised, is the nature of the practice in terms of focus. When one finds presence of awareness in the dimension of sound – sound is the focus. The focus could be the visualisation. It could be the emotional sensation. It could be whatever lies within the fields of the senses.

———— · ————

Let the emotion consume you, like some ravenous beast in full blood-lust. Become the emotion completely, or simply allow it to become you. Don't refer to some other time or place or situation. If you can do this, psychotherapy and psychoanalysis are utterly superfluous.

———— · ————

We need to embrace the energy of our own being with tender ferocity. We need to take total responsibility for each moment of our innately splendid lives, if we are to know the real meaning of Tantra as luminously compassionate abandon.

———— · ————

Vajrayana is not for those without strong emotions and conspicuous feelings. The emotions are the basis of liberation for those with the courage to plumb their own heights and depths in the practice of spaciousness. Vajrayana sees emotions as a dynamic means of finding oneself face to face with the brilliant spaciousness of Being.

The fourteenth of August

Dharma never tires of explaining itself through those who are committed to teaching.

———— · ————

To everyone who has questions or incomprehension; Dharma re-clothes itself in fresh terms.

———— · ————

No *book of truth* can contain Vajrayana. This is because Vajrayana speaks to every style of confusion – and the styles of confusion are as variegated as the cultures, societies, and epochs in which we live. Vajrayana is a stirring anthem to freedom and to the sheer glee evoked by direct insight into the nature of reality.

———— · ————

We could speak of gTérma and it would seem highly intricate – but gTérma is also the expression of every Lama in terms of addressing the questions of students. Every student is a new opportunity to reveal Vajrayana in a new way – with new expressions and new equivalences, resemblances, correspondences, correlations, comparisons, consonances, analogies, similes, and metaphors.

———— · ————

Students were happy enough when I taught in contemporary literary English – but there were malcontents when I brought out the four volumes of 'an odd boy'. *Monothematic memoirs of my life as an Artist* were not Dharma. Students were happier when I followed the fashion – and only wrote familiar, recognisable, identifiable material vis-à-vis Vajrayana. The problem with this approach, is that until one finds Vajrayana in everything; one will find Vajrayana nowhere. Life is Vajrayana – so find it in life, or you may never find it.

The fifteenth of August

We need to be able to stay with the empty dimension of the experience – but also to be aware of the movement; the form aspect of it. When we begin to remain in this way, we discover that form has patterns – and that we can be appreciatively inspired by those patterns in relation to others.

———— · ————

Within the self-created field of dualistic bewilderment, *that which is natural* seems unnatural – and *that which seems natural* is unnatural. On the basis of this primitive prejudice against reality, all other forms of prejudice arise; prejudices against: race, gender, physiognomy, sexual orientation, religion, nationality, class, intellectual capacity, age, and appearance – ad nauseam. Whatever form of distinction has existed in the world, prejudice has existed with regard to it. It is evident from this that the focus of prejudice is always empty of the causes of prejudice. The only cause of prejudice is fear of otherness.

———— · ————

You *could* go back into your childhood with therapy. You could also go back to previous lives in infinite regression. You will have been generating this emotion countless millions of times. There's no *point in time* where it started. The only time is *now*. *Now* is the only time that concerns you – because *now* is when it is happening. That's the time to look at it – not some *previous time*. You could visit that specious time every week with your therapist, until you ran out of life – and that would do nothing to liberate the emotion. Every point in time you look at a past experience – a different person looks back. The past experience will therefore, be different each time you look at it. From the point of view of Buddhism, it's not actually possible to tackle emotional problems in this way.

The sixteenth of August

We desire both liberation and confusion. That is the nature of the path. The path—if it's honest— is one of push-and-pull. That is why Tantra explores ambivalence. Ambivalence is duality on the threshold of non-duality. The illusory split between emptiness and form pans out into simultaneously wanting confusion and wanting liberation. If you realise you want both equally – you have a marvellously creative situation.

—— · ——

Some people dislike my poetry because of its density. I simply direct them to other poets who write according to contrasting criteria. I once ate a large serving of Mississippi Mud Pie in Baltimore. It was the densest food substance that has ever passed my lips and I enjoyed it with fevered relish. I would not recommend Mississippi Mud Pie as anyone's staple diet – and neither would I recommend my poetry in similar vein.

—— · ——

My poetry relates to the inseparability of emptiness and form. In these terms, form equates to linear sense; no matter how metaphorical that it becomes. This is partnered with emptiness as laterality or the collapse of sense-making. With regard to Buddhism form is seen as arising out of emptiness and dissolving into emptiness again – and in this way linear motifs arise out of directionless language or the apparent absence of comprehensibility. This may be unfamiliar as a linguistic form – but it is well accepted in abstract painting. It is also accepted in Avant Garde Jazz – where melody can emerge from and dissolve into a sea of sound. Whenever a person has told me they don't like Avant Garde Jazz— on the basis that there is no melody—I have asked them whether they enjoyed the sound of the wind or the sea. When they admit to liking these sounds, I then ask *"Where is the melody?"* Sometimes this helps.

The seventeenth of August

Yes is the form of the empty *no* – and *no* is the form of the empty *yes*.

——— · ———

We are all responsible for founding the five certainties[3]: teacher, teaching, time, place, and audience. Let us all be enthusiastically and vigorously here. We have the warmth and humour for it – so let us have the wide-awake growl of immediacy.

——— · ———

Lamas may be encyclopædic in terms of Vajrayana – but they are not primarily there to supply information. Lamas are there to describe the way information is employed. Lamas are not Tantric entertainers – or if they are it is the duty of students to strive diligently to be entertained. Students need to ask questions – but not in the 'slot machine' style of asking "*Could you say something about this or that.*"

——— · ———

Guarding the space of Vajrayana and the space of transmission is the responsibility of every practitioner. The atmosphere and ambience in which the teachings and transmissions occur is evoked by each individual. This is the real 'collective wisdom of the sangha' – but not in the sense of a 'conceptual collective'. We are looking at spiritual integrity. Each individual has to feel responsibility for the emotional texture of the environment. One cannot hope to hide out – if one member of an audience has canine fæces on their shoes, the whole assembly smells it. Let us make sure that we have nothing adhering to our shoes or our intentions.

3   ngédpa nga *(nges pa lNga /* ངེས་པ་ལྔ་

276

The eighteenth of August

Considering the writings of Quentin Crisp – it would seem that *finding one's style* is an interesting point to reach in the life of an Artist. It's the *stable shi-nè of sartorialism*. From there, you move into lhatong – and then…

———— · ————

Chögyam Trungpa Rinpoche said *"Our clothing should be a little uncomfortable as it keeps our attention 24 hrs a day. When you come to events, it's good to have your ties done up tightly – as it aids you in cutting through casualness and the casual attitude to Dharma."*

———— · ————

Chögyam Trungpa Rinpoche was highly interested in military costume – particularly the Sam Browne belt. He said that the Sam Browne should feel as if you were in harness to your samaya. He also said that clothing was a suit of armour if manifested properly. He regarded clothing as emblematic of our manifestation in the world — so you should pay careful attention to the details of clothing and shoes. You should choose what you wear as your statement of precision in terms of how it all fits together.

———— · ————

In terms of clothing, you should have the sense of vajra pride in being the yidam. There has to be a sense of appreciation. The whole world becomes degraded if you always settle for second best – it is not that you have to spend a great deal of money on clothing. If you have something old it can be cared for. Your own appearance is an offering to the world.

The nineteenth of August

Vajrayana begins with the premise that dualism is a state of prejudice against nonduality. On the basis of this prejudice against nonduality, infinite forms of prejudice will manifest in order to obfuscate beginningless realisation. The tantric phase of Vajrayana employs the dimension of symbolism in limitless ways – because we are *symbols of ourselves*. We do not experience ourselves as real—whilst we cling to duality—and therefore *what we experience ourselves to be*, is always *symbolic of what we actually are*.

———— · ————

The visionary sphere of empowerment and the nature of conventional reality can flicker and interpenetrate each other. I often experienced Kyabjé Künzang Dorje Rinpoche as a blaze of coloured light. He was highly subtle – and allowed me to become subtle in the context where he overpowered apparent phenomena. Sometimes the transparency of concrete existence is distinctly not an alternative reality. Light essence is a pervasive phenomenon.

———— · ————

When you realise that someone knows everything there is to know about reality – that person ceases to be ordinary in any sense. I felt it in my blood, bone, muscle, cartilage, and nasal septum. The sheer human presence of Künzang Dorje Rinpoche filled me with awe. I had to get over that awe to some degree or I'd never have learnt anything. Awe was necessary in the beginning. Awe was there because study and practice had lifted the veil that prevented me from seeing Künzang Dorje Rinpoche. When that veil lifts – a Lama is likely to nail your head to the wall with a mere glance.

The twentieth of August

When visionary beings emerge in primal space – the invisible character of infinity allows a glimpse of visibility.

———— · ————

One has to be certain of the Lama's teaching and the nature of the practice being given. This means that one has to be able to receive the teaching with an open mind and an appreciative perspective. If one has any doubt in the teacher, teaching, or practice – then transmission cannot occur.

———— · ————

It's possible to enter the world of Vajrayana – whilst remaining English; or whatever nationality you happen to be. You can cross boundaries and live in the tidal margins between cultures. You can be: a gay rodeo rider; a vegetarian firearms enthusiast; a priest who enjoys the sport of pugilism; a pacifist who enjoys war novels; an electric Blues guitarist who loves Baroque chamber music, a Beat poet who speaks BBC English; a minimalist poet who enjoys Shakespeare; or, a Pop Art comic strip writer who reads Jane Austen novels. These may be seen as oxymorons from a conventional point of view – but Vajrayana is not a conventional point of view.

———— · ————

We live in an epoch of adulation to stars of stage and screen – but if we transfer this kind of romantic emotion to the Lama, we will be disappointed. The Lama may well be like a Rock star or film star in terms of their manifestation – but that is simply methodology. That is simply the way they conjure with the perception of their students. The Lama could equally manifest as farmer, road-sweeper, taxi driver, nurse, police officer, restaurateur, accountant, carpenter, electrician, plumber, sanitaryware specialist, traffic warden, grave digger, travel agent, or as some schlemiel you'd rather avoid.

The twenty-first of August

To live life to the full we need discipline. We need the courage to maintain discipline in the face of difficulty and uncertainty. Were we to examine the lives of highly accomplished human beings – we would find resonances with the root vows in their personal codes and mores.

———— · ————

Creative space is called the Great Mother, the womb of potentiality. Because that is the quality of spaciousness – it gives rise to form. The quality of spaciousness is not that nothing is there. 'Nothing' is there – but many 'somethings' are there too, and they're all coming and going. It's a jamboree.

———— · ————

Pride is not far removed from vanity – but some 'mild form of vanity' is not necessarily 'bad'. Enjoying the spectrum of one's manifestation—in terms of body, speech, and mind—can be simple self-reflexive appreciation. It is only when vanity is combined with a sense of superiority—and derision towards others—that it becomes derangement.

———— · ————

Were we to examine the lives of human beings noted as 'great people' – we would find disenchantment, confusion, and despair – as well as idealism, lucidity, and exultation. The failure and perplexity of otherwise admirable human beings occurs almost always as the result of what is missing from their lives in terms of *directives which transcend the individual*. It could be called compassion – but compassion in its complete sense in terms of centreless joy, divisionless desire, pervasive appreciation, altruistic avarice, and self-liberated lust. In less poetic terms, what enables such people to overcome disillusionment is almost always their basic religious conviction.

The twenty-second of August

One of the many excellent *side effects* of Vajrayana is that we are able to *disconnect* any object from its societally ascribed connotations. This is possible because we have the experiential knowledge that these objects are empty of: implications, connotations, meanings, and projected qualities; or lack thereof – because, of course, implications, connotations, meanings, and projected qualities do manifest on a temporary basis.

———— · ————

Everything is free to be what it is – and as Vajrayanists we are free to be what we are in wearing whatever we appreciate. Moreover – if any object we wear or use has negative societal implications, then wearing it or using it, imbues that object or item of clothing with positive causes. It is thus important for tantrikas to have contact with an unlimited range of apparel and associated phenomena.

———— · ————

Dharmakaya, Dharmadhatu, and Dharmata. In Tibetan—our preferred language— these are Chö-ku, Chö-ying, and Chö-nyid[4]. *Chos* means 'as it is'. *Ying* means 'dimension'. *Nyid* means 'nature of'. The quality of Chö-ku, is that it is continually giving rise to differentiated beings. The quality of the Chö-ying is that it continually giving rise to differentiated phenomena. The quality of Chö-nyid, is that it is continually giving rise to Chö-ku and Chö-ying. This may seem complex – but if you have experience of the Four Naljors it will seem obvious. If you have experience even of shi-nè and lhatong—the first and second of the Four Naljors—it will seem simple.

4   *chos sKu* / ཆོས་སྐུ ; *chos dByings* / ཆོས་དབྱིངས ; *chos nyid* / ཆོས་ཉིད

The twenty-third of August

The socially malfunctional and dysfunctional—the neurotic and those with personality disorders—will always be attracted to opportunities which allow them to be as they are. Unfortunately, religion seems to offer an incredibly broad range of such opportunities. The challenge for us, is both to protect the sangha from the aforementioned – whilst remaining open to helping them through tolerance and kindliness.

———— · ————

When 'pride' and 'vanity' are proscribed as improper for Buddhists – what tends to happen is that Buddhists pretend not to be thus afflicted. This pretence leads to the development of cover-up strategies and hypocrisy. Hypocrisy is a worse malaise than either pride or vanity – because at least pride and vanity—when simple, humorous, and overt—can be innocuous and without manipulation. Hypocrisy is convoluted and covert – and tends to an ever-increasing level of psychological malfunction.

———— · ————

Vajrayana is extremely rich and complex. It also has a hierarchy in which it is possible to rise. Those who wish to rise at the expense of others can develop skills in situating themselves in positions which lend themselves to upward mobility. Fortunately, these people do not tend to be attracted to us – because there is no hierarchic future in associating with us. We are a hierarchic dead end. No one is going to be impressed by the fact that anyone is a student of ours. This means that people only associate with us because they like: what we teach; how we teach; who we are; how we are; and, how the sangha is. No one is going to rise in the vajrayana social climbing tree by studying with us. We don't look attractive to anyone who wants to use association with us for self-advancement. This is why we have such a lovely sangha.

The twenty-fourth of August

Please take natural non-referential pleasure in the nature of existence.

———— · ————

Vanity tends to get a bad press in spiritual circles – because, generally, it is narcissistic. A natural vanity which is devoid of narcissism, although rare – would seem to be feasible. Natural vanity is not gross in the way that narcissistic vanity is gross. As long as one admires others to the same degree—or more—than one admires oneself – there is no egregious problem. To deselect oneself from the rest of the phenomenal universe as a subject for admiration is unreal. Nondual admiration has to be unbounded.

———— · ————

It is often imagined that the final goal of practice is the condition in which thought is entirely abandoned. It is not surprising that this idea exists – because many forms of meditation instruction deal with the stabilisation of shi-nè, in which emptiness is the goal. It is not unusual therefore, that little emphasis is given in such teachings as to what lies beyond emptiness. There is nothing false with regard to explanations which posit emptiness as the fruit – and those who explain in this way are perfectly correct according to the view of the specific practices they describe. According to many teachings within the Sutras, emptiness is the goal – but Dzogchen requires subtlety and precision with regard to how emptiness is defined as being an aspect of the goal. This is not particularly controversial, because the Heart Sutra states quite succinctly that '… *form is emptiness and emptiness is form.*'

The twenty-fifth of August

The practice of Drala is a method of becoming aware of the sentient nature of the world. This is important at this time of climate change and increasing pollution.

———— · ————

Drala is awareness of the phenomenal world's inherent magical quality. It is the communicative flow between perceivers of the natural world and the natural world which is perceived.

———— · ————

Drala is feistiness and ebullient vitality which arises from primal purity – the nondual nature of everyone and everything, everywhere.

———— · ————

Drala has a connection with relative time. It is not a neutral phenomenon. There are 'periods of time' which are different in facility – in terms of the communicative flux of the natural world. We change in our perceptual senses. Sometimes we lack openness. At other times we are more sensitive to the efflorescence of what is arising in the sensory fields. There are significant pools of time connected with Drala – and these can be discovered as pluripotential gestalts within the landscape of exactly where we are.

———— · ————

Drala is primal iridescence. It is the beginningless arising of energy from emptiness which is the unimpeded light display of the essence of the elements. This is the nondual world in action: coming into being and passing out of being as the dance of emptiness and form.

The twenty-sixth of August

Thought can no more examine its own nature than a knife cut itself; or an eye, see itself. The only way an eye can see itself is to avail itself of a mirror. The nature of that mirror—vis-à-vis thought—is the natural reflective capacity of Mind, which is beyond thought.

———— · ————

This is our situation. This very moment is Vajrayana – and contains limitless energy. It's ruthlessly and seductively uncompromising. The sheer potency of what we are is overwhelmingly and provocatively inconvenient – but, it is there. It's simply there. When we recoil from it, through any variety of dread, that is also Vajrayana. It is impossible to hide from the manner of our own hiding.

———— · ————

Examining the nature of Mind—employing thought as a tool—is limited by the character of the thought-structures at our disposal. Thought would be examining thought with thought. This is problematic because the thoughts with which thoughts were examined, would have to be examined – and what would examine those thoughts apart from thought (which would also need to be examined)? Thought cannot examine itself. It's a closed system.

———— · ————

Devotion is based on understanding who the Lama actually is. In order to understand who the Lama is, one needs to enter into the Lama's world to some degree – and this requires meditative insight. Without some degree of meditative insight, one could have no inkling as to the nature of the Lama's realisation or lack thereof. This requires study, practice, retreat – and evident results.

The twenty-seventh of August

Mind is misinterpreted as a collage of interwoven cognitive impulses – like the sky, when it is so turbulent with scudding clouds that nothing but clouds can be seen. From this perspective, one might never guess that the sky could be vast.

———— · ————

Elegance is composed of delight and fearless *embracement* – in which we are not gluttonous, timid, or torpid. There is no dank or grimy sense of self-protection involved, and every deranged default impetus is overridden with the sense of splendour, a sense of exquisiteness, the sense of immaculacy in which we understand ourselves as regal.

———— · ————

Tantrikas override pomposity and resentment. Dzogchen is known as the imperial vehicle. From the imperial perspective, the beauty of genuine decorum lies in the non-manipulativeness of its natural etiquette and unpretentious elegance. We should therefore all aspire to appreciate what is beautiful in each other – whatever the clothing, or absence thereof.

———— · ————

Paradox has to be discovered within the *epidermis of everyday detail*. It must be savoured within the *bone-marrow of felt reality*. The vocabulary of Vajrayana cannot be learnt systematically. There is no 'word-for-word translation' – so dictionaries are superfluous. The verb structure of Vajrayana cannot be studied in order to conjugate the emotional temperature of passion into something more spiritually acceptable. Vajrayana cannot be manipulated in order to read the mystery of romance, as if it were a text book for avoiding emotional calamity.

The twenty-eighth of August

The essence of reality is free of dependency on conventional rationality. It cannot therefore be investigated or cross-examined. It is free of demonstrable examples even though examples exist. It is beyond the realm of conceptual mind.

———— · ————

As soon as you discover there's nothing there that is eternal in terms of 'I'— you're free to be there as 'I'. Because some people got so hooked into an ultimatist idea of there being no ego, I used to say *"One day, I'm going to run a course called 'Come Back, Ego, all is Forgiven'."*

———— · ————

Ocean can never be defined by the waves which roll endlessly as its surface. One could study waves into eternity and come no closer to a definition of ocean. All one can say is that waves occur in the ocean and that they are limitless in their forms. As soon as we relinquish our attempts to define ocean according to its waves – we realise that waves and ocean are indivisible. Ocean requires no definition – yet waves continually ornament the ocean with their temporary definitions.

———— · ————

The sky is vast and beyond limits. Within the unfettered space of the sky there is endless movement. Clouds appear and disappear. They appear from out of the sky and they evaporate back into the sky. The sky is not affected by the clouds which manifest within it – even when it is completely overcast and it appears as if its expansive blueness no longer exists. Whether we see the sky or not – it remains there, unaltered by that which appears to occlude it. We could take the blue sky to be the perfect state, and yet to be without clouds is not the nature of the sky.

The twenty-ninth of August

The vajra master is the means by which the broadest spectrum of humanity has access to Vajrayana.

———— · ————

The vajra master provides the truest and most universal, egalitarian context. Vajra masters see the nondual qualities of all their disciples, and allow them access to transmission according to their individual capacities and relative constraints.

———— · ————

Vajra masters appreciate their disciples because of their individual neuroses – not in spite of them. This is because the beginningless nondual state of each individual sparkles through the fabric of their neuroses. Infinite opportunities for realisation exist therefore, as the repertoire of the vajra master's egalitarian effectiveness. Where is the 'egalitarianism' in depriving people of the opportunity to fly beyond the reach and range of dualism? Without the vajra master we are doomed to the slow and painful process of unravelling each minute thread of tortuous derangement.

———— · ————

Some people say that the vajra master is an 'Eastern modality' and that it has no place in the West. These people will obviously know nothing of master classes in music – nor will they know of high-risk sports or the Navy Seals. *Obeying orders* is standard procedure in the armed forces. This does not mean however, the vajra master is like a military commander. There may be certain similarities – but with Vajrayana one is actually entirely free to break one's vow. It happens quite often. People only make this statement about the vajra master because they lack education vis-à-vis the nature of Vajrayana.

The thirtieth of August

If our lives—all of our lives—are not worthy of anecdotes – what shall we bequeath to future generations of Vajrayana practitioners?

———— · ————

The reason I have written autobiographical material is not because I am famous. It's not because I want to become famous. It's because I want you all to be famous. Khandro Déchen and I want to see a generation of yogis and yoginis who will provide stories for the future generation. We have a debt to these people even though they may not yet have been born.

———— · ————

Vajrayana craft work is vital to the continuity of lineage. Craft work was emphasised by Lama Tharchin Rinpoche, Dung-sé Thrin-lé Norbu Rinpoche, Kyabjé Künzang Dorje Rinpoche, and by Kyabjé Düd'jom Rinpoche. The time one spends in giving close attention to detail segues into lhatong. It is also an act of generosity and changchub sem.

———— · ————

The Vajrayana anecdotes which so many people love, do not concern people who followed conservative conventional fundamentalist religious edicts. The stories which inspire people are those which concern Lamas who expressed freedom from limiting legislation by living according to essential Vajrayana. Who will look to conference convenors or conference attendees for inspiration in the future? Who will look to literalist nit-picking academics? Who will look to rulebook referees of realisation or emotionally sterile sacristans? Unless there are a few wisdom eccentrics in this generation there may be no Vajrayana anecdotes for the next generation – unless people look back to the Himalayan countries prior to 1959.

The thirty-first of August

The current trend seems to be towards techniques being practised and disseminated – but, with the absence of lineage. People seem to imagine that there are practices which exist as separate from the quality of the those practising them. People forget transmission. The lineage is the continuity of transmission – but if that is absent then the methods are useless.

———— · ————

A practice which is disconnected from lineage is like a camera employed as a doorstop. If a camera is used as a doorstop, then that's what it becomes – unless someone knows it's not a doorstop. We live in a time of spiritual doorstops when we could all have Hasselblads.

———— · ————

One of the ugliest modern trends is disloyalty. The tragedy is that few see it as disloyalty – because loyalty to others has shifted to a loyalty that centres on ourselves. It is for this reason that some people can abandon Buddhism as a religion, whilst appropriating its methods. The same happened with Blues in the 1960s. Many were excited about Blues – but decided to appropriate its modes and abandon the tradition. I was a Bluesman in the 1960s and I'm still a Bluesman. I was a Nyingma in the 1960s and I'm still a Nyingma. Having lived a life based on loyalty – I have never been disappointed by my choices. I therefore feel confident in promoting the idea of loyalty to others.

Long *(kLong)* – space

September

If one always paid attention to causes and their effects – one's present and future would be worthy and valuable.

HE Ögyen Dro'dül Thrin-lé Kunkyab Rinpoche

རྒྱལ་བ་ཨོ་རྒྱན་འགྲོ་འདུལ་ཕྲིན་ལས་ཀུན་སྐྱབས་རིན་པོ་ཆེ།

There are always two different colours of mind: the red colour of hatred and the white colour of love. It all depends on the colour with which one likes to play at any moment.

Khar-trül Wangchuk Rig'dzin Rinpoche

མཁར་སྤྲུལ་དཔལ་གྱི་དབང་ཕྱུག་རིག་འཛིན་རིན་པོ་ཆེ།

The first of September

From the nondual perspective the rôle of the Lama is to point out that we are sentient – when that is clearly the case.

———— · ————

The connection between nondual beings and dualised beings takes the form of compassionate impressionism. The Lama has to convey approximations—finger paintings—in order to be understood.

———— · ————

Authentic responsiveness occurs as the Lama's natural response. It's a situation of choicelessness in terms of nondual empathetic appreciation. The Lama is dealing with human beings who function at the level of concept – so having realisation, the Lama enters into the conceptual world of students in order to give transmission. Because the medium is concept – the concept is communicated in Tibetan, Dzongkha, English, French, German, Dutch, Swedish, Finnish, Icelandic, Spanish, Basque, Italian or whatever language is required.

———— · ————

Languages are always conceptually based – and each language is tilted according to its cultural history. Languages all contain words which cannot be translated word-for-word into other languages. There is no language in which one can speak simply about that which lies beyond concept. For those who are teaching beyond concept therefore – language has to be augmented by spontaneously inspired theatre. Language has to be augmented by situational choreography and by surprise. This is why the Arts are so important in Vajrayana.

The second of September

One glimpse is not enough? One glimpse is *more* than enough if the facilitator has the facility to provide a glimpse of rigpa – but even a catalogue of several hundred glimpses—if they are re-cycled platitudes—is little better than marigpa[1].

———— · ————

Tantra is said to be 'the short dangerous path' – but this is often misunderstood. The danger of Vajrayana is not the 'mind-explosion' which ends in insanity, or the psychophysical short-circuit which boils the blood – no matter how charming such propositions might be. The danger of Vajrayana is simply that one could merely exacerbate one's tendencies toward narcissism.

———— · ————

Perhaps the greatest danger of Vajrayana is loss of the vajra master. The vajra master allows one to by-pass psychological process. This is a concern expressed by psychotherapists and they are right to be concerned. If a person proceeds on the basis of faith rather than assiduous developed experience – that faith can fall apart. When faith falls apart – one is catapulted back into what has been by-passed. This might not sound so terrible – but that would not be to take into account the stark contrast between the state of faith and the state prior to faith. This is why we do not advocate faith. We advocate that people continue to question and never accept anything they have not experienced personally and directly. Naturally one can take what lies outside one's experience as working hypotheses – but that is how they need to remain until they become factual.

---

1   In Dzogchen terminology, rigpa *(rig pa /* རིག་པ་ */ vidya)* is the awareness in instant presence. The opposite of rigpa is marigpa *(ma rig pa /* མ་རིག་པ་ */ avidya).*

The third of September

Method—in terms of essential Vajrayana—is *whatever* is required.

——— · ———

Method is the exact way of carrying out what needs to happen to fulfil the purpose. In terms of Vajrayana, the purpose is the understanding and growing realisation of the student.

——— · ———

Thabs[2]—method—is the way of unconditioned appropriate responsiveness to nowness. It is the response to space. Because pure perception is not based on referentiality – phenomena are perceived as display, to which unconditioned appropriate responses naturally unfold.

——— · ———

Methods differ widely because practitioners differ widely – and because the condition of duality is complex and comprised of subtle nuances of incomprehension. This is why the gDam ngag given to one student is unlikely to be applicable to another.

——— · ———

Horse riders must respond appropriately in relation to the condition of their horses. Initially this will be based on training and on the application of conceptual information. Eventually however, they have to transcend concept – because riders will need to respond quicker than would be possible through conceptually instigated manœuvres. Perception and response would ideally need to be a nondual dance on the floor of the equestrian arena or in the wilderness.

2   (thabs / ཐབས་ / upaya)

The fourth of September

When a person *fundamentally intuitively* knows how to dress in terms of authentic individual appreciation – they have begun to taste what it means to Wear the Body of Visions.

———— · ————

Individuality is not a frequently used word in Himalayan Buddhism – because it is important to undermine the need to adhere to a fixed identity. Authentic individuality however, is simply the discovery of authentic appreciation. If one discovers authentic appreciation – one becomes unique.

———— · ————

Wearing the Body of Visions in terms of the Art of Sartorialism, is something which is conveyed through the Eight Manifestations of Padmasambhava and the Eight Manifestations of Yeshé Tsogyel. In essence we are all Padmasambhava and Yeshé Tsogyel. The practice of the Art of Sartorialism is one of the many portals of entry into the spatial dimension.

———— · ————

The ambiance of now in which I am being understood is transient. It'll soon evaporate and condensate into another point-instant with its own unique characteristics. Everyone will take something with them: some impression, feeling, or memory – but the only thing that will last, will be what has made sense experientially. No-one can take *the meaning of words* away with them unless they've received the transmission of their meaning. Of course, we can take notes – but if we've not had direct experiential contact with what those words mean, they may not make sense when we read them again. This forces us either to live the understanding or lose it.

The fifth of September

Form is emptiness and emptiness is form. *'Form is emptiness'* is something which is expressed relatedly in terms of Buddhist practice – but what of *'emptiness is form'*? Emptiness as form is the realisation of form as the evanescent self-display of the elements.

———— · ————

This is a time when change is accelerating rapidly and it's vital in this time to communicate and transmit meaning in contemporary language. Meaning is crucial and words are transitory. When we listen or read therefore, we must break open the shell of the words with attuned intent and actualise their meaning – rather than taking refuge in vocabulary.

———— · ————

Emptiness as form is the world as evanescent self-display – and beings are individuated displays within that display. These displays are not ultimately solid, permanent, separate, continuous, or defined – but neither are they vacuous. They are not nihilistically tenuous, fleeting, homogenised, intermittent, or interminably indefinite. The existential display of reality is nondual and reflects both emptiness and form – because emptiness and form cannot be divided, unless by the exigency of hallucination.

———— · ————

The world of perception teeters precariously between existence and non-existence. From the perspective of conventional filtered vision, the phenomena of perception are seductive, provocative, and highly misleading. Substantiality and insubstantiality dance together. It could resemble a fan dance in which the ostrich-plumes of emptiness and phenomena occlude reality, whilst simultaneously being none other than the voluptuousness of being which is being titillatingly occluded.

The sixth of September

There is nothing which is exempt from fashion: politics, philosophy, religion, ethics, morality, medicine, science, and the Arts. The fashion changes in every aspect of life – and whichever way it changes, it becomes normal and acceptable.

———— · ————

The weight of prejudice against personal expression tends to overrule the potential of Vajrayana to address the ethos of *celebrity*. From the point of view of Vajrayana, *celebrity* is not limited to those who are credited with 'celebrity-as-status' due to popular public acclaim. Celebrity, in terms of Vajrayana, pertains to celebrating others as well as to being celebrated by others.

———— · ————

To be someone whose existence is celebrated—in terms of Vajrayana—requires authentic appreciation of other people and their situations. Being a celebrity, as the word is commonly understood, only necessitates distinction or notoriety – and either are possible according to the criteria of fashion. The criteria of fashion are generated by mercantile forces, or the taste of the powerful – but neither can be relied upon to indicate real value or worth.

———— · ————

It is imprudent to understand popularity as a measure of excellence. Excellence can only be measured according to substantial values such as sturdiness, constancy, suppleness, or flexibility et cetera. Where pragmatics are not concerned the question of excellence is personal. Fashion ascribes excellence – and where it does so—and the ascription is generally accepted—one is expected to concur, or be derided as antediluvian.

The seventh of September

Every aspect of dualistic patterning can dissolve by itself. There is actually nothing to do. The Dzogchen view is that we are already realised. We simply need to discover that. We need to leave everything as it is. If we simply allow *that which arises in mind* to move according to its own movement… it will naturally self-liberate.

———— · ————

We're both individuated and non-individuated. Individuation alone is 'divorced individuation'. This means that one's sense of individuation is divorced from non-individuation. Non-individuation alone is 'divorced non-individuation'. This means that one's sense of non-individuation is divorced from individuation. This paradoxical language is fundamental to the understanding of any nondual teaching. Unless you simply enter the felt sense of paradox there is no answer to the question of duality and nonduality – apart from being kind.

———— · ————

The relationship with the Lama is the interplay of nondual mind of the student with the nondual mind of the Lama. It's a Vajrayana game of 'hide and seek' in which the Lama is trying to persuade us that we're not dualistically deranged. The game has been going on for so long that it should be tedious – but the Lama remains as playful as ever. It's this playfulness that is known as compassion. Kyabjé Düd'jom Rinpoche said *"Dualised beings see Buddhas as dualised beings – but Buddhas see dualised beings as Buddhas. This disparity causes Buddhas great irritation – and that irritation is known as compassion."* The Lama gives us skilful remedies for the imaginary illness of dualistic derangement in order that we discover for ourselves that our illness is imaginary.

The eighth of September

The essence of religion is immediacy in the acknowledgement of reality.

———— · ————

Religion is highly valuable to human beings – even though human beings have corrupted religion to a point at which many have become so suspicious of it, that they want nothing to do with it. What is needed is a *Renaissance of uncorrupted religion*. It may not be possible – but it is our responsibility to make it possible.

———— · ————

Religion is a fantastically flexible framework that radiates from the essential discovery of reality. Ideally, religion is the force which animates the Arts and benefits culture. When religion fails in this respect – it is human beings who have caused it to fail through appropriating it for aims which are not religious. The answer is to return to what is authentically religious.

———— · ————

Secret refuge is secret because there is no way that anyone can relate to it unless they have witnessed their being functioning in the dimension of subtle energy. With secret refuge we establish confidence in the actuality of our being as a dynamic matrix of energy currents which are generated and absorbed by the empty essences of the five elements. This chemistry of prismatic vectors only becomes real when outer and inner dimensions of being divulge each other in practices such as 'pho-wa[3] – the transference of consciousness. When an internal practice causes the sutures to open in the cranium — one understands the secret refuge.

---

3 *pho ba* / འཕོ་བ་ / *utkranti)* is the practice of transference of consciousness at the time of death, either for oneself or another. The practice is one of the Six Yogas of Naropa – but can also be found in the Düd'jom gTér, Longchen Nying-thig, and Aro gTér cycles.

The ninth of September

For Vajrayana to be possible, the 'me project' must begin to seem futile.

———— · ————

The vajra world is where people live as tantrikas. It is the ethos or ambience in which the practices exist as operational parameters.

———— · ————

To be a gatherer of Vajrayana information and techniques is bereft of the natural poetry of life and devoid of the wealth of human history.

———— · ————

The death of the 'me project' is the basis of the vajra world – rather than the collection of information and techniques which has become so popular amongst aspirants who follow the fashions of academia, religiosity, or esotericism.

———— · ————

To attempt to practise Vajrayana outside the vajra world—or without intimate personal knowledge of the vajra world—would be similar to going to a place where a Ball and Banquet had been held – and acting out, *what is reported to have happened at a Ball and Banquet.* There may be others attempting the same approximation – but they would be unable to converse or move in time with each other. There would be no music, no feast, and no persiflage, badinage, or banter. It would not be a Ball and Banquet.

The tenth of September

I'm a Surrealist – a non-rationalist. I prefer to go beyond rationality – and make choices based on non-rational perception. I would also call this meditation.

———— · ————

I'm not exactly a great admirer of 'conceptual art'. Writing an extended essay on *why I painted what I painted* would seem to mean that the painting could not speak for itself.

———— · ————

With respect to Art, one can certainly set out with ideas – but ideas are a point of departure. There are, of course, ideational responses to the senses – but they do not have to be intellectual, rational, or linear. The essence of painting is there in the paint and the canvas. Something occurs and continues to occur which is not governed by words. It is highly intelligent but not necessarily linguistic.

———— · ————

If someone were to ask me why I'd written what I'd written – I'd explain in a logical coherent manner. I would not display a picture or painting as an answer to the question. Why therefore, should I be obliged to explain why I painted what I painted – or elucidate in words what the painting means? It's not that one cannot speak about the visual Arts – but the visual Arts should not rely on linguistic concepts in the form of lengthy explanations. The visual Arts are their own explanation.

The eleventh of September

Within the self-created field of dualistic bewilderment – *that which is natural* seems unnatural – and *that which seems natural* seems unnatural.

―――― · ――――

From the perspective of the visionary practices of Vajrayana it is possible to transform every aspect of prejudice against otherness – of every possible description.

―――― · ――――

Because we exist within a dimension of symbolism – Vajrayana employs symbol in order to transform symbol. Even though dualised beings are symbolic, the dualistic symbols that beings are – are radiant with the energy of nonduality. Beings may exist in a state of dualistic distortion – but that which is distorted, is a distorted version of nonduality. Because of this it is possible to employ the energy of duality, to transform what seems to be into what is actually. Beings are self-secret Buddhas – and the powerful methodology of Vajrayana enables the realisation of this, through the empty form of the yidam.

―――― · ――――

Pure vision requires entry into the symbolic world of empty-form, in which practitioners either perceive or become the yidam. To effectuate such a transformation there must be no obstacle to devotion toward the visualised form. The form of the yidam is none other than the Lama from whom transmission has been received. The yidam therefore—whatever the hue, gender, or appearance—must never be separate from devotion to the Lama. The yidam is an anthropomorphic symbol of nonduality, through which the dualistic condition is able to dissolve into luminous recognition of nonduality. The purpose of symbolism is to transform the dualistically deranged symbols of conditioning into the nondual symbol of the yidam, and the kyil'khor or nondual environment of the yidam.

The twelfth of September

Every human being is a nascent Artist – a creatively sensual saint who could change existence with a painting, song, symphony, concerto, poetic canto, novel, play, or sculpture. We don't exclude the nose and mouth – so we include delicious banquets and fabulous fragrances.

———— · ————

We make no distinction between Art and Craft in terms of creative superiority. We make no distinction between painting a canvas and painting a living room wall. Art—in its innumerable manifestations —is the efflorescence of appreciation.

———— · ————

When I look at most of what is termed conceptual art or abstract expressionism – I tend to see more genuine Art in the field of Craft. I often visited the National ResoPhonic 'factory' in San Luis Obispo, California – and found it to feel more like an Art School than many Arts Schools appear at this time.

———— · ————

The Art that lies behind everything has no name or shape. It has no texture, fragrance, sound, or colour. It's simply there as the backdrop of everything. That's probably why I've never sequestered myself within any one discipline of Art. That's probably why I don't see my life as a catalogue of events which dovetail neatly into one another, with every juncture making sense. Appreciation always makes sense, but that which is appreciated is always beyond sense – in terms of cataloguing. Appreciation is not limited by literalism, sophistry, and conventional logic with its indexes, registers, directories, and lists.

The thirteenth of September

To re-phrase Jon Lennon *'Everybody's talking about Bagism, Shagism, Dragism, Madism, Ragism, Tagism, This-ism, that-ism, is-m, is-m, is-m[4] – All we are saying is sit in silence every day.'*

———— · ————

I am always suspicious of today's pressing issues being any different from yesterday's pressing issues. The five dualistic neuroses do not change – even though they may wear different appearances.

———— · ————

We never listen to the news or read the news. People sometimes ask us *"How then are you to know what is happening in the world?"* We reply *"Someone we respect usually tells us what we need to know; sans sensationism and in concise terms."*

———— · ————

Don't invest too heavily in re-living the past. Don't speculate too frequently about the future. Don't complicate the present too often with intellectual cross referencing. Don't dissect and analyse too intensely in terms of what appears to be happening – beyond what seems necessary in terms of pragmatics. Don't strive too hard to control everything. Don't manipulate anyone unless they're definitely intending harm to others. Don't struggle, hustle, hassle, manoeuvre, or stage-manage; as if it was possible to win – and somehow fail to die. Simply enjoy the display of phenomena. It is all there is – and it is entirely marvellous.

4   *John Lennon, Plastic Ono Band, Give Peace A Chance, 1969*

The fourteenth of September

Merely because one is chanting, does not mean that one is practising Vajrayana.

——— · ———

The path of Sutrayana aims towards emptiness. It requires the renunciation of form, or rather the renunciation of addiction to form. Tantra begins with the realisation of Sutra – which is emptiness. The result of Tantra is the nondual state – so its practices deal with re-establishing a relationship with form from the perspective of emptiness. This is far more exciting than people imagine – and it doesn't necessarily involve chanting.

——— · ———

Chanting a Tantric liturgy is one form of drüpthab. Drüpthab—or sadhana—means 'method of accomplishment' – and that method has myriad appearances. In the style of the Mahasiddhas of Ancient India – your Lama could give you the drüpthab of: working as a shoeshine boy at the local airport; training to be a racing driver; learning to knit; becoming a Cordon Bleu chef; losing weight; learning Tibetan, Yiddish, or Mongolian; growing a beard; learning to dress with more panache and aplomb; getting a Heavy Goods Vehicle licence; learning Georgian or Regency dancing; taking an Art Class in portraiture; taking singing lessons; learning to upholster furniture; learning to sky dive or scuba dive; improving your grammar; learning to ride a horse; training to be a comedian – you could even be asked to give up your fashionable exclusionary diet.

The fifteenth of September

Those people who surround us in our world-kyil'khor are all essentially yidams. Everyone is a potential Buddha – and therefore, their forms are the forms which symbolise Buddhas.

—— · ——

In terms of Dzogchen, yogic song—and exercises beyond the remit of silent sitting—are known as secondary means. They are extremely valuable together with the silent sitting. There is a saying *'A stone is not worn away by the same water.'* It is worn away by new water hitting it every nanosecond. Dzogchen has no traditional extended periods of silent sitting in which no other methods are employed. There are always particular methods utilised in order to address what may be causing obstacles to silent sitting.

—— · ——

Seng-gé Dongma is the lion-headed khandro. She has enormous sagging breasts. How can she be visualised if her form is found repulsive in everyday life? Unless the sensuous glory and power of such a woman in everyday life can be appreciated – how can Seng-gé Dongma be approached with pure vision? Dorje Tröllö is the wisdom-chaos manifestation of Guru Rinpoche. He has a copious belly and a hideous snarling grimace. How can one self-arise as such a yidam if one if one finds the form abhorrent? If people revile their own bodies, and they happen to have forms similar to wrathful yidams – how can they have devotion to such yidams? How can practitioners arise as female yidams whilst having prejudice against women? How can practitioners arise as male yidams whilst having prejudice against men? How can practitioners arise as Tröma Nakmo whilst having prejudice against people who reflect the colour of Tröma Nakmo?

The sixteenth of September

It would appear that Vajrayana is not welcome. What people seem to want of Vajrayana is 'Sutrayana with pictures' or an Abrahamic religion with Technicolor superheroes.

———— · ————

The good reputation of Vajrayana will be maintained by those who live in such a way as to give it the honour it deserves. It is therefore up to us – and to all decent, kindly, and honourable Vajrayanists to be the best examples we can possibly be. *How we are* is the only valid criterion in terms of what value we can be to the world.

———— · ————

If people are presented with unmodified Vajrayana – they do not know what to make of it. This is a point worth considering when one looks at the future of Buddhism in the West. There are few people who actually appreciate Vajrayana when they see it. The perceptual psychology of Vajrayana is radical – perhaps too radical for most people to accept.

———— · ————

In answer to a question concerning 'the need to modernise Vajrayana' – Ngak'chang Rinpoche said "*Well I'm a Nyingma which means Old School — and for me, Old's Cool. So, I sing: Gimme that old-time religion / Gimme that old-time religion / Gimme that old-time religion / It's good enough for me. / It was good for the siddhas / It was good for the ngakmas / It was good for the ngakpas – yeah. Lawd it's good enough for me.*" The man got up to leave – but, before he left, Ngak'chang Rinpoche wished him well in finding what he wanted.

The seventeenth of September

Justifiable anger is an oxymoron.

———— · ————

Anger is fear dressed up in an enormous rhinoceros costume.

———— · ————

Anger arises out of fear – so it is preferable to face the fear than occlude it with anger.

———— · ————

It is more natural to be sad rather than angry – when one is confronted with tragedy.

———— · ————

It is a common misconception that the injustice of the world should cause good and honourable people anger. Anger however, does not help to change anything, Anger should not be confused with energy. One obviously requires energy to address injustice – but anger does nothing but cloud one's vision.

———— · ————

Combat—in terms of Ga'tak/Gartak[5]—includes every aspect of life. We will all fight our last fight somewhere – and we will not win; insofar as we will certainly die. We could win if we have no fear of our opponent. We could pass beyond combat, and death would have no dominion[6]. Death would no longer be an enemy. That is the heart of Ga'tak/Gartak. We could continue to have humorous conversations with others. We could have no regrets – and nothing about which we wished to complain. We wait patiently for the show to begin with confidence and dignity. Knowing that the enemy is not an enemy—simply an opportunity to explore the next horizon —represents a wonderful gift to the entire sangha.

---

5   *dGa' sTag* / དགའ་སྟག་ – Joyful Tiger; *gar sTag* / གར་སྟག་ – Dancing Tiger.
6   Dylan Thomas, *And death shall have no dominion*, 1933. The title comes from the epistle of St. Paul to the Romans 6:9

The eighteenth of September

Living the View is the most important practice. If you try to live the view—to hold the view in your mind, and see the world as much as you can in terms of the view—then whatever you do will be valuable.

———— · ————

Orientation, attitude, and motivation are everything. Lack of passion in view and practice leads to distortion of our space quality of being. Our space then becomes vagueness; apathy; spurious ultimatism; directionlessness; lack of motivation; confusion; lack of impetus; conflicting priorities; and undiscriminating tolerance. Undiscriminating tolerance has nothing to do with tolerance, because real tolerance actually appreciates differences and dissimilarity.

———— · ————

Lack of spaciousness in view and practice leads to distortion of the passionate quality of being. Passionate energy then becomes dogmatism, intransigence, inflexibility, sectarianism, fanatism, intolerance, racism, xenophobia, chauvinism, narrow-mindedness, bigotry, distorted fervour, disdain, and contempt for others.

———— · ————

Realisation can be discovered by methods which contradict each other – methods which are the reverse or mirror image of each other. If we don't understand that these methods are mirror reflections of each other, we polarise them – and interpret their respective angles as antagonistic to each other. This kind of paradox is common in Buddhism. If nonduality 'made sense' from a relative standpoint, it would be a relative state of being. The fact that it's not possible to speak in relative terms about ultimate experience without using paradoxes, is what defines the relative view as dualistic – and the ultimate view as beyond dualism.

The nineteenth of September

Although I have great devotion to Kyabjé Düd'jom Rinpoche Ten'dzin Yeshé Dorje and Kyabjé Düd'jom Rinpoche Sang-gyé Pema Shépa – I continue to have dreams of Kyabjé Düd'jom Rinpoche Jig'drèl Yeshé Dorje and to relate to him as my Tsawa'i Lama.

———— · ————

Vajrayanists deal in that which is real and that which is surreal. They deal in that which lies beyond commonly known phenomena. They are not confined by the common parameters of language, sound, colour, or light. Vajrayanists value their Lamas because they know their Lamas have travelled beyond the horizons they are trying to reach. This is the basis of their devotion.

———— · ————

It is valuable to experience devotion toward more than one Lama. One needs to understand that it is the nondual state which is the cause of devotion rather than the assemblage of characteristics which comprise one's Lama. To have the experience of inspiration in respect of a number of Lamas allows the possibility of understanding that they all say the same thing in different ways. It is by this means that one does not merely learn to parrot the linguistics of one's own Lama.

———— · ————

Naturally one loves one's Lama for his or her individual predilections, particularities, passions, and penchants – but that love should become a key to experiencing devotion for other Lamas. If one's love for one's Lama is exclusive, one never knows whether one has devotion or whether one is engaged in primitive cult worship. We have witnessed cult devotion quite often in the world of Vajrayana and are happy to say that it does not appear to be present in any of our current orbits of endeavour.

The twentieth of September

One has to find the razor's edge of existence and nonexistence. One has to rest there – in view and practice.

———— · ————

We need a clear idea of why we are engaged with this practice of Vajrayana. There needs to be some fire burning in us – some dynamic life-spark of enthusiasm which characterises us as members of this tradition.

———— · ————

We hope that the ethos we are attempting to establish will become established in the sinew, bone, muscle, blood, and space of being.

———— · ————

The development of greater passion doesn't mean that we have to engage in more formal practice—there is only so much time in our lives—but we can attempt to live in the fire of Vajrayana; just a little more.

———— · ————

Vajra commitment is the openness to questioning arrogant, unkind, selfish, manipulative, or thoughtless behaviour. This is the only kind of vajra commitment in which we are actually interested.

———— · ————

This is something crucial to apprehend. Inspiration surrounds us continually: in the laughter of seagulls; in passages of music; in the natural beauty of phenomena; in the beauty of the kindness which can flow out of human beings; in the unexpected, spontaneous, and surprising experience of existence.

The twenty-first of September

The Lama's informal symbolic transmission can be anything – it can be any gesture at any time.

——— · ———

If one happened to be locked in a cage with a tiger—even an extraordinarily large cage—one would probably observe the slightest movement of the tiger. Being able to receive informal symbolic transmission could be quite similar. On the other hand, it would be unwise to let anxiety become an obstacle.

——— · ———

Transmission is the key point in respect of Dzogchen. Everything depends on transmission. It can be a highly subtle scenario. Lamas who give transmission need to be understood precisely through whatever means they manifest. Informal symbolic transmission requires both openness and subtlety. The intellect is not sufficient – in fact the intellect can often be an almost insurmountable obstacle.

——— · ———

This Lama'i Naljor of Ma-gÇig Labdrön was first taught by Ma-gÇig Labdrön to her son Gyalwa Thöndrüp. 'Khordong gTérchen Tulku Chhi'mèd Rig'dzin Rinpoche was the incarnation of that son – and although we have received the transmission of that practice from various Lamas, we consider the most important to be that which we received from Chhi'mèd Rig'dzin Rinpoche. This is because he confided "*I still hear her voice.*" When he said that – time disappeared. The 12th Century felt a mere few years away.

The twenty-second of September

The yidam takes infinite forms because there are endless styles of misconstruing nonduality.

——— · ———

The purpose of symbolism is to transform the dualistically deranged symbols of conditioning into the nondual symbols of the yidams – and the kyil'khor; the environment of the yidam.

——— · ———

The nine expressive dance modes[7] are *tranquil—serene; sympathetic—appreciative; humorous—witty; astounding—wondrous; erotic—amatory; heroic—gallant; repulsive—repellent; furious—ferocious;* and, *alarming—terrifying*. Although these dance modes relate to the yidams – they relate equally to those who envision the yidams.

——— · ———

Yidams have infinite forms – because there are endless styles of misconstruing nonduality. These myriad forms however, are classified in three groups – as peaceful, joyous, and wrathful. These three are associated with the three dualistic tendencies: indifference, attraction, and aversion. Body types are associated with these categories. Peaceful forms are thin; joyous forms are voluptuous; and wrathful forms are powerfully large. Because it is common for Vajrayana practitioners to receive empowerments into all three categories of yidam it is necessary for practitioners to have a vital and vigorous appreciation of each form – in whatever colour, gender, body-type, or mode of appearance the yidam displays. Because devotion to the form of the yidam is crucial to Vajrayana, one must avoid negative æsthetic considerations with regard to people who are skinny, curvilinear, or corpulent.

---

7 *gar gyi nyams dGu* / གར་གྱི་ཉམས་དགུ།

The twenty-third of September

Everyone could be an Artist – even in an imperceptible way.

——— · ———

One can be an artist by choosing the colours of one's dwelling – but with love, zest, audacity, and inspiration.

——— · ———

To be an artist one simply maintains the endeavour. One's senses have to cavort with reality – and that voluptuous liaison has to become a dynamic aspect of one's experience of appreciation.

——— · ———

One doesn't have to sell a painting to be a painter. One doesn't even have to have a painting accepted by a gallery. One simply has to paint – to expend effort and be determined. There needn't even be variety in one's work – one could re-paint the same subject, or even re-work the same canvas.

——— · ———

In terms of Vajrayana, creativity is not defined in relation to pain. Vajrayana artists are not required to suffer for their Art. Artists do not have to endure adverse circumstances to create Art. There is no circumstantial mohel[8] – so, *having to suffer in order to create* is an oxymoron. The primary qualification of the Artist—in terms of Vajrayana—is that *the sense fields are open*. One has to have a living appreciation of the fields of the senses. This condition of openness is naturally compassionate. Compassion is naturally communicative – so, there is no reliance on pain to provide its questionable muse.

---

8   Mohel (Hebrew: מוֹהֵל) – a person trained in the practice of brit milah (Hebrew: בְּרִית מִילָה), the covenant of circumcision.

The twenty-fourth of September

Merely because one has a subjective opinion does not give one the right to subject anyone to hearing it.

——— · ———

Although it is not always kind to *say what you mean* – it is always kind to *mean what you say*. Kindness comes before being frank.

——— · ———

Honesty or truth should not be confused with 'speaking your mind'. Idiots generally tend to speak their minds – and what they say rarely has any value. Merely because words exist in one's concept consciousness does not mean they are true – or everyone would be a world-renowned philosopher.

——— · ———

The assertion that 'pride and prejudice are antithetical', is a statement which can only be understood from the perspective of Vajrayana. Vajrayana is based upon the experience of emptiness. Prejudice is predicated on defining otherness as antithetical. From the dualistic point of view *emptiness* is *otherness* – but Vajrayanists are not afraid of *the otherness of emptiness*. *Otherness* holds no fear for those who practise according to the principle of transformation. Tantrikas develop *vajra pride* which—because it is founded on emptiness—allows the possibility of assuming infinite forms of otherness: otherness of colour, otherness of shape, otherness of gender, otherness of disposition – and, limitless other varieties of otherness. Every variant of vajra-otherness is a glorious manifestation of nonduality as it sparkles through the appearance of every permutation of humanity.

The twenty-fifth of September

Everyone is famous for those who like them and enjoy their presence.

———— · ————

You don't have to be famous to be famous – you just have to be real and enjoy existence.

———— · ————

If you ever catch yourself being interested in what is 'trending' – it would be wise to remember that all the war-mongering dictators in history were once 'trending'.

———— · ————

No one should say *"I'm not an artist because I'm not famous – and I'll never be famous."* There were more than a few great artists who were famous after their deaths – and even those who are not remembered may have been greater artists than those who are remembered. Art and fame have nothing in common. If you just want 'fame' there are many easier ways to obtain it than through the Arts.

———— · ————

Hitler and Stalin were famous – but would you want to be either? Who would want to be anyone in the long list of psychopaths who have blighted this planet? Our own considerations around being immortalised have included: discovering—by public consensus— who was the kindest person in any given locality and making a statue of the person. Wouldn't it be wonderful to have a statue of a middle-aged cleaning lady posed with a mop and bucket? An old man in a white coat with a 'Children Crossing' sign. We need to make kindness, generosity, and decency famous.

The twenty-sixth of September

The Lama is both the beginning and the end of the path.

———— · ————

Without the Lama, the situation is either a closed loop or slow progress over a great many lifetimes.

———— · ————

Without the Lama, Vajrayana cannot function. The Lama is the source of wisdom and method, embodying the divisionlessness of emptiness and form.

———— · ————

The Lama provides understanding of the view – and, the method by which that view is actualised. The view is the emptiness aspect. The methods taught are the form aspect. Both are united in Lamas through the dynamism of their presence.

———— · ————

Through having actualised the nature of the teaching, the Lama has the capacity to facilitate that actualisation in others. Actualisation is the condition in which the teaching has become as real as the need to eat, drink, sleep, or breathe.

———— · ————

Although Kyabjé Düd'jom Rinpoche Jig'drèl Yeshé Dorje was my Tsawa'i Lama—my Root Teacher—he sent me to Kyabjé Künzang Dorje Rinpoche in order that I had a Lama who had more time in terms of giving personal teachings. I thus had two Tsawa'i Lamas. Künzang Dorje Rinpoche then had to disappear for 13 years and he advised me in the interim to study with 'Khordong gTérchen Tulku Chhi'mèd Rig'dzin Rinpoche. I then had three Tsawa'i Lamas. This has never posed any kind of problem.

The twenty-seventh of September

Vajrayana can be manifested through any human modality. It could be costume – as Sartorialiam is one of the Arts. Kyabjé Düd'jom Rinpoche Jig'drèl Yeshé Dorje said *"Every tantrika has to be an Artist and manifest all the Arts."* Kyabjé Künzang Dorje Rinpoche said the same. So, one simply has to engage with what is there.

———— · ————

Dining is an Art because taste is one of the sense fields. The sense fields give birth to the Arts so the culinary Arts are part of the spectrum. Cooking, dining, and savouring are Art. Banqueting is therefore simply the Art Exhibition of Gastronomic Theatre.

———— · ————

In the condition of dualistic estrangement, the beginningless nondual state becomes alien – and therefore antagonism to its otherness arises in opposition to every form it assumes. From the basis of this primitive antagonism, every type of prejudice arises: racial discrimination, gender-chauvinism, sectarianism, religious bigotry, bias, intolerance, insularity, fanaticism, and narrow-mindedness.

———— · ————

Duality needs to be continually re-created. If nothing is instigated to create the illusion of duality, the illusion of duality begins to unwind through the psycho-physical elements. This is the heart of meditation. As soon as duality ceases to be re-created, the psycho-physical elements begin to relax into their own condition – because the natural state of the psycho-physical elements is the nondual state.

The twenty-eighth of September

Spiritual materialism means converting spirituality into materialism.

———— · ————

The term 'spiritual materialism' does not describe owning beautiful expensive Vajrayana ritual equipment. This is merely materialism. 'Spiritual materialism' is not the physical ownership – it's what the ownership signifies. It's not merely owning objects. Fundamentally 'spiritual materialism' is using Vajrayana to bolster the 'me project.'

———— · ————

Spiritual materialism applies to collecting. It could apply to collecting objects – but that is a little too obvious. If one has a growing collection of Himalayan antiques – one cannot pretend that one is not a collector. This kind of collecting is relatively honest in comparison with collecting secret teachings and rarely given empowerments.

———— · ————

Every mode of perception or behaviour which makes use of religion as a means of establishing reference points is 'spiritual materialism'. Some modes are trivial—relatively inconsequential— and some are gross. The more obvious or overt the referentiality, the less harmful. The less obvious or overt the referentiality, the more harmful. Those who are able to hide their *spiritual materialism* under the soiled, rank, and fœtid cloak of 'spiritual correctness' are the most depraved *spiritual materialists*. Those who simply delight in possessions or who delight in the excitement of what they receive as teachings and empowerments – are relatively innocent. One can work creatively with such people – but those who imagine they are pure and righteous tend to be extremely hard work as students.

The twenty-ninth of September

Drala is the life and vigour of the land. *Jong* means a mountain valley or meadow. This refers to a place where Drala is more easily appreciated in terms of the elemental presence of the natural world; the earth, water, fire, air, and space of nature.

———— · ————

Drala Jong means 'Sparkling Meadow of Primal Nondual Iridescence'. We asked Kyabjé Künzang Dorje Rinpoche if he would name the retreat centre which he encouraged us to establish. It is traditional to request such a name from one's Lama. He asked us to make a suggestion and we offered Drala Jong – to which he replied *"This is the perfect name for a Dzogchen retreat centre – whoever speaks the name makes a connection."*

———— · ————

With regard to *Drala Jong* – *jong* refers to the sense fields, the perceptual continuum where there is no division between the six sense fields. The experience of their unity manifests a limitless field of perception completely open to the vastness of what is there. From the point of view of nondual perception, we are completely available in terms of our appreciative capacity and fluxing two-way communication occurs constantly.

———— · ————

The practice of *Drala* enhances the capacity to appreciate – leading to an unveiling of the phenomenal world. Drala is the key to pure enjoyment which leads, of itself, to a state of appreciation for the enjoyment of others. When one learns to appreciate phenomena, the sense fields sparkle and an infinite capacity for generosity is born. This connects with others – hence, kindness and appropriate action become effortless.

The thirtieth of September

We like to encourage the primacy of personal choice and personal aesthetics. The Art of life is too often strangulated by fashion and by addiction to convention. Of course, it is also strangulated by addiction to deliberate self-conscious unconventionality and pretentious exhibitionism.

—— · ——

Some people are nervous about 'exhibitionism' – and therefore attempt to blend with the wallpaper of the prevalent culture. The difference between the Art of Sartorialism and exhibitionism is often simply whether one is concerned as to whether one is being noticed or not. If someone accused you of exhibitionism you could simply reply *"Welcome to the exhibition – admittance is free."*

—— · ——

One aspect of being a Vajrayana vow holder is exhibiting an exuberant plurality of appearance through unlimited apparel. The word *exhibit* has no connection with *exhibitionism* – but rather, with Art Exhibitions. Art Exhibitions tend to be held within prestigious buildings where paintings and sculptures can be appreciated with dignity and decorum. One's appearance is a communication of upliftedness – and shows people that they can embrace a greater degree of joy and engender it in others.

—— · ——

Wearing clothes which deviate from *highstreet-drab* or *shopping mall dowdy* is not necessarily exhibitionism. Exhibitionism is far more complex and involves making sure there is an audience. It requires lingering in order to attract attention. It necessitates loitering to entice onlookers. It demands dallying so as to fascinate passers-by. That doesn't mean that you can't be a street performer – but, if so, please collect money for a charitable cause.

Lung *(rLung)* – vital energy

October

One cannot achieve the nondual state merely with study –
one to has to practise the nondual state.

HE Ögyen Dro'dül Thrin-lé Kunkyab Rinpoche

རྒྱལ་བ་ཨོ་རྒྱན་འགྲོ་འདུལ་ཕྲིན་ལས་ཀུན་སྐྱབས་རིན་པོ་ཆེ་

Time and space never change – but mind changes in an
instant. It may have been white in colour moments before.
It may be red in colour in the immediate present. It may
be blue in colour in the near future. Simply be aware of
the changes.

Khar-trül Wangchuk Rig'dzin Rinpoche

མཁར་སྤྲུལ་དཔལ་གྱི་དབང་ཕྱུག་རིག་འཛིན་རིན་པོ་ཆེ།

325

The first of October

Those who take themselves to be *the beginning and end of all they accomplish* are self-circumscribed – and therefore doomed to repeated frustration and suffer bouts of meaninglessness.

———— · ————

Some may be familiar with the idea of the 'dark night of the soul'. Fortunately, a Vajrayanist has no 'soul', no 'atman' – therefore any time of day is fine. The Vajrayana artist consequently takes '... *the dark of the night time and paints the daytime black*'[1] – or vice versa, if it is of creatively æsthetic benefit to beings.

———— · ————

Someone asked me once whether I ever had a 'dark night of the soul' and I replied that I preferred cod – moreover I always made sure I ate fresh fish and had never been dubbed by Her Majesty the Queen. I therefore never had a 'dark knight of the sole'. My apologies if that was less than amusing. My point is that such adages emanate from the prevalent theistic culture – and tend to have no application in Buddhist culture. It is not that *doubt* is unknown – but this adage pertains to fundamental doubt in the basis of everything one had believed. Shakyamuni Buddha advised that we tested his words and only accepted them when they proved true in our own experience – because from that position, such all-encompassing doubt is not feasible.

1   Bob Dylan, *She Belongs to Me*, 1965: *She's got everything she needs, she's an artist. She don't look back. She can take the dark out of the night-time – and paint the daytime black.*

The second of October

Let thoughts of past and future settle in the present moment – and, in that moment, simply experience what is naturally there.
Kyabjé Düd'jom Rinpoche Jig'drèl Yeshé Dorje

———— · ————

Because you're a symbol of your beginningless nondual condition—and because all beings likewise are symbols—there can be no being who is not essentially sacred according to the pure vision of Vajrayana.

———— · ————

Being *symbols of what we actually are* – is explosively creative in terms of Vajrayana practice. We could actually become what we really are in terms of the yidams we visualise. That is the primary function of yidam practice.

———— · ————

You certainly shouldn't be less emotional. You could simply do what you're doing and feel what you're feeling – but not look for security in terms of getting your emotions under control. Your emotions are your means of liberation. They're valuable. If you forget everything we say – please just remember that your emotions are valuable. They contain the energy of your beginningless nondual state.

———— · ————

If you were to fall to your death from a very great height; it would be a shame not to enjoy the view as you fell, or to appreciate the wind in your hair or warmth of the sun on your face. It's good to experience the raw voltage of being alive.

The third of October

There is a difference between *doing as you are told* because you have bought into some kind of a structure for self-advancement – and *entering into the view of the Lama*, because you have a real understanding of that view as being liberating. There is a great difference.

———— · ————

People who buy into cults and commit atrocities at the behest of cult leaders – are those who want personal advancement. Cult leaders may well take advantage of people – but why are people open to being exploited? Some people join cults because they are insecure, frightened, and lonely – but these people aren't the major operatives within a cult.

———— · ————

If you arrive at devotion to the Lama through critical experiential research you understand entirely *'I am allowing myself to be challenged — because I've hit the barriers of my own rationale time and time again. I know my rationale is a closed loop and that the only way out is through being guided by the vajra master.'*

———— · ————

Emptiness is the ground. This is crucial when approaching Vajrayana. Vajra commitment has come from an evolved knowledge that *emptiness is the ground.* If one has evolved that knowledge, then one can enter into relationship with the vajra master. This is definitely not obedience in terms of obeying commands whatever they may be. I have never been asked to do anything unkind, unethical, or immoral – and I have been the disciple of two wrathful Lamas: Kyabjé Künzang Dorje Rinpoche and 'Khordong gTérchen Tulku Chhi'mèd Rig'dzin Rinpoche.

The fourth of October

Vajra commitment does not mean Jim Jones, Charles Manson, or Sogyal Lakar. These extreme examples, taken from the realm of modern cult behaviour are deceitful decoys, employed by those who have never experienced 'vajra commitment'. Such examples are decoys *because* they are extreme – and, *because* there is no sense in which such examples can be understood as teachings. Extreme examples of obedience, are merely a way of discrediting vajra commitment through avoidance of real examples. There are many Lamas and many real examples which are not extreme in any way.

———— · ————

Milarépa could always have walked away from the tasks which Marpa set. He was not Marpa's slave, simply the slave of his wish for liberation. Milarépa ran away a few times – but always came back because he wanted Marpa's transmission. He battled with himself in many ways before he received transmission – but it was always *his* choice. Milarépa is an extreme example. Milarépa is an extreme example because he had been a black magician[2] and caused the deaths of a number of people. Marpa's Teacher Naropa is also an extreme example – but we need not project ourselves into such outlandish situations. No one need cope with a fraction of the pain and discomfort experienced by Naropa or Milarépa. Vajra commitment can only be understood as what is possible within our present society. Vajra commitment has no reason to resort to immorality, unethical behaviour, illegality, violence, or sexual abuse. We have no reason to fear such things – unless we fall prey to cults. We therefore advise people to be aware of 'cult criteria' information. Otherwise, the only thing we have to fear is that our dualism will be demolished.

---

2   thu-gyé jèd-pa *(mThu rGyas byed pa / མཐུརྒྱསྦྱེདཔ)*. Chad-hur bö-tong *(byad phur rBod gTong / བྱདཕུརྦོདགཏོང)* – black magic and curses.

The fifth of October

Dzogchen is the primordial state of the individual – and the ways in which that can be recognised.

———— · ————

Although a percentage of what we teach has a Tantric emphasis, the Aro gTér approaches everything from the view of Dzogchen – in which the individual is primordially free. *Primordial freedom* pertains to 'fundamental goodness', rather than narcissistic or sociopathic potential.

———— · ————

Dzogchen offers the premise that the nondual state can be manifested in every individual. This however, does not preclude having to learn how to balance heaven and hell – on the jet-driven rotary seesaw of tantric discipline. Both approaches are needed if one is to explode the horizon of conventional meaning.

———— · ————

Dzogchen view concerns *self-liberation of dualistic energy*. The inner tantras concern the *transformation of dualistic energy*. Th outer tantras concern the *purification of the energy of defilement*. Sutrayana concerns the *renunciation of form-clinging in terms of dualism*. Dzogchen however, allows all other methods from each of the nine vehicles – as and when they are needed. They are needed far more than some people imagine.

———— · ————

We all have to let go in the end. Even on the way there – every decade ends; every year ends; every month ends; and, every day ends. Everything that begins, ends. This may sound gloomy – but you need to remember that a plethora of phenomena are also continually beginning. The key point is that one has to be there at the beginning – and for that to be possible one has to let go of the previous moment, month, or millennium.

The sixth of October

We're all capable of error. We're all capable of correcting errors – so perhaps we should get on with it.

――― · ―――

At the risk of seeming sacrilegious, we're not required to die for anyone's sins – unless it's absolutely essential.

――― · ―――

Changchub sem is not the overblown sentimentally of pretending to be saintly – but without ever coming into contact with the hard edges of existence.

――― · ―――

With empathy, the same neurosis is necessary in order to empathise. But wherever there's authentic enjoyment, there's a living communication. Changchub sem is communicative. One has to open a channel of communication though appreciation. If there's nothing enjoyable about a person, there's no communication or authentic human contact.

――― · ―――

According to Chhi'mèd Rig'dzin Rinpoche, the word Tibetan word *sDig pa* has always been mistranslated. He emphasised that *sDig pa* does not mean 'sin'. It means error. Unlike sin, 'error' does not carry the charge of being absolutely deliberate. It still means a negative act – but not a negative act that is carried out in the complete knowledge that it is negative. *sDig pa* also means scorpion[3].

3 *sDig pa ra tsa / sDig rwa /* སྡིག་པ་རཚ་ / སྡིག་ར་)

331

The seventh of October

We all have beginningless nondual realisation – so we are all beginninglessly qualified. In the sense in which we experience ourselves as unenlightened beings however – we are all temporarily disqualified.

———— · ————

In terms of Vajrayana as Art – it's important to have as broad an appreciation of 'Art' as possible. We have mentioned interior decoration — but there is also gardening and farming. There is no area of human activity which lies outside 'Art'. In terms of Vajrayana – it's the integrity which matters. It's the willingness not to compromise æsthetics, imagination, innovative judgement, and creative criticality.

———— · ————

Gu-yang[4]—carefree—does not mean careless or not caring. Carefree means not indulging the idea of claustrophobia. Carefree means being open to the texture of reality. Carefree is being simple and having simple dignity. Simple dignity is not conceited, proud, self-satisfied, or complacent – but simply naturally confident. That arises naturally with daily silent sitting.

———— · ————

Ku-nyam[5]—dignity—exists when one cannot be bought with promises of easier, less arduous, approaches to anything. Without dignity the sale representatives of 'meditation without religion' will have you dancing to their mercenary melodies like a meschugganah[6] marionette monkey.

---

4   (gu yang / གུ་ཡང་

5   sKu nyams / སྐུ་ཉམས་

6   Meschugganah – Yiddish, meaning a person who has lost their reason, a senseless or irrational person.

The eighth of October

The first and second Sutric vehicles emphasise the gradual dissection of samsara in which the myriad narcissistic delusions are either individually uprooted, or individually severed through emptiness-analysis.

———— · ————

Mahayana emphasises the experience of emptiness. One sees the emptiness of the subject and object of anger – or one applies the opponent powers. If one experiences anger, one cultivates the feeling of compassion.

———— · ————

In Sutrayana – if one fails to renounce attachment to negative neurotic motivation or behaviour, one would rely on the advice of the spiritual friend[7] with regard to the manner in which one should live the path. The spiritual friend would confront narcissism and give advice on the manner in which one should make amends for narcissism. If one fails in terms of Vajrayana the Lama might do something a little more surprising, astonishing, startling, disturbing, or even shocking.

———— · ————

Tantra emphasises the transformation of the energy of neurotic patterning. Narcissism is transformed through pure-vision of the yidam. If one fails to transform one's neuroses, one relies on the vajra master to 'conjure' with one's dualistic circumstances, in order to destroy one's clinging to self-obsessed fixations. This 'conjuring' requires the play of the four Buddhakarmas: *enriching, pacifying, controlling,* or *destroying.*

---

7   gewa'i shenyen *(dGe ba'i bShes gNyen /* རྒེ་བའི་བཤེས་གཉེན་ */ kalyanamitra)*

The ninth of October

By all means follow the fashion and do what everybody else is doing
– as long as what they are doing is generous, insightful, kind,
energetic, and circumspect.

———— · ————

Authentic appreciation—in terms of the senses and Arts in the
broadest possible sense—is antithetical to the fashion industry and
to fashions of any kind. Appreciation is inherently revolutionary as
it naturally overthrows the conspicuous addiction to consumption
with which we are indoctrinated.

———— · ————

When meditating on Mind, be relaxed and breathe naturally. Gaze
into Space. Space is directly before your wide-open eyes. This is to
look directly into the face of Küntuzangpo. Strongly invoke the
Tsawa'i Lama as inseparable from Guru Rinpoche – and your Mind
will merge with his. Once settled, you may not remain long in clear
awareness. Your mind may move or become restless – and then
what is experienced will not be the nature of Mind but namthogs.
Do not follow the namthogs – because following namthogs is what
will plunge you back into dualism. So, break the chain of namthogs
– and then you will see awareness. When you see awareness, you will
know – because it is translucent, uninhibited, and elated. It is not
circumscribed or delineated by predetermined characteristics. There
is nothing of 'khorwa or 'dé-pa[8] which is not encompassed. It is
beginninglessly what you are. It has never been lacking – but it lies
beyond the reach of engagement, endeavour, and ingenuity. Oral
teaching from Kyabjé Düd'jom Rinpoche Jig'drèl Yeshé Dorje to
Ngak'chang Rinpoche in 1971

---

8   'das pa / འདས་པ་ / nirvana) – the cessation of 'khorwa ('khor ba / འཁོར་བ / samsara) dualistic
    circling.

The tenth of October

In order to let go of patterning, we have to be free of the need of it.

———— · ————

Patterning is self-damaging – because we rely on patterning for security when it has little to offer.

———— · ————

Our patterning is what we recreate – but we don't have to recreate it repetitively. That is the value of silent sitting.

———— · ————

We need to let go of the security of having patterns. Some people would rather be miserable because they're used to the pattern of being miserable. They're identified with being miserable – and would rather be miserable than let go of it.

———— · ————

I have a Sam Browne belt[9]. I wear it cheerfully. I *can* remember being beaten with it as a child – but that has no meaning at this point in time. I'm not trapped by its history. Talk therapy was not involved in being able to wear this belt cheerfully. I didn't have to go back to my childhood to exorcise anything or anyone. I don't blame my father or have any anger towards him – and I'm not in denial. How was this possible you may ask? That's simple. I sat in silence. I practiced Vajrayana. I followed my Lama's advice – and I maintained my vows. I'd recommend it to anyone.

9   The Sam Browne is a wide leather belt, supported by a narrow strap passing diagonally over the right shoulder. 19th Century British Indian Army Officer— General Sam Browne—having lost his left arm in the Sepoy Rebellion, devised a secondary belt which crossed his right shoulder in order to hold his scabbard steady. This attached to the main belt with D-rings for attaching accessories. It carried a revolver in a flap-holster at the right hip. Other officers adopted the 'Sam Browne' and eventually it became standard uniform.

The eleventh of October

Any objectivity attributed to aesthetics is spurious. It is wiser to take all *view-points on aesthetics* as subjective. Then there's no argument. If I meet someone who admires what I find ugly – it's fascinating. And it's not that they're wrong. It's not that I'm wrong. It's not that I'm right. One doesn't have to be right or wrong about subjective opinions.

———— · ————

Tantra is not bland. When you know that your opinion is empty – you can state it with humorous vehemence. You can love and hate in an entirely empty manner. This is a characteristic of essential Vajrayana. We do not have to attribute equal worth or quality to everything as a religious principle. We do not have to be bland in our likes and dislikes as long as we know that we are disporting merrily with empty ideas.

———— · ————

As long as you regard all your opinions as subjective – you are free to dislike anything with hilarious exuberance. It doesn't mean anything. It's simply an empty aspect of personality. Authentic personality can be free to contain like, dislike, and indifference – because each is empty of objectivity. You don't have to argue with anybody – because you're neither right nor wrong – as to whether sweet white wine is good or bad; whether this style of music is better than that style of music; or whether whatever. In this way differences of opinion can simply be fun or fascination. It's when you want to make opinions objective that people have to argue and dislike each other on that basis.

The twelfth of October

'I' is the intangible point between the infinite past and infinite future.

———— · ————

If one is content with this momentary 'I' in the moment, one can have an 'I'. There it is, in the moment. What you can't do with it is make a project out of 'I' – and continue it in time. This is because it continuously changes.

———— · ————

Ego is a verb – not a noun. It is what we do and why we do it – rather than what we are. Ego is not a good translation of bDag as it gives the impression of being a thing that can be detached, removed, avulsed, or amputated. bDag is merely the habit of duality – which, although difficult, can be dropped at any moment. *Ego* was Sigmund Freud's coinage[10] and is not a useful term in the context of Buddhism.

———— · ————

There was a time when I'd teach Tantric practices – and someone erudite in the audience would ask *"Well, who's doing the practice if there's no ego?"* to which I'd answer *"Who's asking the question? Who's hearing it?"* Then I'd have to explain that the non-existence of a solid, permanent, separate, continuous, and defined entity was a Sutrayana issue. The issue was taken for granted in Vajrayana – because as soon as you realise there is no solid, permanent, separate, continuous, and defined entity to call 'I' – 'I' is not a problem. 'I' *does* exist in the moment – just not in the next moment or previous moment. The transitory 'I' is real in the moment – and *that* is the one referred to in terms of Tantric practice.

10 The *id, ego,* and *super-ego* are psychoanalytic concepts which describe interactive agents defined by Sigmund Freud in his structural model of the psyche. **Id** is the instinctive aspect. **Ego** is the pragmatic organising faculty which arbitrates between instinctualism and critical ethical constraint. **Super-ego** is a moral-ethical critical faculty.

The thirteenth of October

We wish you nonreferential joy and gleeful abandon. We wish you passion and spaciousness in the splendid dance of your sense-fields and sense perceptions.

————— · —————

May your life be the cause of laughter and lucence; devotion and delight. May you have the fierce friendship of vajra brothers and sisters. Maybe you have a passionate open heart.

————— · —————

We wish you all great delight. We wish you success in your practice – in order that you generate blazing kindness for the liberation of all beings. May you sample the clear ferocity of primordial awareness which arises from an increasingly vital connection with the Nyingma Tradition.

————— · —————

In terms of Vajrayana desire is only a problem when referential. When desire is referential it centers on 'me' – rather than the free-floating beingness which exists in space with *every other being there ever was and ever will be*. So, when one has experiential space, desire is simply an energy. This means that whether I obtain the delightful focus of desire; or whether you obtain it – is irrelevant. One can enjoy seeing other people obtain what they desire. One can desire on behalf of other beings.

————— · —————

The sparkling through of the nondual state occurs because 'khorwa is a patchwork – a flawed and ineffective system which does not function well even in its own terms. The nondual state sparkles through, due to the failure of samsara – but if one's eyes are not open to witness that sparkling – one sees nothing. This sparkling may secretly animate moments of delight or joy or compassion or fervent lust – but otherwise it is of minute duration.

The fourteenth of October

We simply have to avoid getting in the way of naturally arising kindness. That is one of the functions of silent sitting.

———— · ————

Changchub sem naturally springs from emptiness – and when it does, life will elicit natural responses. For example – you don't have to do anything before you pull someone out of the way of a bus. You just do it. You don't even think. It simply just happens.

———— · ————

The problem with some Buddhists is that they feel constrained to be artificial. They feel that they have to pretend to be what they are not. There is no shame in being dualistically deranged – otherwise we would be eaten by shame. Hypocrisy is always a cause of harshness toward others. It is better therefore, to be open, relaxed, and humorous about personal pride and vanity. We need to own it – so that when we observe it in others, we can apprehend it in a kindly, cheerful, non-judgemental light.

———— · ————

In terms of changchub sem, helping anybody else simply happens. If you build a philosophy out of it, then you have to do something artificial rather than simply being inspired to help – because the situation requires it. If somebody wants help and has to put it into language, they'll ask you for it. So, building a philosophy around it gets in the way of a natural response. A natural response could simply be smiling at somebody on the street. There was a lady walking toward me one day. She had a face like thunder. I thought it might be something to do with our different ethnic origins – but I decided to smile. She returned a smile so brilliant that I can still see it today. She may well forget me – but I will never forget her.

The fifteenth of October

rLung rTa—wind horse—is appreciative vitality, in which the appreciation and vitality incite each other.

———— · ————

If one withdraws, for some reason, from the immediacy of an experience – one loses the sense of changchub sem. One loses the sense of vital connection with the dance of circumstances.

———— · ————

The symbolism of Vajrayana only makes sense when one lives in the culture of changchub sem – and one has to manifest that culture independently as a sangha ethos, within the dominant society. If one estranges oneself from the culture of changchub sem, then its cultural forms can begin to lose their meaning unless one has sufficient experience of practice.

———— · ————

If you start to see yourself as an outsider – you will eventually observe yourself merely 'going through the motions'. This does not happen overnight – but in gradual increments. One could be performing a dance and find oneself confused. *Why am I dancing? I thought I wanted to be here, performing this dance with these other people – but suddenly I find myself bereft of the reasons I chose to do this.'* The meaning of a dance is imbedded in the culture and history of the people who perform the dance, With Vajrayana that culture and history are inextricably bound with changchub sem – with kindness. To engage in a dance, we have to enter the *authentically appreciative world of the dance* – and find the realm of its meaning to be in tune with what we are.

The sixteenth of October

Dharma means: as it is. If 'as it is' is what we discover through practice, then we need to remain true to it – come what may. If we understand the teachings to be the direct expression of reality; then we have to act in accordance with Dharma in spite of insecurity, fear, isolation, anxiety, and bewilderment.

———— · ————

Heroism can be the choice to acknowledge that one is not ready to make vows. It could be heroism to drink less, rather than end up vomiting. It could be heroism to be real and acknowledge one's limitations, rather than taking refuge in one's narcissistic projections.

———— · ————

The most valuable thing to have, is the visceral knowledge that life is not worth living if we do not *live to the fullest in terms of the vows we take*. It is not worth living as vow-breakers – so it is better to be careful and not take vows which we might break. It is preferable to practice *'as if* one had made vows' for some years before taking vows such as vajra commitment.

———— · ————

Kyabjé Düd'jom Rinpoche once said *"Many Western student like helicopter."* By this he was not referring to function as much as shape: large at one end and very small at the other. They come on strong at the start then tail away to nothing. Students are enthusiastic to make vows — but many find they have no *staying-power*, in terms of real responsibility to the lineage which nurtured them. *Staying-power* comes from practice. We do not even have to practise with heroic intensity. If we simply practised regularly – we would reach the point where there was no choice. That *honourable choicelessness* is known as heroism.

The seventeenth of October

Surrealism is an alternative realism that illustrates the fact that everyone's reality is different.

———— · ————

Knowing what you authentically appreciate is an *acquired* taste — *acquired* through the relinquishment of conditioning.

———— · ————

It is always best to go with a developed and advanced sense of diligent personal preference rather than the dictates of societal sartorial fascism.

———— · ————

Kol-chod[11]—slavery—and all forms of subservience, are imposed against the will of those who are enslaved or subjugated. Fashion however, is a form of slavery that is accepted quite willingly.

———— · ————

As soon as I saw I knew. That giraffe-hide in Clifton Antiques Market. It was for sale at a *give-away price* and I knew that it would make a superb greatcoat; especially if it retained the tail at the back. My lady friend at the time—an extremely talented costumier— adamantly refused to take on the project on the basis that she would never be seen with me wearing such a *'farcical abomination'*. I lacked the money to have it made elsewhere – so the chance was lost. That was in 1973. If the chance came today – I would still want to have it made. I hope I am not too brazenly presumptuous in saying that this might be described as authentic appreciation.

11 *bKol sPyod* / བཀོལ་སྤྱོད་

The eighteenth of October

The absence of literalism in Dzogchen is based upon giving emphasis to the natural purity of the phenomenal world – in which all manifestations are perfect *in-and-of-themselves*.

———— · ————

From the Dzogchen point of view there is no distinction between the real substances of 'The Five Meats and the Five Nectars' and the pastrami and Armagnac which can be substituted.

———— · ————

According to Kyabjé Künzang Dorje Rinpoche, to be fruitarian, vegan, vegetarian, lacto-vegetarian, pescatarian, carnivorous, or omnivorous; are all simply *thabs – method*. They are not *den-pa*[12] *truth*. They are not *truth*, inasmuch as they are not *ultimate positions*. *Methods* are relative – and, in being relative, they are all equal as Buddhist practices. Once this is understood one can abandon judgment and censure of others, The world then becomes a friendlier place.

———— · ————

When we partake of Bavarian ham and Calvados – we accept that the *knowledge of the dissolution of the pure / impure dichotomy* is present When this knowledge is integrated into all activity – we cease to make tight-minded moralistic judgments concerning the phenomenal world. This does not mean that we fail in terms of manifesting compassionate responses to suffering. It simply means that we cease to reference ourselves as *people with axes to grind*. The colour, sound, smell, taste, texture, and ideational contours of reality are simply recognised as the display in which suffering occurs. We respond to the suffering of others without becoming the enemies of natural purity of the phenomenal world.

---

12 *bDen pa* / བདེན་པ་ – truth. The two truths are relative truth – kun-dzob kyi-denpa *(kun rDzob kyi bDen pa* / ཀུན་རྫོབ་ཀྱི་བདེན་པ་ / *samvrtisatya*), and ultimate truth – don dam Den pa *(don dam bDen pa* / དོན་དམ་བདེན་པ་ / *param rthasatya).*

The nineteenth of October

Being able to laugh in an unrestrained manner is important. A person who can only giggle is unlikely to achieve anything in respect of Vajrayana.

——— · ———

A woman born and bred in Montana told us a joke.
Question: *What do you call the remaining seconds of life before being mauled to death by an Alaskan bear?*
Answer: *A Kodiak Moment*[13].
Montana can be dangerous if you ride out into the wilderness. Bear roam there—Black bear and Grizzly bear—as well as mountain lion and moose. Moose can be the most vicious. We rode out into the wilderness knowing that the joke was serious to some extent. We went with the inspiration of Kyabjé Düd'jom Rinpoche Jig'drèl Yeshé Dorje who had identified the area as a *hidden land*. The frisson between humour and reality is important in terms of Vajrayana.

——— · ———

Vajra cynicism is indivisible from vajra naïveté. Vajra cynicism is that quality which cuts through fantasy and projection. It rained in Montana on one visit. We got wet. We sludged around in a mixture of mud and horse dung whilst saddling our horses. The mud didn't sparkle with thig-lés – but there was a marvellous reality in the situation. The reality was one in which we could honour the history of the vicinity. People had done what we were doing in the 1800s. Maybe that is vajra naïveté. Kyabjé Düd'jom Rinpoche Jig'drèl Yeshé Dorje had said that the North West of Montana was a *hidden land* – and so we went there to see what we could find. This could be described as the beginning of pure vision.

---

13 The expression 'Kodak moment' came from a popular advertising campaign for American Kodak cameras in the latter half of the 20th Century, produced by Eastman Kodak. The Kodiak Alaskan bear is the second largest bear in the world.

The twentieth of October

As teaching and practice is increasingly collected, the mechanism of dualistic derangement experiences itself as increasingly solid, and incrementally loses the ability to absorb anything that does not rely on substance. Lacking the ability to absorb anything – the mechanism can only mimic. The mechanism tries to appropriate the practice of meditation and the religious way of life – but it merely creates a progressively expanding barrier to reality.

———— · ————

One does not have to be a trülku to be addressed as 'Rinpoche' by a student. All Vajrayana teachers can be addressed as 'Rinpoche' whether they are trülkus or not. The word 'Rinpoche' exists for the benefit of the disciple – not for the benefit of 'the one thus addressed'. Rinpoche becomes part of a Lama's name for the benefit of disciples – not for the benefit of 'the Lama in question'. The word 'Rinpoche' only signifies status in the mind of the disciple who uses that form of address.

———— · ————

With respect to word 'Rinpoche'. If a husband or wife, gentleman-friend or lady-friend, boyfriend, or girlfriend, address their lover as 'darling' it does not mean that the person becomes an official 'darling'. If one were to meet several husbands or wives in India one would not say *"I met the most charming group of darlings in India."* Likewise, 'Rinpoche' is often misunderstood as being a title. 'Khenpo' and 'Lopön' are titles – and so is 'Geshé'. They are degrees awarded for knowledge. 'Lama' can be a title in terms of having completed a three-year retreat – but the word has many meanings according to context. Western people have sometimes referred to the 'Rinpoches' they have met in India. It isn't actually possible to use the word 'Rinpoche' in the plural or to describe anyone as 'a Rinpoche'.

The twenty-first of October

There is magic everywhere if one is open to seeing it. The feathering of the breeze amongst the leaves and tendrils of the wisteria. The sound of the seagulls laughing. The moss amongst the old bricks with which the courtyard is paved.

———— · ————

From the perspective of Dzogchen, the specific nature of practice is governed by the individual. One gains experiential knowledge of the practices transmitted by the Lama. Then, through that knowledge, one becomes capable—with certain highly specific guidance—of applying that knowledge within the stream of one's experience.

———— · ————

Those who know the essence of the elements – see no distinction between Art and Magic. Ordinary artists and ordinary magicians will not be aware of this – and therefore be content to fabricate images and cast spells. Those Artists who know the essence of the elements do not create for popular demand – and those magicians who know the essence of the elements do not need to manipulate anything or anyone.

———— · ————

There is no 'daily round of practice' in terms of Dzogchen. The only daily practice of Dzogchen is to *find the presence of awareness* – through *whatever means*. Dzogchen practitioners should not be limited or conditioned by practice – rather they should seek to acquire precise knowledge of the nature of practice in terms of principle and function. Maybe most importantly in the current world milieu – those who see themselves as Dzogchen practitioners should not be limited by the concept of Dzogchen. The whole nine yanas are there to be practised as and when they are needed. It is important to recognise that we have need of these other yanas – probably far more frequently than we care to imagine.

The twenty-second of October

Practice—from the point of view of Dzogchen—is the texture of life.

———— · ————

If one still has knee-jerk responses—if the five elemental neuroses still dominate—one cannot pretend that Dzogchen is feasible. This does not mean that one has to be entirely free of the five elemental neuroses – but one must have reached the point where one does not take them seriously.

———— · ————

Now that there are Aro gTér Lamas to teach the ngöndro for Dzogchen, the impetus for the rest of our lives will be the three series of Dzogchen – in terms of teaching the specific methods, and creating opportunities for informal symbolic transmission. In terms of how we are with students – we shall become increasingly structureless. We like Vajrayana to be a disclosure which surfaces obliquely when least expected.

———— · ————

With Dzogchen, it is impossible to distinguish between oneself resting in nondual awareness and the nondual awareness one is experiencing. When one rests naturally—nakedly—in the boundless state of nondual awareness, the urgency of injudicious hyperactive conceptuality, memories, and troublesome plans – evaporates and disappears in the spacious sky of awareness. Referentiality collapses and vanishes into nondual awareness.

Kyabjé Düd'jom Rinpoche Jig'drèl Yeshé Dorje

The twenty-third of October

We are happy that our students do not appear to pepper their conversation with Buddhist jargon, cant, patois, platitudes, homilies, stock phrases, or shibboleths[14]. We are happy that individual differences in life-style and diet amongst them are appreciated and respected. These are fairly reliable outer signs that people are beginning to live the view.

——— · ———

Living the view is the central aspect of the Nyingma tradition – but what does it mean to live the view? Sometimes phrases such as these are bandied about until they have lost their meaning. We are happy that our linguistics are not parroted too much. We are also happy that our linguistics are employed. There is a difference between parroting the Lamas' linguistics, and employing them in the context of understanding or explaining the teachings. This is also living the view.

——— · ———

Living the view is a subject which can confuse people. There is a sense in which this phrase appears to be understood – but often on deeper discussion the core of understanding has been found to be vague. 'Living the view' is not the application of Buddhist philosophy as a *spiritual template* by which we condition ourselves into becoming Buddhist androids, programmed to give Buddhist responses on any given subject. To become an archetypal card-carrying Buddhist is merely a parody of what is possible.

14 Shibboleth – 14th Century Hebrew, meaning 'flood, stream', or 'ear of corn'. In the Bible—Book of Judges XII.4-6—it is the password used by the Gileadites to distinguish their own people from fleeing Ephraimites. It was first recorded in the 1630s to mean 'watchword' – but by the 1860s it came to mean 'outmoded slogan'.

The twenty-fourth of October

The *cliff edge*, over which the disciple has to leap, is not perilous – it's merely *self-justification*. It's merely letting go of suffocating infatuation with fixated, fractious, febrile, fatuous, and fancifully flatulent fantasies.

———— · ————

Real examples of vajra command are far more likely to be instances of disciples being asked to question their perception, or to look at their behaviour in a different light, than instances of 'outlandishness'.

———— · ————

The vajra master simply needs to be able to point out that the disciple's view of reality is askew. The vajra master needs to be able to point to instances of arrogance, anger, greed, dishonesty, and deliberate ignorance; and, expect the disciple to take such observations to heart.

———— · ————

The heart of justification has to be torn out. Matari Ékajati[15], the main Protector of Dzogchen, holds a ripped-out human heart – in token of the fact that Dzogchen is impossible whilst self-justification survives. This is obviously a hellish moment. Possibly one would rather leap from a real cliff edge than accept the vajra master's perception that the five dualistic distortions[16] are dominating one's practice. The opportunities for self-deception are so dangerous within Tantra, that the vajra mater has to be able to say *"Stop! Look! See what you are doing! Let go of this delusion immediately."*

---

15 Ngaksrung Mamo Ral-gÇig ma *(sNgags srung ma mo ral gCig ma /* རྔགས་སྲུང་མ་མོ་རལ་གཅིག་མ་

16 Arrogance, anger, obsession, dishonesty, and denial – more commonly *pride, hatred, lust, envy,* and *ignorance.*

The twenty-fifth of October

One of the many problems with fashion, is the desire *to conform in order to be accepted* – rather than follow the nature of individual appreciation. If you desire a piping hot glass of Chablis with your rhinoceros steak; by all means dine on just that. If you desire a Brunello, Barolo, or Barbaresco ice-slush with your turbot or gravy with your oysters; by all means dine on just that – and if you relish it – order another round.

———— · ————

Different shades of red *can* be worn together. Blue and green should *always* be seen – unless your appreciation runs in another direction. Fill your garden with gnomes and name them all after angels and archangels. Collect 'Christmas villages' and populate them with quaint Dickensian characters. Decorate your house in shades of lilac and pink and pose carved wooden eagles at unlikely angles in every room. Go naked on the skyline of Park Slope on cold November nights and throw orchids at passers-by. Sew multi-coloured sequins on your trench coat. Wear Victorian widows' weeds. Wear a voluminous Harris Tweed dress that looks like a coat so that people will keep offering to relieve you of it in Manhattan restaurants. Create a marble monument to Quentin Crisp in your front garden and put a wreath of Arum Lilies down every year on his birthday. Some of these displays have been manifested – whilst some have not. There is no rule apart from appreciation – and appreciation is the efflorescence of wisdom and compassion via the auspices of rolpa[17]. The natural dignity of the Vajrayanist is one of unconventional appreciation – based on the understanding of primordial egalitarianism in which all beings are beginninglessly noble.

---

17 *rol pa* / རོལ་པ་ – energy, play of experience, creative manifestation, enjoyment of the senses, presence excitement.

The twenty-sixth of October

It doesn't matter how much information you acquire – it's whether you possess the logic to make use of it, the curiosity to delve deeper, and the intuition to see what is of real value.

———— · ————

Everyone has to have some realistic sense of themselves in terms of the qualities or skills they possess – in order to be au fait with how those qualities and skills could be of benefit to others. As long as vanity is not mean-minded, haughty, arrogant, pretentious, conceited, supercilious, pompous, and unappreciative of others – there is no horrible harm in it.

———— · ————

Pride in the sense of *self-congratulatory callousness*, is not the same as the *natural pride* in being honourable. Pride is only a negative trait when it is sardonic or misanthropic. Pride is only a negative trait when it is recidivistic in relation to acting in ways that are injurious to the happiness or wellbeing of others.

———— · ————

When 'pride' and 'vanity' are contraindicated as 'improper for Buddhists' – what tends to happen is that 'buddhians' pretend not to be afflicted by these 'sins'. This leads to the development of hideously embarrassing cover-up strategies and rank hypocrisy. Such people are always the first to judge others in respect of pride, vanity – or any one of a number of reprimandable, yet possibly harmless foibles.

The twenty-seventh of October

To *live the view* is to be open in perception – open to seeing emptiness and form at play. This is something which cannot be constructed and imposed.

———— · ————

One cannot merely make *valiant attempts to live the view* – or to use effort to see in this way. One cannot ask oneself questions, as one observes reality – with regard to *how emptiness is reflected* and *how form is reflected*. One simply has to be open to these realisations. Living the view has to be spontaneous and arise as a result of practice.

———— · ————

If we try to see emptiness and form at play intellectually – this is not living the view. We are not however, making an injunction that you should not try to see in this way, as an exercise. We are merely pointing out that this does not constitute to 'living the view'. Living the view is a spontaneous accomplishment which arises from having imbibed the view through the transmission of Lamas.

———— · ————

One receives transmission of Inner Tantra and Dzogchen through listening to the teaching with spatial-empathy. The potential is thus seeded within the dimension of the perceptual continuum; to suddenly see in exactly the way that such seeing was described by the Lamas. This functions in very much the same way as receiving transmission for visualisation in an empowerment – and in this way 'living the view' could be described as 'the yidam practice of Dzogchen'. The space of one's life is the space of practice – and the drüpthab or sadhana is the realisation of living the view which suddenly arises in terms of one's confrontation with the phenomenal world.

The twenty-eighth of October

History is the Artistic evolution of manifested forms. These forms are each an oscillating biographic and autobiographic pattern, in terms of artistic intentions and how those intentions are interpreted. The nature of the oscillation is the richness of associations evoked by Art. This is why we are all Art – and why we are all Artists.

———— · ————

Reading about history and seeing its cultural patterns in the natural effulgence of human society is not separate from looking at the Arts. History is a *manifestation web*[18] of endless simultaneous stories which interconnect and rhyme at their theatrical interconnections.

———— · ————

History is a theatrical play with a hundred thousand million actors who miraculously always remember their lines – even when they forget them. History is dramatic irony. History is poetry. It is moving images. It is every form of Art in an interconnected web – which is always the Present Moment.

———— · ————

Shakespeare knew that *Art is life*, when he wrote '*All the world's a stage – and all the men and women players. They have their exits and their entrances – and everyone, in their time, playing many parts.*'[19] But life need not be a play. It could be a film, book, or poetic epic. It could be a symphony, concerto, or opera. It could be Baroque, Classical, Blues, Jazz, or Avant Garde. It could be an exhibition of paintings or sculptures – an installation or wardrobe of ensembles. It could be a fecund festival of fragrances or a gastronomic gourmet extravaganza.

---

18 Kün-trol *(kun khrol /* གུན་ཁྲོལ*)* describes an infinite series of patterns which arise and dissolve into each other. Kün-trol is not a philosophically monist fixed design. With regard to Buddhist nonduality, form is necessarily empty and therefore no fixed pattern can ever be held to have permanent existence.

19 William Shakespeare, *As You Like It,* Act II, scene vii, 1623

The twenty-ninth of October

What prospective students need to do, is discover—for themselves —what is possible with a Lama. This requires practice. The same is true in terms of judging an equestrian instructor. If you never ride – you can never know how competent the equestrian instructor might be.

_____ · _____

The Lama cannot enable anyone to discover dad'dun as an act of will. The Lama cannot even assure you that dad'dun is there to be found in relation to themselves. It has to be a personal exploration and a possible personal discovery. It requires study, practice, and retreat.

_____ · _____

That Lama is one with whom one can establish vajra commitment. To enter into vajra commitment is to leap from the perfect precipice – to find oneself in the radiant space of choiceless choice that is the heart of Vajrayana. To enter into vajra commitment is to leap open-eyed into the shining emptiness of the Lama's three displays[20] – and to experience the ecstatic impact of each dynamic gesture.

_____ · _____

There are famous and highly revered Lamas – but it is no easier to experience dad'dun in relation to them than to experience it for passing monastics members of the gö kar chang lo'i dé. It is far easier to experience a highly charged emotion in relation to revered Lamas – but this should not be mistaken for dad'dun. Dad'dun is what occurs when one has practised to the extent that one actually recognises—to some degree—the realisation of the Lama. If one has no meditation experience it is not possible to have dad'dun.

---

20 The Three Displays of the Lama are: Presence Display (chöku / _chos sKu_ / ཆོས་སྐུ / _dharmakaya_); Personality Display (long-ku / _longs sKu_ / ལོངས་སྐུ / _sambhogakaya_); and Life-circumstances Display (trülku / _sPrul sKu_ / སྤྲུལ་སྐུ / _nirmanakaya_).

The thirtieth of October

We do not blather about humility, temperance, modesty, abstinence, patience, virtue, tolerance, sanctity, devotion, piety, and the need to destroy 'ego'. We would find such a discourse distasteful. So, be as exuberant as you like. Be vivid. Be naturally glorious, magnificent, spontaneous, extemporaneous, whimsical, delighted. Laugh often and be the people you are.

———— · ————

We would not be much use to people who wanted pious, reverend, revered, priestly, venerated Lamas. That is not who we are. We are not noticeably humble – unless we speak of Kyabjé Düd'jom Rinpoche Jig'drèl Yeshé Dorje, or of Kyabjé Künzang Dorje Rinpoche and Jomo Sam'phel Déchen Rinpoche. We are more used to those who'd like to live life to the hilt. So simply be the people we love and cherish – but, be aware. Practise with determination and take practice to heart.

———— · ————

Spiritual ambition spells disaster. To want status or recognition of any kind, is doomed. Obviously, some kind of recognition from the Lama is important – but that 'recognition' has to be a greater level of intimacy, in terms a *sign of being understood*. For that to occur, one has to authentically enter into the nature of practice. Intimacy with the Lama isn't constituted through being offered a merit badge, or being told *'You can lead the practice every morning'* or *'You can have your very own special seat.'*

———— · ————

One does not always have to have a reason for doing anything – because reason—conceptuality—is only one of the sense fields. There are also the visual, olfactory, gustatory, and tactile senses – and these sense fields each have intelligence. Often one's reason for doing anything is merely a fabricated means of justifying one's choices to the criticality of socially indoctrinated judgmentalism.

355

The thirty-first of October

To practise Vajrayana is to plummet into wisdom-fire[21]. Fire transforms solidity into emptiness. Fire displays the empty nature of the phenomenal world. Fire fascinates. Fire is both tangible and intangible. It's intangible and yet it destroys or devours tangibility. The Fire of Vajrayana is the form of the yidam.

———— · ————

One's loyalty to the vajra master and lineage—and to Vajrayana— cannot be based on a 'deal'. Loyalty is not negotiable. That kind of loyalty is for mercenaries – soldiers of fortune. Loyalty tends to be based on having lived in a coherent society – and we no longer have coherent societies. A coherent society is one in which honour is universally understood. If one is brought up in a society, engaging in life-pursuits which are time-honoured – then one has a better ground for honour. Fortunately, we still have movies which depict honour – so maybe we could start there.

———— · ————

The teachings of Mahasiddhas must be as *unusual* as their behaviour. If their teachings are nothing out of the ordinary, then one might be inclined to ask *'Where is Mahasiddha – apart from certain questionable behaviours?'* There are limitless ways of ruffling people's feathers without having to be unethical, immoral, abusive, or criminal. Someone once said to us *"You can't really have a vajra master in the West; because of all the laws and rules."* Khandro Déchen replied *"That would mean the vajra master is a cultural paradigm. If the vajra master is limited by a cultural paradigm – the vajra master cannot be realised. Realisation has to be able to manifest whatever the prevailing conditions – whatever the cultural paradigm. The vajra master must be infinitely adaptable, and endlessly creative with regard to disrupting dualism in whatever the circumstances."*

21 yeshé kyimé *(ye shes kyi me /* ཡེ་ཤེས་ཀྱི་མེ་)

Jalu *('ja' lus)* – rainbow body

November

Devotion, is dedicating yourself to your Lama and tradition – whilst equally respecting other Lamas and their traditions.

HE Ögyen Dro'dül Thrin-lé Kunkyab Rinpoche

རྒྱལ་བ་ཨོ་རྒྱན་འགྲོ་འདུལ་ཕྲིན་ལས་ཀུན་སྐྱབས་རིན་པོ་ཆེ

We—as the confused and complicated animals of the world—must always endeavour to find appropriate information by 'updating' with presence of awareness.

Khar-trül Wangchuk Rig'dzin Rinpoche

མཁར་སྤྲུལ་དཔལ་གྱི་དབང་ཕྱུག་རིག་འཛིན་རིན་པོ་ཆེ།

The first of November

There are—and always have been—people who are *Lamas in name only*. It is therefore wise to be as cynical as one is open – and to be wary of being gulled by cult gurus or subverted by ecclesiastical academics, pious dogmatists, and institutional religious pontiffs.

———— · ————

Other than residing in nondual awareness – there is no point at which one could say *'This is the* **actual** *reality; the others are distortions.'* All one can say is *'This is human vision according to my individual perception – as modified by my culture, class, age, gender, and life experience.'* It would seem there are as many different realities as there are perceivers of reality.

———— · ————

When substantial, elaborate conceptual patterns appear, it is easy to distinguish them – but when insignificant, intangible movements ensue, it is difficult to apprehend them immediately. This is the undercurrent of conceptual meandering[1] , so it is important to observe carefully. If you can be continuously present in meditation and post meditation, when walking, sitting, eating, drinking, and sleeping – that is the principal point. *Kyabjé Düd'jom Rinpoche Jig'drèl Yeshé Dorje*

———— · ————

Essential Vajrayana is the proclivity of those who have courage of heart and subtlety of mind. It is for those who have audacity of determination and outrageous endurance in the face of nihilist materialism. The weight of three million years is massive – and to stage a personal rebellion on behalf of everyone and everything, everywhere is a challenge that few would wish to accept if it were not for the inspiration of those who have accepted the challenge with colossal integrity: the heroes and heroines who are the authentic Lamas who hold the lineages of Essential Vajrayana.

1   namtog gyo gyü *(rNam rTog g. Yo sGyu /* རྣམ་རྟོག་གཡོ་སྒྱུ*)*

The second of November

Dzogchen is not simply a body of transformative techniques which facilitate the realisation of the nondual state. It is part of a religion called Buddhism – of which it is the innermost of the Six Tantras of Vajrayana.

———— · ————

If you want to cultivate an understanding of emptiness, you need to look for the reflections of emptiness within the mirror of the world of form. You need to look at the moments when your experience is transitional – when one sequence of events seems to conclude and the beginning of another has not yet become obvious. There is a gap there – and that gap is emptiness.

———— · ————

Seeing Vajrayana merely as a methodology is a mechanistic view – which is ignorant of the fact that a practice does not exist as separate from a practitioner. Vajrayana practices depend on the motivation and perceptual personality of the practitioner. Dzogchen practices performed by those who practise for their liberation alone, are Pratyekabuddhayana[2] practices. They are divorced from Dzogchen by virtue of failing to function in terms of Mahayana. Those who merely reads books about Dzogchen—no matter how convinced they are that they are living the view— are practising Shravakayana[3].

2   Rang-gyal thegpa *(rang rGyal theg pa* / རང་རྒྱལ་ཐེག་པ་*)* – solitary or self-centred realisers.

3   Nyan-thö-kyi thegpa *(nyan thos kyi theg pa* / ཉན་ཐོས་ཀྱི་ཐེག་པ་*)* – listeners. This would equate with readers and workshop attendees.

The third of November

Lama'i Naljor is the heart of Vajrayana – so nothing can be practised beyond Sutrayana unless the experience required to relate with a vajra master is present.

———— · ————

A liberated Mind warrior[4] is a revolutionary in terms of appreciation. This appreciation is the functional dynamic of compassion. To walk populated pavements or mountain tracks—as an authentic individual whose display arises from genuine non-referential appreciation—is the greatest act of compassion.

———— · ————

Without some sense of the inseparability of 'emptiness' and 'form', Vajrayana could come to feel like a monolithic, phantasmagorical menagerie – a mediæval escape from reality. Vajrayana however, has nothing to do with escaping from the supposed harsh reality of the world. These are not merely *ancient teachings*. They may have been practised for over a thousand years – but their efficacy is due to the fact that their essence is beyond cultural patterning.

———— · ————

Lama'i Naljor experience requires kindness that is free of artifice, the direct appreciation of emptiness, the natural desire to facilitate the liberation of everyone and everything, everywhere. It is necessary to have relinquished the sense in which personal identity can be protracted beyond the moment. In other words, the 'me project' must have come to seem futile. This then is the basis of the vajra world - rather than the collection of information and techniques that has become so popular amongst aspirants who follow the fashions of academia, religiosity, or esotericism.

---

4   Changchub sempa *(byang chub sems dPa'* / བྱང་ཆུབ་སེམས་དཔའ་ / *bodhisattva)*. The syllable *dPa'* relates to hero or heroine *(dPa'bo* / དཔའ་བོ་ or *dPa'mo* / དཔའ་མོ་ / *vīra or vīruṇi)*

The fourth of November

Cheerfulness is uncomplicated. What could be simpler than putting others first?

———— · ————

To be a gatherer of information and techniques is bereft of the natural poetry of life and devoid of the wealth of human history. The vajra world is where people live as tantrikas. It is the ethos or ambience in which the practices exist as operational parameters.

———— · ————

It is extraordinarily simple, ordinary, and direct. Magical maniacs of all religious denominations have been doing it for thousands of years. They all did the same thing. They let go of self-interest and were therefore free of the strategising ploys which inhibit cheerfulness.

———— · ————

The word *friend* seems to have lost its original meaning. It now seems to mean acquaintance or some unknown person in a social media setting. This is sad because a friend should be someone for whom one would make great sacrifices. If one's husband or wife is also one's friend – one will be as happy as it is possible to be short of nondual realisation.

———— · ————

The vajra world is co-created by the Lamas and students - or by the Lamas and the sangha. Lamas and students co-create each other – and it is this co-creation that allows the vajra world to come into being. In terms of a play – it is the actors who bring the play to life. This is never truer than with Shakespeare - and to some extent Vajrayana is similar to Shakespeare inasmuch as the language is symbolic. Try reading a Shakespeare play without having witnessed the play. It requires the Lama to give life to Vajrayana texts and practices.

The fifth of November

Once one begins to move beyond the tight constraints of dualistic conventions – phenomena begin to perform like a firework display

——— · ———

When we sit, we should sit without purpose – without hope or fear; praise or blame; gain of loss; or finding and losing. The eight mundane concerns[5] should cease to concern us.

——— · ———

Motivation propels you into practice – but there it must stop. If you fill your sitting space with the desire for progress, you'll stifle the development of insight. So, letting go of motivation is critically valuable.

——— · ———

To have perfect Lamas - students must allow their Lamas to *be* what they *can* be. Lamas are not going to confirm that they have nondual realisation. They are not particularly going to volunteer anything about themselves at all. Actually no one should waste anyone else's time by explaining themselves – either with braggadocio or disingenuous humility. We are who we are – and people can make what they will of us. So, it is for students to see their Lamas, understand what they have to offer – or not. As Dung-sé Thrin-lé Norbu Rinpoche said *"It is the students who say you are a Lama. No one else can do that. Even if some important famous Tulku says you are a Lama – it makes no difference; if you attract no students. So it is the students' own recognition of your qualities that makes you a Lama."*

---

5   jigten chö gyed *(jig rTen chos brGyad /* འཇིག་རྟེན་ཆོས་བརྒྱད་

The sixth of November

You can imitate the nondual state by cultivating kindness in thought and activity. This will open you to the discovery of beginningless changchub sem.

——— · ———

Romance—falling in love—is a reflection of emptiness for a Vajrayana practitioner. There are many aspects to romance that require one to be a better practitioner. One has to be kind and open-minded. One has to be generous and appreciative. One has to put one's own needs aside – and to a certain extent be selfless. The opposite approach would tend to terminate romance.

——— · ———

The people of a country can only be as proud of themselves as they are proud of their monarchs and their country. The country is the kyil'khor of the monarchs. The monarchs—as good and worthy Kings and Queens—care for their people's welfare. They have noblesse oblige.

——— · ———

There are many similarities between a monarchy and a sangha and its Lama. Lamas do not need to have the wealth of monarchs – but they need to have a rich sense of the kyil'khor over which they preside. It is a question of investment. What we invest in our country— through service to the monarchs—allows us to reap the interest of that investment. It is a poor people who have poor monarchs - and an impoverished monarch whose people are lacking in the attributes of a good life. Good monarchs measure their wealth by the wealth of their people.

The seventh of November

Common sense—for many people—is merely the sum total of prejudices acquired from parents, associates, and society in general.

———— · ————

When people say *'Buddhism is not a religion – but a way of life.'* It is because they do not understand the meaning of the word *religion* or what it essentially implies. Those who reject the idea that Buddhism is a religion usually, eventually, abandon Buddhism. We have seen it too many times to be uncertain about it.

———— · ————

The splendour of Tantric Lamas—as *vajra monarchs*—is measured in appreciation rather than financial terms. *Vajra monarchs* should have beautifully patched clothing; clean, starched, and precisely ironed rags; and, a full array of mismatched silverware. *Vajra monarchs* appreciate quality to the extent that they repair whatever has value. They know the art of polishing shoes and caring for leather goods. They set the example in terms of how to live with dignity even in a hut composed of hammered-out tin cans.

———— · ————

We witnessed Tibetan refugees living with natural dignity in McLeod Ganj in 1971. They were poor – but their homes were surrounded by flowers growing from painted tin cans. The doors to their huts were salvaged wooden frames over which flattened ghee cans had been nailed. The doors were painted - and emblazoned with flowers and mantras. In contrast - some of wealthier homes we saw were drab and somewhat squalid. There was an impressive lesson to be learnt from witnessing this disparity

The eighth of November

Whatever arises in mind, simply arises – it does not substantiate one's existence.

———— · ————

A common problem that is rarely acknowledged is that 'I' want to watch 'myself' becoming 'enlightened' in the epic thriller movie of 'me'.

———— · ————

There's no requirement for extravagant ostentation, luxurious overindulgence, or rococo ornamentation in the vajra world – simply enthusiasm, precision, and innate dignity. The vajra court can be a cave or tent as much as a palace or stately home.

———— · ————

We tend to want to get as close to the liberated state as possible without surrendering dualism. We want to find ourselves suspended fractionally above the surface of the ocean of nondual experience. This is amusing because it's the 'sparkling through' of nonduality which prompted practice in the first place.

———— · ————

Without a precise knowledge of Vajrayana, one cannot follow its logic. Logic is involved with Vajrayana   even though it transcends the intellect. Vajrayana has certain precise principles which can be employed to understand whether Vajrayana is being distorted – but these principles have often not been adequately understood by those who have argued these matters in the public domain.

The ninth of November

There can come a point where one begins to suspect that one might not actually be able to relate to nonduality through the mechanisms of duality.

———— · ————

When one realises that nonduality cannot be approached according to the dictates of conventionalism it becomes somewhat less disturbing to consider the possibility of letting go of the reluctance to dive into the sea of direct experience. This is because, when one dives without abandoning duality – the instant rewind cuts in and one finds oneself back on the edge of the sea with some vague memory of wetness.

———— · ————

Kyabjé Künzang Dorje Rinpoche drilled me in the understanding of 'principle and function' in order that nothing within Vajrayana would remain a mystery. There are various principles – but the primary principle is nonduality: *form is emptiness* and *emptiness is form*. Many functions are based on that principle – such as the interplay of compassion and wisdom: compassion is form and wisdom is emptiness; compassion is male and wisdom is female. These nondual binary correlates are to be found in every aspect of Vajrayana – and, when this is understood, Vajrayana unravels itself. If one understands principle and function there is nothing that cannot be understood—intellectually—within Vajrayana. The understanding of principle and function also opens up an understanding of other religions, philosophies, and even political systems.

The tenth of November

Ethics and morality are valuable and absolutely necessary – until the point at which one rests in rigpa. Then they are entirely superfluous.

——— · ———

Secrecy is not merely an inscrutable device designed to keep power in the hands of an elite – even though this purpose has not eluded certain misguided individuals during the course of history. Secrecy with regard to Vajrayana concerns the power of intimacy – and the exceptional conditions which need to prevail in order that authentic intimacy can occur. These exceptional conditions are known as the five certainties.

——— · ———

As a fundamental principle, the 'guarantee mentality' is not a hopeful start to vajra relationship. One cannot say *"Yes – I will take vajra commitment as long as I don't have to have my ideas challenged."* Having one's ideas challenged is the fundamental position. It's worse than any 'cliff'. Worse than Abraham slaughtering Isaac. Allowing one's rationale to be challenged is the whole terrible truth of the matter. That is the very worst thing that can ever happen in terms of vajra commitment. There is no Kool Aid scenario in authentic vajra commitment – only the terrible fact that one's vision of reality may have to fall apart. There is only the dreadful knowledge that one's justifications may be suspect. There is only the knowledge that one cannot hide. The vajra master will say *"Stop—look—see what you are doing."*

The eleventh of November

The vajra world is co-created by the Lamas and the students and the sangha.

—— · ——

If one cannot be free to give up the sovereignty of one's narcissistic rationale, Vajrayana becomes meaningless. If we fail to recognise the compassionate nature of vajra relationship as the heart of Vajrayana, then we are left merely with an esoteric Baroque pass-time. In terms of Baroque – I far prefer JS Bach.

—— · ——

Real examples of vajra command are likely to be instances of disciples being asked to question their perception, or to look at their behaviour in a different light, rather than any kind of 'outlandishness'. Vajra students simply require the openness to question their arrogant, unkind, selfish, manipulative, or thoughtless behaviour. The vajra master simply needs to be able to point out that the disciple's view of reality is askew. The vajra master needs to be able to point to instances of arrogance, anger, greed, dishonesty, and deliberate ignorance; and, expect the disciple to take such observations to heart.

—— · ——

If one's approach to vajra relationship can be characterised as having 'joined a vajra commitment club' then practice will bear no fruit. The teaching of the vajra master must be understood through *presence display, personality display,* and *life circumstances display.* This is to *take the three kayas of the Lama as the path.* To denigrate the Lama is to lose the opportunity of transmission. One enters into a crude and degraded form of relationship in which one destroys oneself. The Lama is a dangerous vehicle – like an æroplane. If one has the confidence initially to book the flight, there is no sense in taking one's leave of the aircraft in mid-air sans parachute.

The twelfth of November

If a 'meditation technique' is merely learnt – the mechanism of self-definition will regard it as a focus of fascination. It will then merely entertain the dualised identity of the 'meditator'

———— · ————

We do not concern ourselves with the flourishes of your personalities. We do not even disapprove of your neuroses too much - why should we? Your neuroses are the basis of realisation and so we prefer to conjure with them. We only disapprove of neuroses which lose track of kindness. This is what is dangerous.

———— · ————

We work in a Vajrayana paradigm in which everyone is allowed to be as they are. The Vajrayana paradigm allows exuberance, but it demands attention to detail. It demands impeccability. It allows mistakes, but they need to be instantly corrected. If we are not open to instant correction, the problems can become enormous. The danger of Tantra is that we can make the mistake of taking refuge in our mistakes as the manifestations of our authentic being.

———— · ————

We've always been interested in presenting Vajrayana to artists. The idea concerning Buddhism in the West, is that the most natural crossover lies with philosophy, psychology, and science. Unfortunately, that mainly concerns Sutrayana Buddhism. The Arts are a far better bridge in terms of Vajrayana Buddhism – because Vajrayana deals directly with the sense fields through ritual, visualisation, and voice. All the Arts are employed within Vajrayana – and so the most receptive audience for Vajrayana should be Artists. Unfortunately, Artists don't often seem attracted to Vajrayana.

The thirteenth of November

There is no massive problem with occasional lapses into 'common or garden' selfishness - as long as we are always prepared to own up to them in relation to our relationship with the Lama and with our vajra brothers and sisters.

———— · ————

Often, people speak in *stock phrases* – and expect *stock phrases* in response. When replies based on stock phrases are not forthcoming, there is a tendency to feel wrong-footed or alienated. The same applies to using words according to the correct meanings when the meanings have been popularly misunderstood.

———— · ————

Vajrayana is not emptiness-biased. It's the path of transformation, as distinct from the path of renunciation. The goal of Vajrayana is nonduality – and therefore the path embraces both emptiness and form. This is why Kyabjé Düd'jom Rinpoche Jig'drèl Yeshé Dorje speaks of the infinite purity of the phenomenal world.

———— · ————

There is too much at stake in Vajrayana to wallow in the indulgence of self-satisfaction. It is important for those with high hopes of Vajrayana to remember kindness. If one forgets kindness one is lost. Kindness means listening to those we may have offended by our acts. Kindness means caring about the fact that others have been hurt by what we have said or done. Kindness is the ability to feel real shame when we have acted without awareness or consideration for others. We all make mistakes. We all have times when we feel the raw edge of existence more than at others. When under pressure we all have less time, space and awareness of the sensibilities of others – but we must remember kindness even under the most abominable pressure. That is what it means to practise Vajrayana.

The fourteenth of November

Tantra is the hot blood of kindness; and in essence – vajra commitment is the ultimate acknowledgement of that.

———— · ————

No one is advantaged by arising as a 'schmuck manifestation' – so the Lama exorcises such demons through raging kindness. Kindness is always preferable to *arrogant face-saving, self-defensive aggression, indulgence in myopic comfort, paranoid posturing, or determined unwillingness to acknowledge reality*. Each one of these strategies murders kindness – and cripples the capacity for realisation. Each one of these drags us further in the direction of callousness and lack of connection with the suffering of others.

———— · ————

Kindness is not always comfortable in life situations; but through kindness we gain the respect of our vajra brothers and sisters. Through kindness, we become people of honour. Through kindness people believe our word, when it is given. Through kindness people learn to trust our motivation, and co-operate with us in our endeavour to create a better world. Kindness gives confidence to others. Kindness encourages self-respect and authentic dignity.

———— · ————

For there to be ideal Lamas – their disciples must permit their Lamas to manifest what they are capable of manifesting. There is however no way of discovering a Lama's capacity by asking a question. No Lama is going to affirm their realisation. Lamas are unlikely to designate the nature of what they have accomplished. No Lama is going to waste their time—or anyone else's time—with rhodomontade or insincere self-effacement. It is the responsibility of students to discover what qualities their Lamas may have – and that can only be ascertained through study, practice, and retreat[6].

---

6   Retreat *(mTshams / མཚམས་)* in this case is not intended to mean years or months – simply regular short retreats of a number of days.

The fifteenth of November

There is a tendency to project quotidian attitudes onto Vajrayana. In the modern world a great deal of effort has been expended on making life easy – so people approach Vajrayana as if it should be easily accessible. Vajrayana however, has nothing to do with the quotidian limitations of instant availability.

——— · ———

Naturally it is necessary that lively or frivolous banter between friends should blur the edges of an otherwise constrictive etiquette – but one should always be aware of the possibility of employing one's greater wit in an unkindly or ungenerous manner.

——— · ———

Few realise that the opinions they hold are those with which they have been programmed by society, by their families, and by their peer groups. Few come to their opinions through personal investigation or unbiased research. Rather than questioning ourselves we would rather reassure ourselves that we were right.

——— · ———

It is a modern convention to feel that one has the inalienable right to make one's opinion known and to supply whatever information one imagines has credibility. To speak the truth has come to mean to give one's opinion – but opinion is merely opinion and all opinions may be said to be equal. Naturally the opinions of an altruistic genius may be considered to have more value than the opinions of an ignorant bigot – but such distinctions can be decidedly murky – and evaluations are best savoured privately rather than broadcast – unless harm would result.

The sixteenth of November

The five-fold spectrum which illuminates being is the quintessence of the emotions. They are the essence of the elements which comprise materiality and the phenomena of the world. The five coloured lights are the essence of earth, water, fire, air, and space.

——— · ———

People—all too frequently—fail to understand that it is ludicrous to denigrate a partner. If someone were to say that their husband or wife was a fool, we might feel tempted to say *"Look at the fool who married the fool."* It is possible, of course, to make a bad choice – but there are remedies. One is no longer at risk of social opprobrium for leaving an undesirable partner – especially in the early stages of a relationship before children become part of the equation.

——— · ———

One enriches the quality of life by the respect and appreciation extended to friends, relatives, and partners. If one has no honour with regard to the quality of one's associates, one deserves the 'ill company' one keeps. If people have no honour and no appreciable qualities, one should not keep company with them. There is no sense in having any form of association that is without respect and appreciation. A basic sense of honour is fundamental to civilised life. Politeness, courtesy, and appropriate manners, are important to human society – and one should only be aggressive in one's speech in order to protect others from malignment or harm. It is a sad statement of modern politics that people have descended to the level of verbal abuse – and that voluble acerbity and tabloid sarcasm have come to be equated with intelligence. It is yet sadder that internet discussion of Buddhism engages in the same sort of degenerate wrangling.

The seventeenth of November

We believe in encouraging adulthood rather than infantilising students.

———— · ————

Adulthood has responsibilities. Adults keep promises to themselves and others. Adults balance spontaneity with circumspection. Adults balance: self-expression with reserve; freedom with responsibility; awareness with kindness; personal style with group sensitivity; honour with tolerance for others; self-respect with respect for others; and, desire with discipline.

———— · ————

Having an attitude of cheerful and discerning appreciation, does not mean that one cannot express one's confusion, or ask any question that is deemed important. If one cannot ask one's teachers any question, with regard to the texture of one's practice or living-the-view, it is possible that doubts may not be clarified, storing up problems for the future. However, when asking questions of the Lama, one should not take the approach of offering one's own value judgements. If one has chosen to become a disciple one should never approach one's Lama in a manner which is closed to learning or seeing one's behaviour or motivation in an alternative light. To denigrate the Lama is to denigrate one's own spiritual path. If one has chosen to be a disciple, one will have done so on the basis of one's spiritual experience. If one then denigrates the Lama, one calls one's entire spiritual life into question. If one criticises one's Lama, one criticises oneself for having accepted such a Lama – and one's entire spiritual practice and experience of transmission from such a Lama becomes devoid of meaning.

The eighteenth of November

To combine theocracy and Vajrayana is a spirituo-political problem and necessarily partakes of the art of the impossible.

—— · ——

Vajrayana does not function perfectly within a theocracy – because a hierarchy of Lamas implies a hierarchy of realisation.

—— · ——

Most religions prefer their ecclesiastics to conform to recognisable legislated codes – even though the realisation expressed by mystics of all religions has gone beyond the boundaries of ossified hierarchic sanction.

—— · ——

As a Vajrayana practitioner, the poetry I compose mocks, ridicules, parodies, lampoons, derides, and caricatures duality. To celebrate nonduality takes far fewer words – and celebration doesn't need commentary. My poetic satires are frequently composed as *counterfeit zealous harangues* against tyrannical fetishistic spiritual fashion – and I am aware that I am not entirely absent from the target audience.

—— · ——

If there is a Vajrayana hierarchy then it can only be the head of the hierarchy who can give transmission. To receive transmission, one has to regard the empowering Lama as a realised being – because only a realised being can give transmission. If a Lama is not the head of the hierarchies – then how can transmission be given? Every Lama gives transmission, so there is no practical problem – merely a theoretical one. The problem with having theory and practice which do not coincide, is that it causes confusion – and confusion can lead to aggression. There is therefore no hierarchy beyond one's own Tsawa'i Lama.

The nineteenth of November

Most religions prefer to venerate saints who are safely dead.

——— · ———

Sem[7]—conceptual mind—is a prison – but it offers the escape from prison.

——— · ———

The appropriate way to question your Lama, is from a position in which you are confident that your Lama will clarify confusion. Question the Lama from an argumentative or self-righteous stance, in which you're attempting to vaunt the validity of your own position means that you don't have a Lama. Should you appear to succeed in proving your Lama wrong, one would immediately lose your Lama. He or she would become a 'tantric lecturer'. If your Lama is no more than a 'tantric lecturer' then you merely receive the transmission of an ordinary person. If one sees one's Lama as a realised being, one receives the transmission of a realised being.

——— · ———

A dictionary explains what words mean – but that is not always a guide to how they are used. When people said *"We'd like to share something with you,"* I always took it to mean that they actually had something – and were going to give me a part of it: their sandwich, their pizza, their bottle of wine, or whatever. But, no! I was wrong. There's a new meaning of the word 'share'. It works like this *'I have a vapid idea and I want to bend your ear with it for half an hour.'* So the new meaning of 'share' seems to be 'take'. *"I want to take your time with my vapid idea."* So, when I hear someone say *"I have an idea that I want to share with you."* I reply *"No thank you. You are too generous. You must keep it for yourself. Far be it from me to leave you with less of your idea."*

---

7 *sems* / སེམས་ – conceptual mind, as distinct form sem-nyid *(sems nyid* / སེམས་ཉིད་*)* – the nature of Mind.

The twentieth of November

Vajra relationship is the heart of Vajrayana. Any attempt to dilute this relationship to the anæmic taste of the congenitally timid, is to siphon the fuel from the engine of the indestructible vehicle in order to avoid the danger of explosion. A vehicle without fuel is undoubtedly safer – and we can only bid those who wish to travel in such a vehicle 'bon voyage'.

———— · ————

Viewing the five elements of the psychophysical body as impure or defiled is an impediment to understanding Dzogchen. Dzogchen sees nothing as intrinsically impure. According to the view of Mahayoga, the human body is the dKyil'khor of the 108 peaceful and wrathful awareness beings. According to Anuyoga the human body is the dimension of rTsa, rLung, and thig-lé. According to Ati yoga the human body is the compassionate dimension of existence in which association and interaction are self-fulfilled in their own arising.

———— · ————

The sixth of the fourteen root vow concerns never denigrating other spiritual systems. This is not merely an ethical principle in terms of respect for other religions. The act of denigration is one in which we have to ignore the possibility of seeing the principle and function of a path for an individual. Tantrikas needs to be open to seeing the principle and function of everything. As a matter of pragmatics, it is vital to enact this vow within one's own religion, in terms of the teachings of other Lamas. This vow is therefore important within Himalayan Buddhism in all its different traditions. If one cannot be tolerant of others within the same religion, how can one ever hope to extend respect to religions other than Buddhism?

The twenty-first of November

The art of life is concerned mainly with simplicity – in terms of direct non-referential enjoyment of the sense fields.

———— · ————

The traditional image for a Vajrayanist is of a snake which is entering a bamboo tube – it can only go forwards. Lateral movement is not possible, neither has it adequate musculature for going backwards in such a situation. Doubt is appropriate only when considering the step of entering the path of Vajrayana – but once doubt has been overcome, and confidence has arisen, doubt must not be indulged. This does not mean that doubt will not arise – but that *the sensation of doubt* must be regarded as a practice – in terms of *finding the presence of awareness* in the sensation.

———— · ————

Non-theistic magic is based on the primacy of sems nyid – the nature of Mind – rather than on the lent power of a creator God or his Bête Noire, Lucifer – or even Bette Midler. Mind—sems nyid— is powerful. Even conceptual mind—sems—is powerful. Sems can imagine destruction and proceed to destroy. Sems can imagine creation and proceed to create. Whatever sems intends can occur. Sems can imagine an enemy and want to destroy that enemy through tactical manœuvres. Sems is capable of infinite imagination with regard to the destruction of enemies. Sems can equally imagine a friend and have countless ideas of how to relate with a friend, how to cultivate a friendship or engage in shared interests with a friend. We exist. The nature of mind exists. The intelligence of sems—non-informationally informed by sems nyid—exists without need of theistic structures.

The twenty-second of November

With regard to Vajrayana and the Arts, everyone is an actor on the living stage and a moving exhibit in the gallery of society.

——— · ———

'Khordong gTérchen Tulku Chhi'mèd Rig'dzin Rinpoche was a life-style choreographer. He was a play director on the living stage and film director on the living film set.

——— · ———

When we speak of the Arts and the Art of being an actor in everyday life circumstances – we do not mean acting as in 'pretending' or 'being false' – but manifesting personality as the display of changchub sem. When we see creativity in each other, we can become inspired to be as worthy and kindly as we can be. That is acting. Through this acting, appreciation grows for others—and towards others—in the impeccable theatre of generosity and precision.

——— · ———

The need to seek personal reassurance from the Lama is problematic. Simply accept the fact that this is what you feel you want. You do not have to act on what you feel. If you absolutely must seek reassurance – you have a simple option and a complex option. The simple option is that you can ask for reassurance. The complex option is to attempt to obtain reassurance without seeming to ask for it. That is sneaky, underhanded, and generally doomed to failure. The reason why a person might attempt to obtain reassurance by sleight-of-hand would be because refusal might be painfully embarrassing. It might be humiliating to be seen as needing reassurance – and if it is, do not ask for reassurance.

The twenty-third of November

Chaos and pattern—when united—manifest in terms of the nondual state. There is no separation between chaos and pattern.

———— · ————

Our longest standing students are all eminently tease-able because they know that it is a sign of affection, and a conduit of transmission. The principle and function of reminding apprentices of small details of attire is that *detail* is important in respect of practice. As the tantras proceed toward Dzogchen the instructions become increasingly subtle and it becomes increasingly important to be exact. One cannot be exact in one area of one's life alone – one is either exact or not exact.

———— · ————

One cannot be exact in practice and slipshod in every other area. The results of being slipshod may not necessarily advertise themselves in disaster unless it is a horse who is slipshod and then – a broken leg and death might result. One false move when defusing a bomb and all the other careful work is to no avail. Details are therefore important. Finally, we come to leather. It is always good to remember that leather goods came from animals – and we should therefore, take care of them as a matter of respect for the animal whose life was forfeit so that we could wear the belt, shoe, jacket, or coat. If we care for the phenomena in our charge, the phenomena last. If phenomena last, there is less waste in the world. If there is less waste in the world the world becomes a better place for beings. It is a question of wisdom and compassion.

The twenty-fourth of November

We live within a work of Art which creates itself in relation to our participation.

———— · ————

The more we participate in the Art of existence the more its quality as Art becomes apparent.

———— · ————

When we learn to allow our senses to make direct contact with the fields of the senses – we learn how to enjoy the Art display of everyone and everything, everywhere.

———— · ————

Maybe it is a sign of the times that anyone could see me[8] as elegant. What I try to encourage is appreciation. True elegance is, of course, appreciation – the fundamental appreciation of phenomena, in the very nature of appearances – the phenomena we apprehend from the replete sense fields which animate being. Elegance is composed of delight and fearless embracement in which we are not gluttonous, timid, or torpid. There is no dank or grimy sense of self-protection involved. Every deranged default-impetus is overridden with the sense of splendour and exquisiteness. This is the immaculacy in which we understand ourselves as regal beyond the remit of mere rank. Tantrikas override pomposity, portentousness, pretention – so when Dzogchen is described as the imperial vehicle; it pertains to what is natural. From the point of view of the imperial vehicle the beauty of genuine decorum lies in the non-manipulativeness of natural etiquette and unpretentious elegance. We should therefore all aspire to appreciate what is beautiful in each other – whatever the clothing or absence thereof.

8 Ngak'chang Rinpoche *(sNgags 'chang Rinpoche /* སྔགས་འཆང་རིན་པོ་ཆེ*)*.

The twenty-fifth of November

This dimension of experience with the Lama concerns *'cutting through spiritual materialism.'* We need to be discriminative in terms of *what is thought to be spiritual* and *what is thought to be secular, temporal, or non-spiritual.*

———— · ————

In terms of Vajrayana—with regard to the Mahasiddha Tradition of the Inner Tantras—there is no 'spiritual' as opposed to 'secular' or 'non-spiritual'.

———— · ————

In the company of the Lama everywhere is a gompa and every moment is the quintessential moment of the dBang. This is made gloriously possible by Vajrayana.

———— · ————

To watch a boxing match with Dungsé Thrin-lé Norbu Rinpoche is evidently not the same as to experience exactly the same external manifestation in the company of someone who was not one's quintessential exemplar. To attend a ballet performance or opera with one's Lama needs to be experienced as a teaching and as a practice. To take a parachute jump with one's Lama needs to be experienced as a teaching and as a practice.

———— · ————

Being in the presence of one's Lama is a bewilderingly wonderful catalyst. One doesn't have to go to the East. One does not have to sit in an imposing gompa perched on an impossible crag in the Himalayas. One does not have to sit in a fabulously decorated shrine room. Not that there's anything wrong with these possibilities—they are all as excellent as each other—it is simply that the Lama opens up the entire fabric of the phenomenal world and therefore we are unrestricted in our access to the vajra world.

The twenty-sixth of November

In the past, the best examples of successful vajra commitment have manifested according to the way we have been able to work with apprentices' interpersonal difficulties.

——— · ———

Whenever people have allowed us to guide them—and they've followed the guidance wholeheartedly—they have found that it proved worthwhile putting their rationale on one side. These occasions, even outside vajra commitment, have been true examples of how vajra commitment can work with people.

——— · ———

The only thing which makes people 'special' in our eyes is their kindness. Deranged 'disciples' who are prepared to abase themselves to cult leaders in return for power to make others abase themselves, have nothing whatsoever to do with vajra relationship.

——— · ———

Our idea of vajra commitment, is simply the openness to look at one's neuroses. It is simply a matter of having honour – in the old-fashioned sense of the word. Anyone who really has honour, understands this. Anyone who has honour will know that honour is not comfortable. Honour does not always mean winning. Winning has no meaning if one's honour is lost.

——— · ———

The director of the play has an idea of how to present the play and the actors cooperate together in order to create a vital ambience that invites the audience into the world they create. With Vajrayana the actors and the audience are the same people and the director is often at the centre of the stage. The stage is anywhere and everywhere - and the play is an open-ended artistic endeavour in which the play is written and performed simultaneously.

The twenty-seventh of November

As Buddhists we have no class – class is a refuge we have abandoned.

———— · ————

Refuge comes before everything – before gender, age, ethnic group, nationality, class, and political persuasion. There is no 'working class Buddhism' by virtue of which one can cling to offensive attitudes to others.

———— · ————

Something strange happens to people when they become involved with religions. It seems that some people start out with an idea of being kinder and wanting to understand the way things work at some sort of universal level – and then gradually they forget about altruism and wanting to be better human beings. They gradually become *professional religionists* who no longer care about anything but their religious hobbies. They then develop convincing arguments as to why it is acceptable to *practice for the realisation of all beings – whilst having sympathy and empathy for none.*

———— · ————

'Rinpoche' is a term of respect and endearment used by Vajrayana disciples when speaking to their teachers. It is not a title and has no specific meaning beyond 'precious jewel'. The German word for 'jewel' is 'schmuck' – and of course there is the Yiddish variant, pronounced with a 'hard u'. As I'm half German, maybe I should be addressed as 'schmuck' – but schmuck is not a title either. At the hospice where Ngakma Yeshé[9] used to work there was a German paper shredding machine which bore the following caution 'Achtung Schmuck!' She found it amusing because it appeared to read 'Pay Attention Dickhead!' I explained that it meant 'be careful of your jewellery' but it remained amusing nonetheless.

9   An American Aro gTér teacher and disciple of Ngak'chang Rinpoche and Khandro Déchen.

The twenty-eighth of November

Changing Lamas is a perilous procedure if the desire stems from the wish to evade the Lama-student process.

———— · ————

The line or argument that some people adopt when they criticise Lamas suggests that they are fully conversant with the modus operandi of nondual realisation. If you can dictate the parameters in which a realised master functions – you would be a realised master. If you comprehend the nondual state you have no need of a Lama. If you are not a realised master than there is no way in which you can comment on realised masters. All you can say is *'This is the Lama with whom I wish to study – and this is not.'* You do not have to study with masters whose manifestations seem alien to you – but neither can you judge them. If you set yourself up as a judge of realised masters then either you are claiming to be a realised master – or you have set yourself outside the remit of Vajrayana.

———— · ————

There is no way that you can just destroy your neuroses. It's not a matter of destruction – and in any case, who would destroy what? 'Your neuroses' are not separate from the 'you who wants to destroy your neuroses'. As long as you cling to that bifurcation – nondual realisation will elude you. You have to be able to practise with your entire situation *as it is*. You cannot begin from any other position. You have to accept the entire situation – or it can never be transformed or self-liberated. Your personal situation is all you have – and there is actually no other way to proceed. Your neuroses are the best situation you could have. It is the only starting point. From this point of view, we have to celebrate the situation as it presents itself – and simply, wordlessly, observe the play.

The twenty-ninth of November

What is important, is not so much the ferocity of practice – but rather whether this practice and commitment and connection to Lama and Lineage is maintained up to the point of death.

———— · ————

Tantra means continuity – so our advice is 'continue'. Continue to hold the living quality of the view of Vajrayana within the fabric of your life. It is not always possible to practise every day—but it is always possible to maintain the feeling of being primarily involved with practice. We're not advocating pretence – but rather the feeling that there's a continuity of involvement threaded through the sequence of events which constitute your lives. This feeling will lead to an acceptance of yourselves as intrinsically good people—people with infinite potential. Do not indulge in judging yourselves in terms of fleeting phenomena of moods and personal crises. Do not identify yourselves with personal histories or characteristic limitations—rather, identify with Guru Rinpoche and Yeshé Tsogyel as being your real nature.

———— · ————

Terminology can be problematic. Meditation is not a progression through stages – nor is it advancing or climbing. Meditation is a process – not entirely dissimilar from maturing or growing older. We celebrate our birthdays on particular days – but that does not portend that, as soon as we wake up, or as soon as the birthday candles are extinguished, we are a year older. The timing of a birthday party is arbitrary. In maturing as a human being, there is a process of evolution. Development occurs over a period of time – but it is not gradual. This is precisely what occurs in terms of meditation. Meditation is not based on stages as heavily defined segments of an established spiritual framework - but upon a process that is taking place in those who meditate, and that process takes place in the context of our living situations.

The thirtieth of November

Originality is not a major Buddhist theme – but in terms of essential Vajrayana it connects directly with changchub sem. Being original has nothing in common with doing something no one has ever done before or creating something no one has ever created. It means freshness. It means being free of influence through enjoying all influences.

———— · ————

In terms of originality – one could eat a boiled egg with well buttered granary bread. One could wash it down with a pint of espresso. That could be an original act every morning. One hundred thousand others could also engage in the same original act. There'd simply have to be freshness of approach.

———— · ————

There was a great emphasis, early in the second spread of Dharma in Tibet, on Vajrayana being presented in the language of Sutrayana. The Inner Tantras were outlawed for a period – and, by the time they were allowed to be taught, the language of Dharma had settled into a Sutrayana style. It is now a little rare for Vajrayana to be taught directly *as* Vajrayana. Vajrayana has always been secret – but the secret quality of Vajrayana has come to pervade the entire structure in such a way as to obfuscate the structure. This is why Chögyam Trungpa Rinpoche's books 'Dawn of Tantra' and 'Journey Without Goal'—amongst others—are so extraordinary. He revealed the structure and the essential paradigm without revealing that which should remain secret. There is much of Vajrayana that does not need to be secret. There is much that could be disclosed which would be of great benefit to a wider audience. That approach however, has not gained wide-ranging favour.

Nyingje *(sNying rJe)* – kindness

December

Seeking refuge in Guru Rinpoche is the most important practice during this degenerate period.

HE Ögyen Dro'dül Thrin-lé Kunkyab Rinpoche
རྒྱལ་བ་ཨོ་རྒྱན་འགྲོ་འདུལ་ཕྲིན་ལས་ཀུན་སྐྱབས་རིན་པོ་ཆེ

Pay attention to simple phenomena – because they provide useful information which is required throughout one's entire life.

Khar-trül Wangchuk Rig'dzin Rinpoche
མཁར་སྤྲུལ་དཔལ་གྱི་དབང་ཕྱུག་རིག་འཛིན་རིན་པོ་ཆེ།

The first of December

Buddhism is not a *religion of truth* – it's a *religion of method*. The *method* takes you to what is true – or rather, to *reality*. The practices are not reality in themselves – they're methods for realising the nature of reality.

———— · ————

A yidam is not an archetype. People have started describing yidams in this way – but it is neither accurate nor helpful. An archetype arises out of the human psyche, whereas yidams arise from *mind that is identified with primordial space*. Yidams do not arise from concept consciousness – no matter how extraordinary that consciousness may be.

———— · ————

If one imagines that a hammer is a saw – one will not merely fail to drive nails into wood; one will damage the saw. Buddhism is a religion of method – but if you think it is truth, you will both fail to make use of it as method and you will cause yourself and others a great deal of needless confusion. The confusion will arise from the fact that methods contradict each other – whilst being entirely concordant with recognising the nature of reality.

———— · ————

Chhi'mèd Rig'dzin Rinpoche told me this story. A scorpion arrives at a river bank and, unable to swim, asks a kindly frog whether a ferry ride was possible. The frog replied *"I'd like to help – but you're a scorpion. You'd sting me and then I'd die."* The scorpion replies *"But If I stung you, I'd die too – because I'd drown."* The frog sees the logic and allows the scorpion a ride across the river. Half way across the scorpion stings the frog. Just before dying the frog asks *"Why?"* to which the drowning scorpion replies *"Because it's my nature."* Khandro Déchen and I have often thought of this story in respect of human relationships we have observed.

The second of December

Talking merely to hear yourself speak is like eating merely to watch yourself defaecate.

———— · ————

It's not that you have to make every idea a physical reality; not every idea is feasible. If, however, your ideas merely remain conversational, you will find a decreasing audience for your ideas.

———— · ————

Bringing one's creative ideas into the nirmanakaya is important in being a mensch. To be a person who merely talks about their wonderful ideas without ever making them a reality is a sad waste of time.

———— · ————

When sitting in meditation, you let the emotion consume you, like some ravenous beast in full blood-lust. You become the emotion completely, or it becomes you. You don't have to refer back to some other time or place or situation. Analysis is utterly superfluous.

———— · ————

There's no need to be concerned about whence emotions arose in one's life. That's merely a therapeutic concern – and psychotherapy has no real place in Vajrayana. It's the immediate emotion that matters. When it's fresh, it has a sharp dynamic – and it's more difficult to be slippery about what it is. Comparing an emotion to other times such an emotion arose doesn't help with addressing what is happening now. It's the raw texture of what is happening that is vital. Comparing an emotion with a previous emotion is a way of avoiding the moment, by way of investigating how the moment could make sense. It's a way of stealing the space of the situation and converting it into a claustrophobic form of comfort.

The third of December

Education doesn't end when your school days are over – it doesn't even start when your school days commence. The educational system, where is it is valuable, trains you to read and write – the rest is up to you.

———— · ————

We have to accept responsibility for educating ourselves. It's a human duty – and a humanitarian duty. No educational system will provide the education necessary to becoming a fully-fledged human being – and if you are not fully fledged, you cannot fly. If you cannot fly you can never see that far – and you remain parochial.

———— · ————

Education is the outcome of appreciation. One appreciates the phenomenal universe – and one proceeds in terms of particulars. Exploring any particular takes you in the direction of other particulars – and you explore further. Obviously, one explores more than one particular – and this leads to fascinating cross references in terms of the development of one's education. Each human being could evolve a unique educational referencing system which would be a work of Art in itself. Such a work of Art could weave itself with the threads of Shakespeare, Norse legends, American 19th Century history, and the evolution of revolver handguns, Beat poetry, Surrealism, Dutch pottery, Turkestani carpets, Hindustani Classical Music, Baroque composers, and early 19th Century clothing. Another person's Art work could include an entirely different list of phenomena – but each exploratory Art work would comprise an education. It is education in this sense which makes human beings fascinating. It's what makes us authentically human – and enables us to manifest changchub sem.

The fourth of December

Nothing has ever come easily to me, other than putting on weight.

———— · ————

Life is either hard or it is hard. When one understands that and accepts it – it becomes easier to live life like a mensch.

———— · ————

Most of what is of value in our lives has been achieved through hard work – often hard unremitting work. That however, is not to say that it wasn't enjoyable – and, at times, utterly delightful.

———— · ————

I don't come from a privileged background. I'm working-class. I attended a sub-standard school – albeit with an excellent English teacher. I'm not naturally talented other than having an enormous appetite. I have an IQ of 66[1]. If I have accomplished anything in my life it has been entirely due to enthusiasm and persistent hard work.

———— · ————

We have to change ourselves in order to accommodate the imperatives of Vajrayana – not the other way round. The outer aspects of Vajrayana will change over time – but the essential teaching can only continue, or it will stop being Vajrayana. People should not be in such a hurry to change what they have so recently received. I have heard people talk about Buddhism changing in the West, and the need for change – but that position can be rather unappreciative and arrogant.

---

1 Ngak'chang Rinpoche (sNgags 'chang Rinpoche / སྔགས་འཆང་རིན་པོ་ཆེ་).

The fifth of December

We are committed to practice and we are committed to death. They're the same phenomenon.

———— · ————

When we commit ourselves to practice and to opening, we commit ourselves to change. When we change, we die. We have to die in order to change. If we cannot die, we cannot change. This is a simple, blunt, uncompromising statement of fact.

———— · ————

The elements manifest through the sense fields: through the body; the intellect; the emotions; and. the subtle body. Nyams are convulsions within these fields. They convulse according to the patterns of convolutions created by the continual struggle to re-create duality.

———— · ————

It is not who 'he' or 'she' may be. It is what people may be manifesting in the moment – in terms of reacting to their lovers. It is how people might catch a glimpse of the manifesting elements which characterise them in the moment. It is how this enables people to see that their reactions to lovers are dictated by the way they distort their intrinsically immaculate arising elements – in the moment.

———— · ————

Spacious confidence enables one to forge ahead in making decisions – rather than constantly hesitating and anxiously altering choices for some specious 'good outcome'. Knowing that the direction of life cannot be extricated from infinite chains of preceding incidents provides a curious ground. It could be called *optimistic pessimism*. *Optimistic pessimism* is knowing that *independent choices* are *dependent* on the *interdependent* nature of existence.

The sixth of December

Vajra commitment does not mean that we cannot have physical limitations which the Lama takes into account. It means that we have to be enthusiastically open to whatever offers itself next in the company of the Lama.

——— · ———

In terms of *taking the three kayas of the Lama as the path* – personality display is concerned with one's observation of the Lama. One cannot merely observe the Lama's personality display and be open to it as 'incomprehensible dharma'. One has to enter into the spirit of the activities suggested. One has to enter fully into what is being created. If one retracts into the cosy comfy snug limitations of one's own preferences – then one misses the opportunity.

——— · ———

The word tralam-mé is difficult to translate - because it has different meanings according to context. Just as the word field has different meanings in English, the word sky has some of those meanings and others that are more profound in the Tibetan language. In Tibetan vocabulary which is not specific to Dzogchen, the word tralam-mé pertains to meteorological phenomena. In the Tibetan understanding these are classed as 'sky phenomena' – thus rainbows and meteors both class as tralam-mé.

——— · ———

In terms of Dzogchen long-dé, tralam-mé pertains to the subtle meteorology of being – and the weather conditions of vajra romance. Tralam-mé can be translated as poetic turbulence: the vivid fire of resonance or energetic reciprocity of individuals who fall in love. Tralam-mé is the energetic movement within the subtle atmosphere of the body – and is thus linked to the zap-nyams described in the Dzogchen long-dé practice of sKu-mNyé. These poetic turbulences facilitate mirroring through the rhyming of coruscations.

The seventh of December

From the perspective of the visionary practices of Vajrayana we become able to transform every aspect of prejudice against otherness in terms of vibrant appreciation.

———— · ————

Morbid obesity is beautiful in terms of the sphere of intangible appearance. This is something that some people find difficult to understand. Merely because one understands that obesity is a serious health risk does not mean that one has to find its appearance repellent, derisible, or shocking. That health education and aesthetic sensibilities have to run in tandem is a primitive form of perception. As Hamlet points out *Why, then, 'tis none to you, for there is nothing either good or bad, but thinking makes it so.*[2]

———— · ————

The elements of the world are at once factual and mystical. *Earth, water, fire, air,* and *space* are inexhaustible dimensions. They inspire both the materialistic sciences and the sciences of human meaning. The elements inspire the Arts, and they inspire the dance in which romance is experienced. The human body displays the implications of the elements. *Earth* is the skeletal structure, hair, and flesh of physical being. *Water* is the blood and lymphatic system. *Fire* is the heat of living tissue and the rhythms of visceral vitality. *Air* is the breath which animates life. *Space* is the unbounded non-intentional primal alertness through which awareness illuminates being or through which dualistic contrivance attempts to dominate the natural flow of the elements. The senses are the communicative quality of the elements in which the dance of existence and non-existence allows 'self' and 'other' to be both separate and non-separate.

2   William Shakespeare, *Hamlet*, Act II, scene ii

398

The eighth of December

Fashion is a vile voracious vampire which sucks the individuality out of life. The fashion industry is a pack of jackals. They tear the living flesh from people – and convert it into jackal meat.

——— · ———

William Shakespeare had a few comments on fashion. *"He wears his faith but as the fashion of his hat."*[3] / *"What a deformed thief this fashion is."*[4] / *"All this I see, and I see that the fashion wears out more apparel than the man. But art not thou thyself giddy with the fashion too, that thou hast shifted out of thy tale into telling me of the fashion?"*[5] / *"A man in all the world's new fashion planted, That hath a mint of phrases in his brain."*[6] / *"New customs, though they be never so ridiculous, yet are followed."*[7] / *"I'll be at charges for a looking-glass, and entertain a score or two of tailors to study fashions to adorn my body: Since I am crept in favour with myself, I will maintain it with some little cost."*[8]

——— · ———

If you meditate, you will gain conviction – but if you do not meditate with joy, you will not recognise the natural state. So, meditate with resilient joy – and signs will appear. Signs will appear that display your familiarity with remaining in the natural state. Then tight obsessive cohering will gradually loosen. Obsession with the eight worldly dharmas will lessen. Authentic devotion to the Lama and the Lama's instructions will mature. Anxious fixations will evaporate. Diamonds and broken glass will then appear equal.
Kyabjé Düd'jom Rinpoche Jig'drèl Yeshé Dorje

3   William Shakespeare, *Much Ado About Nothing*, Act I, scene i, 1623

4   William Shakespeare, *Much Ado About Nothing*, Act 3, scene 3, 1623

5   William Shakespeare, *Much Ado About Nothing*, Act 3, scene 3, 1623

6   William Shakespeare, *Love's Labour's Lost*, Act 1, scene 1, 1594

7   William Shakespeare, *Henry VIII*, Act I, Scene iii, 1623

8   William Shakespeare, *Richard III*, Act I, scene ii, 1594

The ninth of December

Sexuality is the primary image in Himalayan Buddhism – but the sexuality of which it speaks is the *penetrating/engulfing nature of reality* itself. From this perspective, the manifest universe exists through spontaneously and continuously engaging in the act of making love.

——— · ———

It is not easy to remain in love indefinitely. It is far easier to continually fall in and out of love. It is easier to live in the marital mortuary of moribund ardour. It is also easier to live a turbid, stagnant, loveless coexistence. The single difference is that there is little self-determined effort or courageous openness involved in the inevitable deterioration which afflicts many relationships.

——— · ———

For romance to transpire is not unusual. It occurs daily in ordinary circumstances – yet romance also tastes the energy of existence and non-existence: the incandescent alternating cyclic blaze of being. Falling in love initiates the dissolution of fixated personal boundaries. Being challenged or threatened by the outrageous transmission of romance is the living blood of Vajrayana.

——— · ———

Vajra lovers are bedazzled by the sun and moon within each other. These radiant spheres are realised as the self-same fields of luminous experience which fulfil themselves individually within lovers. This self-recognition unifies self-dividedness – and enables the realisation that individuals are complete in themselves. Yet 'the other' is also there: as the perfect resonant reflex of the personality of a lover. Each glows for the other – defined yet undefinable.

The tenth of December

The only problem with *agoraphobia* and *claustrophobia* is the *phobia* – without that, they could easily become nondual.

—— · ——

In order to experience vastness, one has to abandon the need to indulge in experiential agoraphobia. Before that is possible however – one has to discover the nature of 'the payoff' in terms of agoraphobia.

—— · ——

The elements should be approached as a lover would be approached – before the first naked caress. The elements are not merely categories – just as men and women are not merely male and female. There is no secret as to what will be found when a lover disrobes for the first time—men and women are anatomically predictable—and yet, each person is utterly and profoundly – physically mysterious.

—— · ——

Vajrayana relates directly to the emotional texture of life – through the very fabric of the dualistic neuroses. Neurotic infatuation—posing as passion—is capable of generating scenarios of deliverance and disaster; salvation and damnation; or heaven and hell. As such, neurotic infatuation provides continually provocative junctures. One such juncture is that acceptance or rejection has the possibility of becoming spiritually catalytic. The prospective lover becomes larger than life, as the neurotic distortion of the khandro or dPa'wo – but even within this neurotic paradigm, there is an enormous opportunity to leap beyond the confines of dualistic neurosis. This is the ground level—or experiential platform—from which any serious practitioner can aspire to vajra-romance.

The eleventh of December

Vajrayana is not for the rigidly sensible or pusillanimous – but neither is it for the foolish or unstable.

———— · ————

To engage with the challenge of Vajrayana – emptiness and form need to 'dance' as the conflagration of personality. Emptiness and form are the most important terms in attempting to establish a relationship with the structural symbolic aspects of Vajrayana, both as theory and practice.

———— · ————

A Pavane is a stately dance in slow duple time, performed in courtly clothing – popular in the 16th Century. Having observed dances of this type in the BBC adaptation of Jane Austen's 'Pride and Prejudice', we can see that there is something quite wonderful about performing movements with grace and elegance in a formal setting. Maybe this is one of the reasons Rig'dzin Chögyam Trungpa Rinpoche encouraged ball-room dancing amongst the other spiritual disciplines he advocated.

———— · ————

Everyone who has fallen in love—and experienced the tentative nature of initial courtship—will have experienced the wild expectancy in which anticipation and culmination oscillate. Hope and fear arouse each other. Gain and loss excite each other. Meeting and parting stimulate each other. The electric tension of these powerful ambivalences—in tandem with commitment to the Lama —is a sparkling texture in which particulars can be released. Fixed positions and definitions can be allowed to dissolve. The energy of the romantic context can thus be experienced simply and directly.

The twelfth of December

Essentially Vajrayana is a one-to-one religion – Lama and student. If there is a sangha however, it cannot comprise of more people than one would find at a wedding.

——— · ———

The creation of the vajra world sets Vajrayana apart from societal religions. Vajrayana may be a social religion in sufficient ways to classify it as such – but it's not a system suitable for large congregations.

——— · ———

There was never a sangha around Kyabjé Künzang Dorje Rinpoche as far as I ever saw. In my entire time with him, the only other student I ever saw was Khandro Ten'dzin Drölkar. He did have other students – but they came to see him individually. That is how it was with the Mahasiddhas.

——— · ———

Beauty is in the eye of the beholder – as are ugliness or bland featurelessness. These are also in the ear of the listener; the olfactory sense of the fragrance inhaler; the gustatory sense of the diner; the tactile sense of the textural investigator and, the ideation sense of the theorist. The is no absolute definition of anything that exists outside the momentary frame of reference of each individual.

——— · ———

Desire habitually promotes self-seeking. The desire which drives romantic pursuit is no exception to this – apart that is, from the fact that *something else occurs*. When drawn to a person – desire is communicated to the one who is desired. When this occurs – the romantic couple are unsuspectingly lured into Buddhist practice. The practice, into which they are enticed, is that of wisdom and compassion. The couple begin to display unusual open-mindedness and uncharacteristic kindness – but what is more extraordinary, is that they feel inexplicably unthreatened in so doing.

403

The thirteenth of December

There are many external similarities between monarchy and the monarch — and a gö kar chang lo sangha and the presiding Lama.

———— · ————

Lamas do not need to have the wealth of monarchs – but to function as vajra masters, they need to have a rich sense of the kyil'khor over which they preside. It is a question of mutual investment. The mightier the sangha make their vajra monarch – the mightier they become individually as practitioners.

———— · ————

The time, effort, and ingenuity we offer in service to country and monarch – ennobles us as individuals. People who are destitute in terms of willingness have destitute Lamas. Destitute monarch are those whose subjects are destitute. The wealth of real monarchs and authentic Lamas can be measured their wealth of their subjects or sangha.

———— · ————

Magnificence with regard to gTértöns—as vajra monarchs—is gauged in terms of their wealth of appreciation rather than their fiscal wealth. Visionary emperors should wear pristine schmatta[9]. Visionary emperors appreciate quality in terms of repairing whatever can be repaired. Their lives are an example in terms of living with dignity – under whatever the prevailing conditions. This was made clear in the life and circumstances of Kyabjé Künzang Dorje Rinpoche. He was the undoubted King of the Universe in his sun-bleached threadbare clothing. Whatever he wore was superior to kim khab[10].

9   Schmatta – Yiddish (שמאַטע / *shmate*) –rags
10 *kim khab* / གོས་ཆེན་ – gold brocade

The fourteenth of December

The Lama is at once a very ordinary and completely extraordinary person. The Lama is able to witness the perceptual habits of students at a non-cultural level. The Lama is able to establish highly personal contact with students – even if they come from other age groups, backgrounds, or cultures.

——— · ———

With regard to getting to know the student, the Lama operates at a level which doesn't require biographical information, of any sort. Even when teachers ask questions about past events, there is no particular reliance on the details provided. It is more a matter of how the details are presented – and the Lama's consequent clear understanding of the student's perceptual constructs and conditioned frames of reference.

——— · ———

One has to manifest patience with the seemingly endless stream of thought and the seemingly endless series of repetitive movements. If one is impatient there is no hope. Patience arises out of generosity. One has been generous. One has said *"This time is given for all beings."* What can one do then – but manifest patience? What else can one do but experience the results of generosity and tolerance? Whatever happens, happens. We've agreed to that. We've given the ground. We've allowed the theatre of phenomenal reality to open. It's the first night. It's always the first night. The players are fresh and excited. The performance is magnificent. All that generosity floods back. One is patient as the play reveals itself. One is tolerant of whatever manifests.

The fifteenth of December

We want people to feel empowered in seeing themselves as artists— without—necessarily being able to earn their living as artists.

_____ · _____

People who attempt to make a living as artists but fail, are not 'failed artists'. They've just failed at inaugurating 'careers in art'. That they've failed in a commercial sense does not mean they have failed in a creative æsthetic sense.

_____ · _____

At first, there is some sense of sacred and secular. Initially it is valuable to concentrate on the sacred domain – but unless one comes to see the sacred in the secular, one will remain immured in duality. At first the sacred Arts are the prime arena for practice – but once one has evolved familiarity and skill in the sacred Arts; one needs to see that the same energy exists in all the Arts. There is essentially no division.

_____ · _____

The lovers' open-mindedness equates with wisdom – inasmuch as lovers cannot remain lovers if they become closed-minded. To be unaccepting and opinionated, is to shut off. This interrupts the life of passionate communication. Lovers do not like to disagree – because opposing each other would create distance where closeness is essential. This forces lovers to re-appraise any belief which is antithetical to the other. The lovers' kindness equates with compassion inasmuch as lovers cannot remain lovers if they can entertain the possibility of causing each other pain or distress. To be unkind or uncaring is to repudiate the energy of the other – and, to interrupt the life of compassionate concatenation. To oppose each other would be to author discord in a relationship where harmonious affection is primary.

The sixteenth of December

There's always a chance factor with approaching Vajrayana –
because there has to be a unique connection. It's not entirely
dissimilar to falling in love. It could be anytime, anywhere, with
someone quite unexpected.

———— · ————

There are aspects to one's connection with the vajra master which
are similar to the process of falling in love. You could say *I want to
achieve realisation for the benefit of all beings so I will receive teachings and
transmissions from a Lama. I will then practice and eventually achieve
realisation.'* That is like saying *I want to get married and have children, so I
will pick a man or woman from those I see or from a catalogue and proceed.'*
That might not be practical. You cannot decide to fall in love with
somebody – that has to happen by itself. The man or woman has to
be more than merely attractive to you – they have to have the right
personality and there has to be some sort of chemistry.

———— · ————

We attract each other through liberated potential. This is visible,
according to the spectrum of appreciation our lives portray. The
more naturally that personality is expressed – the more relaxed
people are with their capacities and capabilities. The more *unaffectedly
articulate* people are – the less they engage in artifice. The more that
personality is conveyed unpretentiously – the less people concern
themselves with the projection of a calculated persona. The more
the need to make demands is abandoned – the more open people are to
the mysterious arising of khandro - dPa'wo mirroring.

The seventeenth of December

Romance plays the part of an unseen spiritual treasure – living in the heart of the common culture. Esoteric teachings are sought through clouds of incense and the rich spectacle of brocade – yet most people appear blind to the vast and subtle sensory spectrum of romance.

———— · ————

Vajrayana is constantly performing itself: in us; through us; and around us. We can either acknowledge it, by taking hold of the bare electric cables of existence and non-existence – or we could try to pretend that it's not happening. Whether we like it or not – Vajrayana is what is happening as the warp and weft of reality.

———— · ————

The yidam is an anthropomorphic symbol through which our dualistic condition is able to dissolve into luminous recognition of the nondual state. The purpose of symbolism, in practice, is to transform the dualistically deranged symbols of our conditioning into the nondual symbol of the yidam, and the kyil'khor or non-dual environment of the yidam.

———— · ————

Ngo sprod[11] mere indication.] applies to a method of transmission in which words are used to convey the nondual condition. These statements cannot be elaborated – they are either comprehended immediately or they remain incomprehensible. The danger with such statements is that people can imagine they understand them, when in fact they are very far from understanding. Addiction to such statements as the only meaningful aspect of teaching is usually a mark of incomprehension.

---

11 *ngo sProd* / ཌྱོ་ཧྥོ་

The eighteenth of December

One could say that Lamas were croupiers – and that their casinos were venues where winning and losing were ro-Çig[12]—one taste—as in *the one taste of emptiness and form.*

——— · ———

Vajra masters may be the monarchs of their kyil'khors – but their majesty is never haughty, arrogant, imperious, or desirous of droit du seigneur. Vajra monarchs are vastly wealthy in terms of appreciation of the phenomenal world and therefore have no desire for excessive conventional wealth.

——— · ———

Kyabjé Künzang Dorje Rinpoche was also known as Drüpchen Karma Gyalpo – the Mahasiddha Monarch of Mastery. That he was a monarch was obvious to many people – and not only to Himalayans. Western people—some of whom were antithetical to royalty—would say *"He was just so obviously the King of the Universe."*

——— · ———

Because we are all symbols of the nondual state – there can be no form of being who is not essentially sacred according to Vajrayana. Although we all have predilections with regard to what is attractive – we need to implement a vision of wider scope. We need wider scope in terms of how we see our world – and, the many beings who ornament its environment. We can accept the limits of our styles of appreciation for what they are – but as practitioners of Vajrayana, we need to recognise that we have to be able to take the pure vision of the yidam practice into the nirmanakaya. We need to practise to become open to the dimension of the everyday world as nirmanakaya – the kyil'khor of the yidam.

12 *ro gÇig* / རོ་གཅིག

The nineteenth of December

Life is full of surprises – but that is to be expected, in terms of emptiness and form.

———— · ————

There are many variables. If it was just a matter of pointing the gun and shooting, there would be no problem – but keeping still is not easy. Keeping still is not difficult either – it is merely that no-one can remain physically still for very long. In the short period of time when you find yourself physically still – it is simply a matter of knowing that stillness.

———— · ————

If realised beings did not manifest personality – they would not be able to communicate personally with individual people. The personalities of realised beings—with their concomitant predilections—are not fixed. Realised beings do not self-identify according to their momentary displays. Personality is an appreciative gestalt through which communication occurs. This is not a matter of hardwired likes and dislikes. The likes and dislikes are mere display.

———— · ————

Tantrikas live their lives with an utterness that is captivating. It's not that they would not relish a relationship – but their lives are not vacuous. What makes neediness so unattractive is that the neediness is the main image one projects – and that is not interesting. In terms of 'how can you not be needy when you are single and wanting a relationship', the answer is simple: If you have a variety of needs which are being met by a thoroughgoing involvement with the phenomenal world and the need for a partner is simply there – it will not manifest as overt, overarching, overwhelming, overbearing neediness.

The twentieth of December

Buddhism is actually entirely pragmatic. It's not an imposition on reality.

———— · ————

Buddhism is not a constructed philosophy which forces human beings to proceed according to rigid directives which take no account of the diversity of experience.

———— · ————

To proceed through the yanas you simply have to get 'some' taste of the goal of each yana. You have to reach a pragmatic point for take-off into the paradigm of the subsequent vehicle.

———— · ————

You don't have to pass the cycling proficiency test of Sutra, as it were, before climbing astride the *Harley Davidson* of Outer Tantra or the *Vincent Black Lightning* of Inner Tantra. You simply have to be able to *experientially comprehend* another vehicle. With Dzogchen there is no motorcycle analogy. Kick starting the engine, top speed, and destination – are identical.

———— · ————

Vitality is the sense of being alive in one's practice. I'm not a dead body. I'm not a vajra android who sits on the floor and gets up again repeatedly, day after weary day – because retracting presence is a method of avoiding pain. One doesn't mumble mantra as if one was an inmate at a mental hospital – chuntering in order to maintain a comforting dullness. We're alive – so we need to be vital in our practice.

The twenty-first of December

We practice because we're Nyingmas. That's a deliberately banal statement
– but entirely meaningful because it functions for us. Because it
functions for us – it may function for you. But then you have to
know what Nyingma means. Being Nyingma is being associated. It's
a sense of devotion. After a while, the whole sense of having a goal
has to disappear. It's quite enough to be a Nyingma.

––––––– · –––––––

The possibility of experiencing the one taste of desire and fear, is
the heart of many experiences. When falling in love however, it
suffuses all the senses. Not only is there taste – but felt-texture,
fragrance, seeing, hearing, and ideation. The senses blend into it.
The senses become alive to each other – and a space occurs in
which the senses can begin to speak in each other's languages. They
speak with touch. They hear through tactile sensation. Lovers taste
each other's words – and inhale the perfume of each other's dance
steps.

––––––– · –––––––

Tantric sexuality is a vast field of living knowledge in which coital
union is infinitely modulated in terms of all the sense fields. It
voluptuates in: the soft silence of falling snow on bare branches; the
succulent stickiness of budding twigs; the glorious unreserved
unravelling of blossoms; and, the cool moist fire of autumnal
foliage. It is the art of the way in which the eye sees. It is the poetry
of the way in which the ear hears. Eyesight penetrates visual
phenomena, and is engulfed by the field of vision. Hearing
penetrates sound and is engulfed by the auditory dimension. Every
sense-perception and sense-field performs – and is performed by,
the same ecstatic dance.

The twenty-second of December

Faith, in Buddhism, is described either as 'blind faith' or 'learning faith'. Blind faith is romanticism. It is, however, also rather powerful. One can go a very long way with blind faith – one could even achieve realisation through blind faith – but (and this is an enormous 'but') if you have faith in the wrong person; it could be a huge disaster. Having misplaced ungrounded faith is a problem for obvious reasons. I don't think we need to tire anyone's patience with a description of cult atrocities.

———— · ————

Having *blind faith* in a truly wonderful Lama – *can* be a problem. The reason for that may need some clarification. Blind faith in the perfect teacher is a problem because one doesn't see who the Lama actually is. One is not experiencing the reality of the Lama. Blind faith can therefore become an obstacle. Because of this, Buddhism advocates 'learning faith' – in which one's confidence is based on experience. For example: *you approach a Lama; you get to the Lama; you receive advice; you take the advice; you have further experience; and then, you receive further advice on the experience.* If everything holds true, then you are probably in touch with something real. If yet further advice holds good, you become capable of taking advice which is further and further from the norm. This continues until you become able to accept advice which lies outside your rationale. You are prepared, in those terms, to go further and further. You are prepared to go out on a limb, so to speak. You are able to say *'I'll do whatever I'm instructed to do. That is the extent of my confidence. Because I know it's not worth being doubtful any more. Doubt is holding me back. I know what it's like to obey my own rationale as the final yardstick as to what I'll do and won't do. I have tested that time and time again. Every time I fall back on my own rationale I end up in the same dreary place. I have pushed my rationale to the limits and found it to be severely wanting.'*

The twenty-third of December

Reciting mantra is a process of tuning oneself like a musical instrument. One begins to resonate with the power of the mantra.

———— · ————

In yogic song 'sonic identification' is the principle; but with recitation of mantra, rapidity and numerical drive is the principle.

———— · ————

By taking the recitation of a mantra to completion, one experiences a profound state of resonance with the yidam. This is not to say that anything 'magical' happens, it is simply that the power of the mantra becomes manifest in one's life in terms of the active compassion of which one is capable.

———— · ————

Power of mantra is interesting. There are texts which indicate that after so many million recitations, you can manifest siddhis – but in some sense you could miss the point by approaching mantra with that idea. Mantra is the sense of terminal intimacy with the sound – through which one's capacities become 'self-apparent'. Mantra is a 'carrier wave' on which the unique frequency of the yidam travels. By reciting mantra, one tunes oneself to the 'frequency' of the yidam.

———— · ————

What started my interest in poetry? Learning to speak. It seemed fantastic that there were words – and that they could be used in such different ways. Maybe it was having an English father and a German mother – and learning that there were no equivalent words in German for every English word. It made me realise that ideas were beyond words. Language was an approximation of what occurred perceptually. I realised that words were objects which pointed at meaning. They could be used to suggest things that couldn't be spoken or written in a normal linear way.

The twenty-fourth of December

Happy Yuletide. Have fun – but keep the chemistry of the four naljors in mind. See the space in which phenomena play. Fun will then naturally manifest, with or without Santa Clause – but never without presence.

———— · ————

It can be claustrophobic to be a practitioner. When you start to *live the view*, it makes personal neurotic games increasingly self-transparent. You can't enter into them with the same degree of gusto. You can't quite pout with the same degree of strength in the lower lip. You can't quite enjoy slagging off your enemy with the same degree of energy and linguistic volatility.

———— · ————

Vajrayana is dangerous. Life is also dangerous. One can avoid being foolhardy, intemperate, rash, imprudent, impulsive, or reckless — but one cannot put safety before all else. There are dangerous pursuits such as horse-riding, skiing, sky-diving – but even driving a car is potentially lethal in terms of possible collisions caused by the irresponsible or intoxicated. Life kills us all in the end and accidents cannot always be avoided. It is preferable therefore to face life like a hero or heroine.

———— · ————

The nature of sexuality can be delved as a metaphor for Tantra – and, Tantra can be researched as a metaphor for sexuality. This theme can be followed throughout the array of the sense-fields, in which sexuality becomes the texture of all living experience. It then becomes possible to explore the parameters of relationship as a metaphor for Tantra – and Tantra as a metaphor for relationship. The same sumptuous interface is there. It is within this vivacious dialogue that instantaneous translation begins to take place – and Tantra articulates itself as the fabric of life.

The twenty-fifth of December

Conceptuality is a sense field as much as the other senses – but apart from artists, most people prioritise the linguistic aspects of thought.

——— · ———

Men and women, as nondual beings, are endowed with the capacity to display exactly the same activities. There is no sense of difference beyond that which is obviously biological.

——— · ———

Duality, in whatever human context, always produces division. The ways in which 'division' expresses itself are endless. Each way in which 'division' expresses itself also provides a method of dissolving that division.

——— · ———

Intuition is commonly acknowledged – but usually it is seen in terms of insight into conceptually comprehensible subjects or situations. In this sense artists and lovers have much in common. Lovers are consummate spheres of ultimate artistry.

——— · ———

When you gaze into a mirror you see reflected images of whatever exists in front of the mirror. You do not see the reflective nature of the mirror. What is this reflective nature of the mirror? What is this capacity to reflect which is defined as clarity? What is that quality which allows the manifestation of reflections? The nature of the mirror is not visible – you can only see it through the images reflected in it. In the same way, we only see the reflections of the realised nature of body, speech, and mind. Through these reflections however – we have a method of discovering the nature of that which reflects. This is why Khyungchen Aro Lingma holds a mélong[13].

13 *me long* / མེ་ལོང་

The twenty-sixth of December

The rôle of the Lama is to manifest the goal. One has to observe the Lama and ask oneself *'Would I like to be like this person?'* If not – one may possibly have to look elsewhere. One has to come to an understanding of the qualities of the Lama; and one can only do that through practice. One has to explore the situation. One has to discover the quality of the Lama.

———— · ————

Tantra addresses the unification of emptiness and form, rather than attending to the dichotomy of 'self' and 'other'. It addresses duality; or perhaps better: it undresses duality. Tantra undresses dualistic fixations, as they portray themselves, within the divergent aspects of gender. Tantra seduces duality into revealing the illusory shapes to which it clings. Tantra seduces duality to reveal the nakedness of its empty nature. Tantra delves the interplay of emptiness and form with delicious deftness – according to the manner in which these dualised figments of nonduality reflect themselves in men and women.

———— · ————

The creation of the vajra world sets Vajrayana apart from *the religions of society*. Vajrayana is a religion in sufficient ways to classify it as such – but it is not a system that is suitable for large congregations. In the epoch of the Mahasiddhas of ancient India, the vajra master worked one-to-one with students. Even when Vajrayana was taught in Tibet and Bhutan—during the First Spread—the student-teacher ratio was often limited to a handful. Guru Rinpoche and Yeshé Tsogyel had twenty-five disciples. There were maybe thousands who took Guru Rinpoche and Yeshé Tsogyel as their inspiration – but they were composed of small groups around individual Lamas.

The twenty-seventh of December

To be a yidag[14] means that there is no empathy in one's relationship with *positive phenomena*. One is always hungry – but whatever one devours is experienced as poisonous.

———— · ————

Yidag are traditionally depicted as beings with gargantuan mouths and thin throats. They cram such a great deal into their enormous mouths with the result they cannot swallow anything. Whatever they see looks wonderful. They want it all because they experience themselves as starving. They try to consume it – but whatever they try to consume turns out to be inedible. It turns out to be inedible because of the manner in which they attempt to eat it.

———— · ————

As a yidag, I might go to a superb restaurant. The food is fabulous – but I slather over the table cloth and snatch food from the waiter before it has been placed before me. Then I stuff it into my mouth so indecently that I choke on it. I spit the contents of my mouth across the room and vomit on the carpet. Half-digested food lodges in my nostrils, and I have to be beaten on the back to prevent choking. No matter how delicious the food – it causes me pain because I am a malfunctioning human vacuum cleaner. I cannot swallow food as quickly as I feel I need to swallow it. There is so much in my mouth that I cannot swallow – but I cannot remove it, because I am starving. This is a yidag. Some Buddhist intellectuals are yidags – they gorge themselves on information and then regurgitate it over each other.

14 *yi dags* / ཡི་དྭགས་ / *preta* – hungry ghosts – one of the six realms or dualistic cycles of experience.

The twenty-eighth of December

The yidam is the Lama manifesting in visionary form, as the method of practice. Through empowerment, the Lama describes the manner in which the sphere of apparitional appearances[15] is experienced.

―――― · ――――

To experience empowerment is to be put in direct communication with the sphere of energy; the dimension of personal experience in which the horizons of human possibility are endless.

―――― · ――――

To arise as the yidam is to realise that one is not confined to a crippling codified image of what is personally possible. The least one could discover is that one does not have to identify as a victim of childhood trauma – or of any societally pre-conditioned formulation.

―――― · ――――

Awareness-spell is the natural resonance of the awareness-being; the way in which a visionary symbol of the innate nondual state reverberates or communicates the power of its capacity to transform. This *enchantment* is the method of singing power into being. This is the method by which one gives voice to the dynamic of one's actuality – and vibrates in sympathy with primal creativity.

―――― · ――――

The rapturous visionary context of Vajrayana is no place for the sequestered rationale of conventional pedestrianism. Within the poetically pristine polemic of Vajrayana, the only viable vector is immersion in the efflorescence of the sense fields – as it is only there, that it is possible to learn directly from the energy of being which exists in relation to a lover.

15 long-ku *(longs sKu /* ལོངས་སྐུ */ sambhogakaya)* – Sphere of apparitional appearances.

The twenty-ninth of December

It's not what you do, it's the way that you do it – that is to say, either with kindness or without.

———— · ————

When all is said and done, academic knowledge and intensity of formal practice *can* mean almost nothing. It is 'who you are as a human being' which matters. It is your level of kindness and consideration of others which is significant. It is your ability to relax with your situation and to find humour in your own crises which is worthy of respect.

———— · ————

Remember to breathe air. A great deal is said about 'compassion'. People seem to like to hear about 'compassion' and feel moved to comment on the profundity of statements on 'compassion'. We rarely mention 'compassion' because we take 'compassion' as a 'given'. Why would anyone follow any religion if they had no sense of kindness? It is what we expect of our students. We rarely mention 'compassion' for the same reason we do not remind people to eat, drink, sleep – or to breathe air. Please don't forget to breathe air.

———— · ————

We prefer to use the word honour rather than ethical discipline. There are sometimes puritanical implications involved with ethical discipline. Honour means the same thing – but there's a sense of valour. We have to be brave to practise shi-nè and lha-tong. We have to be brave if we are to stare into the face of emptiness and form and find the presence of rigpa. Honour means doing what one says one will do. It means sitting when one doesn't particularly want to sit. It means persisting in one's practice and not being seduced by other alternatives.

The thirtieth of December

Being natural is not the same as being predictable in terms of common societal mores.

———— · ————

Being natural should not be confused with the inability to: behave with decorum; adapt to different social codes; address others with courtesy; speak with good enunciation; employ good grammar; or maintain adequate personal hygiene.

———— · ————

Being natural is ideal – but what is 'natural'? Some feel it is natural to be angry when insulted. Some feel it is natural to feel any one of a number of emotions in response to life circumstances. What we would ask, is where this information was acquired and why it came to believed?

———— · ————

If there is excessive discipline, there is great energy. You might call that 'tension' – or you might call it 'nervousness'. You might call it 'anxiety', or you might call it 'fear'. You might certainly feel that it is not what you want from a spiritual path. In some ways you might be right—few would want such a spiritual path, and those who did might be suspect. We have no desire to recruit sado-masochists. If there is excessive looseness, there is no energy. You might call that 'relaxation', or you might call it 'fun'. You might also call it 'naturalness', or you might call it 'friendliness'. You might feel that this is exactly what you want from a spiritual path. Perhaps in some ways you might be right. There is certainly nothing un-spiritual about having fun, being relaxed, or being natural—but as Dung-sé Thrin-lé Norbu Rinpoche said, *'Pigs are also natural.'*

The thirty-first of December

It may not be Lo-sar[16] – but we wish everyone a Happy New Year. To wish others *kindness, merriment, and freedom* is always both cheerful and cheering.

———— · ————

When empowerment is authentically experienced, the nature of the unbreakable bond between vajra brothers and sisters[17] becomes apparent.

———— · ————

To be vajra brothers and vajra sisters does not mean that you will not at times feel critical of each other – but that critical perception needs to be taken as a self-reflection. It is good to use every context of perception as a practice, rather than as an immediate impulse to be right.

———— · ————

Namthogs flash into appearance like lightning – or, like waves swelling on an ocean. There is constant movement. This arising must be recognised immediately. If merely *thoughtless blankness* is experienced — it must be *clarified* with *presence*. This *clarification through presence*[18] must occur repeatedly – otherwise meditation will sink. If many namthogs arise, do not be discouraged. This is not the failure of meditation. This is a sign of awareness. The failure is when namthogs are unnoticed. Noticing – is not failure. Namthogs must not be suppressed or eliminated. Whatever happens – be without hope or fear. Be without uncertainty or anticipation. Keep this essential instruction in your heart – and everything will be fine.

Kyabjé Düdjom Rinpoche Jig'drèl Yeshé Dorje

---

16 *lo gSar* / ལོ་གསར་ – Himalayan Buddhist New Year is celebrated on various dates depending on location *(Bhutan, Sikkim, Tibet, Nepal, and India).* It is celebrated on the 1ˢᵗ day of the lunar calendar *(February or March).*

17 dorje ché dang *(rDo rJe mChed dang lCam bral/* རྡོ་རྗེ་མཆེད་དང་ལྕམ་བྲལ་)

18 ngon du *(mNgon du /* མངོན་དུ་)

Tsa *(rTsa)* – subtle channel

Appendix I

Extract from:

The White-robed Dreadlocked Community – an Introduction to and Defense of the Ngakpa tradition

by Dr Nida Chenagtsang

In 'The Ornamenting Flower of the Mantra-Holders: An Explanation of the Enjoyment (Body) Accoutrements, Clothing, Jewellery and Music of the Ocean of Awareness-Holders of the Ancient Translation (School) Vajrayana' it states:

'In this, one ought not to look merely to the most sublime of the Vajra (tantric) Awareness-holder mantra-holder's clothes – it is an essential teaching (gNad dam pa) that not only these but even regularly worn clothes and clothes of enjoyment are inseparable from tendrel or interdependent, auspicious connection.'

As it says in the Great One of Oddiyana's (i.e. Padmasambhava's) 'Embodiment of the Lama's Realisation or Enlightened Mind/Intention/Perspective ('bla ma dGongs 'dus kyi de nyid):

'Clothing has the auspicious or inter-dependent connection of the yidam. Fasten yourself without impurities or defilements to what possesses magnificence, spontaneous and natural dignity, and brilliant radiance (bag dro lhun chags bKrag mDangs can).

Improper clothes are those which are unattractive (literally, which don't 'come into the mind') and which possess a form displeasing to the eye: they are made of impure materials, they are badly made, they exceed their proper proportions, they have ugly colours, they are rough in texture, and so on. When one wears sumptuous clothing (phun sum tshogs pa'i gos) one imagines that one is putting on the Dharma-robes of the body of the yidam which possesses the clear or vivid appearance of the Creation Stage.

With this, hold the View of Interdependent or Auspicious Connection (knowing that) the clothes worn externally as a mantle are the manifestation of the Father Daka or tantric hero, those wound around the inner body are the manifestation of the Mother tantric Heroine, those that cover the upper body are the manifestation of the peaceful yidam, and those which wrap around the lower body are the wrathful deities.

Since the collar is auspiciously connected with the life-span, don't make its length too short all around! Since the encircling hem (lJags ri cha) is connected with merit and riches be careful to bring together the ends! Since the qualities of construction of the garment are inter-connected with one's own (moral) qualities or character make sure to make it to proportion! Since the dyes and colours are connected with one's feelings (of loving-kindness or hatred) towards beings make the oil (pigments) bright! Since the adornments are linked with the retinue and students, decorate it beautifully! Since the way one wears it is connected with the accomplishment of one's actions, abandon improper behaviour like wearing it crooked, having one side (pulled) below the other, wearing it inside out or upside down, letting the front sag down or trampling the back of it underfoot, and don it properly!'

(Cf. gSang rNying rGyan dang rol mo'i bsTan bCos, iron block-print sha 22, tha 13)
(Ref: https://perfumedskull.com/2017/05/30/the-white-robed-dreadlocked-community-dr-nida-chenagtsangs-introduction-to-and-defense-of-the-ngakpa-tradition/)

426